LUST FOR JUSTICE

LUST FOR JUSTICE

The Radical Life & Law of J. Tony Serra

Paulette Frankl

Lightning Rod Publications
Santa Fe, New Mexico

Lust for Justice
The Radical Life & Law of J. Tony Serra

Lightning Rod Publications
PO Box 22749
Santa Fe, New Mexico, 87502

Cover Art: Inspired and stylized from a photo by Jeffrey Newbury, *Los Angeles Times* magazine, article "The Ballad of Hooty Croy" by David Talbot, June 24, 1990.
Further Credits: "J. Tony Serra Fits Big-Screen Rebel Image," *The Recorder*, February 17, 1989.
"Semantic Warrior," Nikki Meredith, *Pacific Sun Weekly*, August 8-14, 1986.
Jan Sluizer for her Tony Serra radio interview tape, 2006.
Nicholas Wilson for his Tony Serra victory photo in the Bear Lincoln case.
Bernadette Zambrano for her photo of Tony Serra by the lake.

Dedication

For each and every one of us who needs a champion in our court,
a voice to say what we cannot say for ourselves, validation of
our dignity, and a helping hand against the powers that be.

Acknowledgements

This book is in its 17th year. It owes its existence to the many people along the way who have carried the torch of support when I failed to see how it could ever see the light of day. I give thanks to those who have given of themselves to help make it happen and whose vision validated and inspired me not to give up.

Cathy Scott, true-crime author and award-winning journalist, for her extraordinary friendship, networking, generous assistance and encouragement, time, and Internet expertise. This book would still be buried in my despair had it not been for you, Cathy, kicking me in my sorry ass of little faith. Thank you! Your energy is a force of nature that surpasses all resistance. And thank you for connecting me with Deke.

Deke Castleman, my editor par excellence, who truly gets it. A book owes its life to the ones who breathe their own life into it. This book reflects your caring, patience, grace, and sensitive touch. Your heart, soul, and DNA are all over it. It waited 17 years to be born in your hands.

Mary Neighbour, author of *Speak Right On: The Story of Dred Scott*, for detecting this book's strong heartbeat and whose vision and editing made it so much stronger. Thank you also for convincing me that I was *not* a fly on the wall in this book, but a voice worth reading.

Lady Laurie Buckley, lusty soul sister, for giving this book its title: *Lust for Justice*.

Ann Yeomans Ann Yeomans, Archetypal Therapist, for being such an inspiration and true friend.

Nicholas Koenig: my brilliant artistic son, founder and creative director of NK & Associates Design, artist and sculptor, whose artistic savvy vastly improved some of these drawings.

Josiah "Tink" Thompson: author of *Six Seconds over Dallas, Gumshoe, Kirkegard,* who was the *real* investigator on the Chol Soo Lee case from which the fictionalized film *True Believer* was made, whose close association with Serra and whose knowledge of the law and inspiring conversations and insights about Serra helped to shape my artistic style of courtroom art.

Penelope Rose and Stephanie Brown, whose office assistance and friendship made all the difference.

Bernadette Zambrano, Native-rights activist and kindred spirit, for ongoing soul-sistership.

Christine McKellar, author of *Port of No Return,* for giving me shelter and friendship all during the Binion re-trial.

Karen Signell, author of *Women's Dreams*, and her partner, Ann McLeod, author of *Being Someone* and *The Lost Dogs of Shoretown,* whose literary encouragement and assistance gave me a leg up.

Allison Evans, author of *The Voice of Flowers*, and Dennise Ferry, whose ongoing informative support solidified my path and helped in so many ways.

Annice Jacoby, whose priceless seeds of language fell on fertile soil.

Marjorie Blaire whose chance encounter, validation of my writing, and connecting forces have became a major conduit in the manifestation of this book.

Hart Sprager, author of *Hear the Earth*, whose humble spirituality encouraged and reminded me that there are no accidents.

Margaret O. Ryan, for hauling me through the longest breach birth of writing and editing imaginable, for the hard laughter of late-night phone calls that pitched us both into realms of inspiration.

Early editors Allice Klein, Celia Bolem, and Nancy Palmer Jones for keeping the integrity of this book while hacking through the brambles.

Lazaris, whose teachings about manifestations really work!

Helen MacLeod, poet and needlepoint artist par excellence of authors and other animals, for her referrals to so many people.

Tara Kronenberg, without whom I never would have set foot in that

Acknowledgements

first courtroom on that first day and thus become a courtroom artist, the path of which led me to J. Tony Serra.

Gerry Spence for proving his true greatness.

And first and lastly to Tony Serra for saying yes! It's been a long hard haul, but here it is, Tony!

THANK YOU ONE AND ALL! This book owes its life to you!

Contents

Foreword

I don't like the man, Serra, very much.

I have always wanted to be brave and reckless, especially facing judges and the enslaving moguls of corporate America. But I admit, I have never fully succeeded, not to my satisfaction. I have wanted to fight for the poor and give up any hint of economic security and put aside all striving for worldly things. Once I said to my darling, Imaging, I think we should sell everything we have and give it to the poor and live without devoting any of our lives to things, and she said, "All right. I'll go with you." I looked around and saw all of the possessions and comforts we have and I said, "Forget it."

I have wanted to take on the government, especially the IRS that sucks us dry for a government that spends our money killing many innocent people in false wars, but I dutifully write my check each year with little more than a passing whimper.

I have wanted to fight pro bono in deserving cases that have begged for my attention. But like every law office, we have bills to pay and the loyal folks who labor with us have theirs to pay as well, and as a consequence too many deserving cases go wanting for proper representation.

These are a few of my major failures, and the reason that I don't like Tony Serra much is because he does not suffer the same.

He has vowed poverty and I suppose he will sleep under the bridge if he must. He comes into court looking like a lost tramp in a dirty unpressed suit and tennis shoes. He isn't afraid of judges or opposing lawyers. He doesn't respect those who aren't deserving of respect and isn't hesitant to say so. He will fight an often evil, broken, judicial system like a mongoose fights snakes. He will defy the IRS on moral grounds and go to prison. He looks for a fight as if his breathing will stop without one.

This book is a story of his life. I am glad there are a few (and there are only a few) audacious miscreants such as he around. He gives meaning to the word courage.

It must also be said that sometimes, Tony Serra is a role model for poor judgment.

But as Justice William O. Douglas once quipped, "If you want to be a successful outlaw, you have to live within the law." I remember Race Horse Haines, one of the great lawyers of our times, who said that when he faces a troublesome problem in the courtroom, he asks himself, "What would a real lawyer do here?" When I face a tyrant judge or an overpowering opponent, I ask, "What would Tony Serra do here?" But rarely do I have the courage to follow the answer.

—Gerry Spence

Preface to the Art

I first became aware of Paulette Frankl's art in the year 2000, while I was serving as Curator of the Las Vegas Art Museum. At the time she was busily engaged in drawing courtroom scenes during the first trial of the alleged murderers of casino heir Ted Binion. During this period, Ms. Frankl happened to meet my landlady, Jean d'Agostino, a retired textile designer from New York, who lived directly across the street from Ted Binion's house on Palomino Lane. As it happened, I lived in Ms. d'Agostino's carriage house at the time. (Tony Serra himself, in fact, eventually represented one of the two defendants in the later retrial of this complex case.)

Encouraged by Jean, Paulette brought her sketches to me at the Museum. I was curious about them, having often seen such drawings on television, and was pleased to learn of the artist's presence in Las Vegas. Soon thereafter, Paulette moved to Santa Fe. However, a fortunate result of this move was that in 2005, I included eight of her paintings in an exhibition I curated at LVAM, *Fifteen Santa Fe Artists*. This show was accompanied by a full-color catalogue published jointly by the Museum and Bell Tower Editions of Santa Fe. In the catalogue's introductory essay, I argued that the work was more advanced than the range of international contemporary visual art: an audacious claim, but standard thought when coming from me.

I now confront a body of work quite different from her paintings. Let me say that straightaway, I was riveted by the images of Tony Serra in action. I have leafed through them now countless times, with always-increasing admiration. Taken together, the drawings in this book exhibit a considerable range of styles, and Ms. Frankl has many more at her command, as I know from having seen most of her work over the past decade. Due to the 20th century's gradual but successful analytic dismantlement of the former tradition, a distinct consistency of style is no longer a term of praise, but may be in fact a weakness, one which Ms. Frankl's work transcends with ease and great versatility.

I would say that the dynamic qualities of the Tony-Serra-in-action drawings, in particular, are perhaps made possible more by the practical example of Italian Futurism (c. 1909-1915) than by other precedents. However, her ad hoc use of it employs figuration much more clearly. The multiplication of the head, arms, and hands of Mr. Serra in a single work are like a kind of cinematically combined fast-forward and freeze-frame depiction of a sequence of split-seconds. But there is nothing superficial about this work's intellectual penetration. The effect of the technique is quite brilliant, both expanding the perception of time and concentrating a picture's expressive intensity.

As he makes his witness examinations and larger arguments, Mr. Serra's courtroom behavior often has him assuming and acting out the various roles of a given trial's principal characters. This book's drawings convey the relentless attorney's basic nature, through these one-man yet diverse personae, with overwhelming visual and psychic force. The facial contortions and emphatic dead-aim gesticulations that the works depict ultimately give one the sense of both the character and physiognomy of the man himself, and yield results that are as real and moving as portraiture is capable of achieving.

Speaking for myself, the drawings virtually transcend portraiture into lived experience. Collectively, they form an oeuvre that is unique, superior, and emotionally unmerciful. What they add up to, in terms of illuminating a human being's questing spirit and devotion to justice through his personality, appearance, and physical movement, leave me with a deep and honest admiration for both the artist and her subject. Or, I should modulate, leave me with a great degree of respect for both the author and the man who has inspired her to create this amazing book.

—James Mann, Ph.D.
Curator, Las Vegas Art Museum 1997-2001
Curator-at-Large, LVAM 2003-2005

Chapter 1

The Voice of the Drums: The Bear Lincoln Case

Police cars with sirens screaming pulled up alongside the Pier Five Law Offices of famed criminal defense attorney J. Tony Serra, located on the San Francisco Embarcadero. The sirens blended with the even pulse of drums beating inside the office on the evening of August 16, 1995, when Eugene "Bear" Lincoln voluntarily turned himself over to the authorities for the alleged killing of Mendocino Deputy Sheriff Robert Davis. The sirens signaled where Bear was heading; the drums signaled where he came from.

Bear had been hiding out in the wilds of the mountains of Mendocino County for four months eluding a nationwide manhunt and the Sonoma County SWAT helicopter patrols, the FBI, the California Highway Patrol, officers from city, county, and state agencies, freelance posses on horseback, and bounty hunters on dirt bikes eager for the $100,000 reward. He could have disappeared forever into Canada, but he chose to stay and face his day in court, once it was confirmed that J. Tony Serra—the legendary political-cause lawyer who had won a death-penalty acquittal on a retrial for a fellow Native American, Patrick "Hooty" Croy—would take his case.

This trial appears at the beginning of this book, as it represents the conflicting cultures that Tony Serra has spent his life mediating. On the one side is the powerful culture of law and order and its voice of authority: the nearly omnipotent forces of mainstream society protecting the status quo of the haves against the have-nots. On the other side is the impotent culture of the disenfranchised, the dispossessed, and a voice so muted that it can hardly be heard: in this case a Native American whose mere prosecution for the alleged killing an officer was tantamount to conviction. This trial represents the clash between a Native American— a member of society's most maligned outcasts versus officers of the law— society's most highly venerated members.

In the foyer of the Pier 5 law office of Serra, Lichter, Daar, Bustamante, Gilg & Greenberger, police officers, media, lawyers, and tribesmen were gathered to witness the surrender of Eugene "Bear" Lincoln to the authorities.

The 41-year-old Lincoln, accepting his transfer to the officers with inner strength and quiet dignity, made this statement: "I'm coming in to litigate this, because I'm innocent. And the reason I delayed was because I was fearful for my life."

A large poster dominated the room. An upright grizzly bear, its front legs stretched high above its head and bound in handcuffs, was superimposed against the background of a round drumhead with feathers. The text read, "Free the Bear."

With a nod of grateful acknowledgment to his supporters, Bear Lincoln exchanged his hand-sewn ribbon shirt and red-bandana headband with its eagle feather for the orange jail issue. To counteract the officers' protocol for arrests, the Native Americans endowed this critical turning point with *their* protocol of a spiritual rite of passage to empower Bear, their Wylaki tribesman, to persevere in his new life as a member of the U.S. government's penal system on a death-penalty charge.

Tony Serra walked stiffly through the dense crowd, head down, stoop-shouldered, to the central clearing. He wore his long gray hair, usually tied back in a ponytail, loose and free, as a sign of solidarity with the Native Americans in the room. The orange evening light highlighted his high cheekbones, his prominent aquiline nose, and the lines of his deep humanity, giving him the appearance of having Native ancestry.

Addressing the crowd, he seemed to pull in the energy of the room and draw himself up to full size as he spoke vehemently of the egregious injustice that had been committed, confirming Eugene Lincoln's innocence, and vowing his determination to set Bear free. His words felt like spears aimed at close range at the officers of the law. The energy of the room changed as Serra spoke, and the police officers suddenly looked like tin soldiers in the presence of this man of true personal power.

. . .

Bear was locked away behind concrete walls topped with barbed razor wire, iron bars, and iron doors. Although the geographical distance from Bear's people on the Round Valley Indian Reservation in the northeastern corner of Mendocino County wasn't far, prison was a universe removed from the nurturing spirit of nature and Mother Earth. Here, no receptive ground lay beneath his feet, no tangy fragrances of pine woods. There was only the stench of sweat, urine, and disinfectant, only catcalls, curses, and threats. This was a world of hard surfaces, harsh light, and hardened spirits, of deprivation, violence, and revenge. Guards stood by with guns and billy clubs at the ready. The only light was from bare bulbs glaring brightly 24/7, themselves imprisoned in tiny metal cages.

But beyond the prison, the beat of the tribal drum never ceased. Drums beat to gather people for fundraising rallies in cities all over California. Drums beat to welcome people to benefit concerts starring John Trudell, Native poet, musician, film star, and political activist. Drums beat for spiritual gatherings and for purifying sweats. Drums beat to summon the spirits of the ancestors on behalf of their native son. The drums called, and the people came.

. . .

Two and a half years passed before Bear Lincoln's case went to trial. Death-penalty cases take a long time to prepare, even for six active lawyers and six paralegals. Tony and his defense team submitted every possible motion. They went to the Appellate Court. They went to the District Court. They went to the California Supreme Court.

The team worked well together. Though they had different points of view on specific issues, they were all like-minded people. After discussion, they voted and on reaching consensus, they proceeded with one mind. No dysfunction, no infighting, no personality conflicts. No one went home angry. No one dropped out.

Even though Serra himself took the case *pro bono*, the lawyers, paralegals, and witnesses all needed to be paid, as did court fees, travel expenses, and the countless other costs associated with a trial.

The trial took place in Ukiah, in northern California. Too far from San Francisco to commute daily, lodging was an issue. Serra tries to stay with friends whenever possible to cut down on costs. Hesh Kaplan, a supporter of Bear Lincoln, offered to share his house with Serra's team during the long course of the trial. A revolving dozen or so people stayed there. They cooked their meals together and slept in sleeping bags wherever there was space: on beds and couches, on the floor, or outside under the stars. They carpooled to court. They worked and worked and went way beyond the norm in terms of operating well together.

As Tony Serra's courtroom artist for this trial, I was part of the team, so I, too, enjoyed the camaraderie in the communal house. Hesh Kaplan, our host, seemed to enjoy it most of all. When I thanked him for his generous hospitality, he assured me that *he* was the lucky one to have encountered so many extraordinary people and to have been in the position to accommodate them.

Bear Lincoln's Native supporters held rituals in preparation for the trial: gatherings, prayer meetings, sweats, purifications of body and spirit for verbal combat. Native women sewed prayer shirts for Bear to wear in court. They hand-stitched a beautiful deerskin vest, embroidered and beaded on the back with a large circle hoop, symbolizing unity and bear-claw paw prints pointing in the four directions; it was crafted to "protect" Bear against the semantic warfare that occurs in the court.

Tony invited me to attend one of the spiritual gatherings in Round Valley, California's largest Native American reservation. I'd never driven with Tony at the wheel before and I wondered if he drove like he spoke—in elliptical lurches of accelerated passion and unexpected lane changes. I fancied it would be like "Toad's Wild Ride." I wondered if such a risk-taker bothered to wear seat belts. To my relief, Tony was a comfortable driver, mindful of the speed limit and courteous of other cars on the road. His huge old junk Buick, a cherry car in its day, still had its original velvet interior, though mildly trashed. Its vintage preceded the advent of seat belts. He drove it with the kind of patronizing care one would take leading an elderly person across the street.

We traveled with Diana Samuelson, Tony's co-counsel and specialist on death-penalty cases, Bia, one of the six Native American paralegals on the case, and Phil de Jong, the local Ukiah lawyer.

We took Highway 101 north, driving into the night, then onto narrow winding roads that took us backward in time. Just south of Laytonville, we turned onto Highway 162. The sinuous two-lane road snaked through the mountains along Outlet Creek and the Wild Eel River, known by the Natives as the River of Blood.

Bia told us that this name memorialized the slaughter of thousands of Native people by white invaders. According to legend, so many people were killed that the river ran red with the blood of Indians for three days.

Just before the road's final plunge into the valley basin known as Round Valley, we paused for a moment at Inspiration Point to note a historical plaque that read, "This valley was discovered by Frank M. Azbill, arriving from Eden Valley on May 15, 1854," and it listed the area's first Anglo settlers. Bia told us that Azbill ruthlessly killed the first 40 Yuki Indians he encountered. She added that the day the official plaque was installed, local members of the Round Valley Indian Reservation put up a handwritten sign of their own: "A Brief History of the Round Valley Area: 1853-1874. White settlers, instead of bypassing the valley as ordered by D.C., slaughtered 11,600 of 12,000 native people and stole their land." The hand-painted sign may be gone, but history doesn't forget. To this day, a river of animosity runs red with rage between the Native people and the white inhabitants of the valley.

From one green mountain vista to another, the basin measures nine miles across. It is home to the tiny town of Covelo, as well as the Round Valley Indian Reservation. Ironically, since the reservation cannot support its own tribal police, it relies on the local sheriff's department to handle the frequent domestic disputes that flare up. One survey reported that 30% of Round Valley's middle-school students had already had some contact with the criminal-justice system or were on probation. These run-ins with the law deepen the disparities between whites and Natives in this beleaguered region where violence is the only common means known for settling disputes.

. . .

Bear Lincoln had himself been a troubled youth with a history of encounters with law enforcement. Mendocino County court records show that drug and alcohol-related offenses had landed him in county jails at least 20 times in several states by the time he was 25. In 1979, he was convicted on a felony charge for the alleged beating of a two-year-old girl. It was later revealed that he hadn't beaten the child, but took the rap for her mother. In the early 1980s, Bear turned over a new leaf. He embraced not only traditional Native American sources of spirituality for guidance and strength, but also Christian beliefs. He became instrumental in the movement to acquire the Sinkyone Wilderness as the first Native American Park and he took an active role in the park's mission to teach Native American youth about their history and culture. Bear earned the reputation of being a gentle intelligent man with a green thumb.

This shooting situation changed everything.

I'd never experienced the prejudice or deprivation that were ways of life for Bear and his people. So I had difficulty comprehending just how deep and widespread separatism impacted whites and the Natives with attending fears and furies. This fractious reality became immediately apparent upon arriving at our motel in Round Valley's town of Covelo, when Bia, the Native American paralegal who was a young-looking grandmother in her fifties, refused to join us on a short stroll to the local bar. She was terrified to be seen in public with a group of white people. It didn't matter that we were her friends, allies, and colleagues. She knew much more about this town than we did. Tony finally talked her into coming with us by pointing out that she was safer with us than alone in an all-white motel.

Although the bar was less than three blocks from our motel, Bia walked in the shadows as far from the road as possible. I had my arm around her the whole time, shielding her, reassuring her, coaxing her along. As soon as we arrived at the bar, Bia bolted for the back room where Native Americans hung out. It was the equivalent of the back of the bus. She remained there until it was time to go. Later, in our shared motel room, Bia barricaded the door with a large upholstered easy chair and slept out of sight from the window, even though the curtains were pulled. The next morning, she flatly refused to join us for breakfast. Her fear was far stronger than her appetite. She didn't relax until we were safely on the reservation.

For me, the walk to the bar was a refreshing change from sitting for hours in the car. Inside, a clap of stinking air stifled my breath. We took a centrally located table and ordered beers all around. Tony had his usual non-alcoholic O'Doul's.

We were a table of new faces in this town of old racial issues. Tony's broad face and high cheekbones caught the attention of some local punks in this segregated room; his gray hair was a sure sign that he was an easy target for racial confrontation. One of the locals in a tight tank top staggered over to our table, posturing drunken dominance, his sights set on Tony. I wondered how he'd handle this bull of a man who was half his age. Tony simply lowered his gaze so there was no eye contact, then offered the challenger no response. Having been a champion boxer in his day, he probably could have knocked the drunk's lights out in a one-two punch, but instead he withdrew his presence to the point of emanating zero energy.

"Gimme your beer," the guy demanded, his foul breath stinking of cigarettes and bitter brew. Tony quickly pushed the non-alcoholic beer in his direction. The fellow's corded neck and muscled arms were combat-ready; his small eyes blazed with a daring malevolence. He provoked, postured, and challenged, but Tony never even looked up. Finally, the guy just left, all played out.

"What just happened?" I asked Tony, surprised by his total passivity in this confrontation.

"We came very close to having a racial incident, and it could have gotten ugly with all the guy's buddies standing around. I didn't want to create a scene in this town, so it was better to allow him nothing to hook onto. It's a Zen trick I learned in my travels," Tony explained quietly, a residue of his "cloaking device" still apparent.

Round Valley in the daylight is heartbreakingly beautiful. Protected by mountains on all sides of its nine-mile span, its fertile well-tended pasturelands appear to reach into an emerald eternity. Its majestic oak trees are said to be some of the grandest and oldest in the country. White settlers took the fertile heartland, leaving the Indians with the unwanted arid acreage to the north. The valley's beauty sharply contrasted the animosities that charged the town's atmosphere. The toxic waste of racial turmoil tainted this self-contained basin.

Covelo, the only hamlet in Round Valley, possessed a grocery, bank, bar, liquor store, gun shop, motel, and school. There was no apparent form of culture, industry, or entertainment, not even a movie house. The total population was less than 3,500.

About 11 miles beyond the north end of town, we turned off the main road to the entrance to the reservation, where a long lane of gracious oak trees flanked both sides of a dusty rutted dirt road. Tony parked the car in the shade of an oak; we opened the car door and stepped into a different world.

Life on the res is different things to different people. For those who romanticize the Indian image, the reservation is a sanctuary for Native people, a place where they can practice their ways and carry on their lifestyle. For those who know better, the res is a ghetto, a form of confinement without walls for a once-proud people who were overtaken, conquered, plundered, and annihilated. Their land was stolen, their culture pillaged, their language beaten out of them. Children were rended from their families and sent off to the white man's boarding schools where electric-shock treatment was the preferred form of punishment. In short, they were forced-fed the cruelties of a culture they could neither understand nor accept. The res serves the double purpose of keeping the Indians in their place and pacifying the white man's guilt. Out of sight, out of mind. It breeds alcoholism, crime, diabetes, and depression. The great American dream of the Land of Opportunity does not apply to America's Native people.

Their abject poverty was immediately apparent. This was not the well-manicured emerald pastureland of the white farmers on the other side of the valley. Here the land was gray, barren, and poor, etched away by weather right down to its bare hard bones. There were no gardens or productive fields. The shacks were in serious need of repair. Windows were boarded up to keep out the weather; doors hung on half-hinges. The occasional rusted armature of a car resting on its axle near the road where it had been abandoned was a metaphor of the ruin of a discarded life devoid of hope, going nowhere, suitable only as shelter from the relentless sun for the stray dogs.

The vibrations of the drums throbbed through the soles of our shoes; we followed the hypnotic rhythm to an open meadow. The setting was simple enough: a cleared circle of space with a hand-hewn pulpit for the speakers and bales of straw for everyone else. About 40 people were present. The defense team was introduced one at a time to an elder of the tribe, who placed his hand on that person's chest and looked him or her directly in the eyes for a long silent moment to confirm purity of heart. We were the only outsiders at this gathering on the res.

The speakers were mostly women, recounting a litany of injustices perpetrated against their grandfathers, fathers, husbands, sons. These women's faces had been ploughed with hardships. Their ancient eyes had weathered too much suffering, witnessed too many funerals. They each ended by confirming, "We must become stronger; we must endure."

I thought of my own privileged life in a culture where self-betterment, a decent education, career, success, health, happiness, creature comforts, material gain, even wealth were all available to me. Here, the only reward seemed to be the grim determination to survive another incident and endure for another generation. These once-proud and vital people, whose very essence was freedom itself, whose rich cultural imagery appears everywhere as part of the American heritage, were now housed like cattle in holding pens, marking time till death by their own hand: alcohol, drugs, unemployment, rage, despair.

Bear's case was only unusual in that he had a top-notch lawyer and a cracker-jack defense team. As such, he had become an icon for the Indian Rights movement. Tony Serra was introduced as lead counsel on the case. In his speech, Tony insisted that Bear Lincoln had acted in self-defense in the death of Deputy Bob Davis. "*Ho,*" affirmed the entire crowd in unison and three hefty grandmothers came forward to engulf Tony in a big hug. He disappeared into their embrace like one of the family.

By then, dinner, largely provided by the defense team, was ready—hamburger, ribs, salmon, corn, beans, fry bread—and the children ate as if there was no tomorrow. Afterwards, a few of the boys tossed around a football and Tony ran out for a pass. He easily caught the ball with one of his large hands, caressed the grainy pigskin for a brief instant, then tossed back a perfect spiral. Little did the boys know that they'd received a pass from a once-all-star defensive end for Stanford University.

An important part of the agenda was to visit the scene of the shoot-out on Little Valley Ridge. We walked in silence up the dirt road, Tony in the lead, outpacing us all like the athlete he'd once been. One would never guess his age of 60-something, or that he had recently undergone a double hip replacement. Once we reached the junction at the summit where Little Valley Road crossed a thin fire track, Tony and his team reviewed the events of April 14, 1995.

The crime scene itself had been grossly mishandled on the night of the event, and evidence had been destroyed. Ninety-five people reportedly tramped through that scene, in which some 200 rounds of ammunition were fired. The crime-scene photographer quit when his camera ran out of batteries and it started snowing. He didn't bother to record where the bullet casings were located, nor did he triangulate the position of each casing so he could replace them. This was an appallingly unprofessional investigation, considering the number of spent rounds and two deaths.

I sat on an embankment watching intently as Tony and his team consulted sheaves of the evidence. They pantomimed the shoot-out, leveling pretend rifles at one another from various locations. They examined every bush for its potential cover, every tree trunk for tell-tale bullet marks. They measured distances, considered angles. Based on Bear's detailed description, Tony and his team were forming visions of what had transpired. Once this case went to trial, these visions would have to be so clear that a jury would almost perceive that they were witnessing the event happen before their own eyes.

· · ·

There was nothing good about Good Friday on April 14, 1995. That day brought only death, terror, and heartbreak to the Round Valley com-

munity. Age-old intra-tribal rivalries over issues of harassment and tribal roots and values came to a head on that day. The Britton clan and the
Peters and Lincoln families had a long history of being at odds with one
another. The Brittons, though Native, were known as a wannabe white
family with white values who curried favors from white law enforcement, while the Peters-Linclon family adhered to traditional values. An
altercation between Reginald "Gene" Britton and Arlis Peters erupted
into a shoot-out in the parking lot of the Covelo High School. Gene Britton, 48, was fatally shot by Arlis Peters. Peters fled the scene. That much
was indisputable.

Word of the shooting quickly spread throughout the small community of Round Valley and police officers of several agencies were summoned to swarm the reservation in an all-out manhunt for Arlis Peters.

That night, two officers—Deputy Sheriff Dennis Miller, a former
Marine, and Officer Bob Davis, a former Navy Seal commando who had
served in Vietnam, Beirut, and Grenada—staked out a position on a dirt
road along a ridge not far from where Bear Lincoln and his mother Lucille lived in their cabins. Officer Davis was called "Covert Bob" by fellow
deputies, because he enjoyed surveillance and liked to drive around the
reservation at night with his lights out; it was revealed at the trial that
Davis was himself part Indian from an undisclosed region. He always
carried M-16 automatic and 9mm semi-automatic weapons with him. On
this night, the deputy sheriff's 4X4 was parked on a narrow fire track out
of sight from the dirt road leading to the summit where Bear and Acorn
Peters were walking.

The trial revolved around two sharply conflicting versions of what
transpired that night. According to the police report, when the call went
about the shooting of Gene Britton and the escape of Arlis Peters, "Deputies Miller and Davis drove to the ridge top and backed their car off the
road. Davis alerted Miller that someone was coming. Both deputies got
out [of the vehicle], and Davis shined a flashlight on a man carrying a
rifle, and announced loudly three times, 'Sheriff's Department, drop the
gun.' The man shouldered the rifle and fired a shot, and both deputies
opened fire with pistols. The man went down, and it was quiet.

"After a few minutes, the deputies heard sounds in the brush and
thought someone might be preparing to attack them from behind. They

decided to take cover in a climb of small oaks across the road. Davis wanted to check the fallen man to make sure he wasn't playing 'possum.' As Davis bent over the body, Miller saw motion down the road and fired a burst of full-automatic fire from an M-16 assault rifle. Almost simultaneously, he fell over an embankment, rolled on his shoulder and came back up. When he looked up after his fall, Davis's head had been partially blown off. The horrific result of a high-velocity bullet, such as one from an M-16, fired at close range. [Miller] saw more movement down the road and fired another burst."

According to an article in the *Albion Monitor* by Nicholas Wilson, many residents in Round Valley questioned the deputy sheriff's version of events. Neighbors readily reported that "it sounded like a war zone, with heavy automatic weapons fire." Residents listening to police scanners reported they heard a shoot-to-kill order issued when Bear Lincoln became the prime suspect. Within hours, a nationwide alert had identified Bear Lincoln as wanted for murder. Yet he still didn't know he was a marked man.

Deputy Dennis Miller's story changed over the course of his retelling it, each variation attempting to accommodate the facts as they were revealed. Bear's story, in contrast, remained simple and unchanged, from his first recounting at the time he turned himself in, to his last telling of it, in court, under oath, some three years after the event.

· · ·

The day began like any other. Bear Lincoln was sitting out on the porch of his hand-built cabin, drinking coffee on the beautiful spring morning, when his lifelong friend, Leonard "Acorn" Peters, drove up in his small pickup truck. The two buddies often spent the day just hanging out together, tending to kids and horses, taking target practice, and drinking beer. Life on the res wasn't fueled by the hustle-bustle of ambition, but rather by making the most of nothing special going on.

That evening, Bear and Acorn got word that Acorn's brother was wanted for the murder of Gene Britton. They armed themselves with rifles and set out on foot to search for Arlis, whom they feared was in hiding or possibly dead. Acorn and Bear walked cautiously in silence, listening for any unusual sounds that might direct them to the whereabouts of Arlis Peters. Acorn was in the lead. A sudden staccato of machine-gun fire exploded the silent darkness with jagged bright blotches of light. It seemed to come from out of nowhere and everywhere. Acorn, lurching backwards, was fatally shot.

Bear, thinking it was the Brittons shooting at them, returned fire, shooting blindly at the intersection of the ridge and fire roads. With bullets flying all around him, he ran for cover by the side of the road. Jumping over an embankment, Bear scrambled to safety in a nearby creek bed. There he lay in fear of his life, shocked, scared, confused. In the warp of his racing thoughts and pounding heart, he replayed the scene and concluded that the assailants had to be the Brittons. He didn't know how long he remained in the creek bed, bothered the whole time by the thought of his friend Acorn lying there in the road, not knowing if he was alive or dead.

A hat worn by Acorn had belonged to Bear; it was found in the road with a bullet hole through the crown. So the story evolved that Bear had initiated the gun battle, since evidence showed that Acorn's rifle had not been fired that night.

Bear waited till the night relaxed back into silence before venturing to check on Acorn. Back on the road, Bear was still thirty or forty yards from Acorn's body, below the ridge, when the sharp crack of automatic gunfire again illuminated the darkness, showering the road with a hail of bullets. Whoever was shooting was closer to the road than before, closer to the intersection, since Bear could now see the muzzle flashes. Bullets flew by him and he returned fire, shooting from the hip. He didn't have time to aim and he didn't have anything to aim at, so he kept pulling the trigger. Only one round went off before he was out of ammo; then the gun just clicked.

Again, Bear dove for cover. The rain of gunshots ceased as suddenly as it had begun and in the silence, Bear heard what sounded like a man shouting the 10-99 code of a police radio call, reporting that Deputy Sheriff Bob Davis was down, shot in the head. There was no mention of the Indian lying in the road. Once back in the underbrush, Bear ditched his empty rifle as he ran toward his mother's cabin.

Lucille Lincoln, Bear's 65-year-old widowed mother, was at home with family members, including grandchildren, when the shooting took place. She had heard the shots coming from the direction of Bear's cabin. She didn't know who was doing the shooting, but it was close enough to feel the danger; she knew she had to get her family somewhere safe. After loading her grandkids and other family members into the truck, she was about to drive away when Bear came running up the road.

"Get out! Get out! They'll kill us all!" he shouted. "They killed Acorn. They shot him dead for no reason. You better get out of here. They'll come and kill you, too!"

Hyped up with emotion, Bear told his mother not to take the road. Acorn's body was still lying there and he thought it would be safer for them to walk out the back way. But that was unrealistic, considering her age and arthritis and the young children with her.

Remembering his dad's old .303 riffle in his mother's house, Bear grabbed it for protection before running to a friend's house, where he learned for the first time that an officer had been killed. He felt the urgency to tell his story about the ambush on the ridge and the killing of Acorn to as many people as possible before he, too, was killed.

Driving out with her grandchildren, Lucille Lincoln slammed on the brakes of her truck when her headlights suddenly illuminated the body of Acorn lying across the road. Equally suddenly, in the darkness of that night, she was caught in a blinding spotlight. Loud male voices shouted at her, "Turn your fucking lights off or we'll blow your fucking head off!" One of the men shouted, "We'll jam the gun up your ass and pull the trigger!" These same men, highway patrolmen, ordered her out of her truck, then dragged her along the road, past the body of Acorn, where they threw her face-down into a muddy ditch. A patrolman handcuffed her while pressing his boot on her neck.

Mrs. Lincoln and her grandchildren were hauled to a makeshift command post in the valley, where they were questioned and eventually released. Lucille then drove to her sister's house, where she found Bear in the back room, writing out his will, a letter to his girlfriend leaving her two of his horses. His mother took the letter as Bear lit out for the hills. She didn't know where he was going or if she'd ever see her son again.

Residents of the reservation issued a news release within a few days saying they had been "living in a state of terror at the hands of the Mendocino County police." According to tribal council member Ron Lincoln, a relative of Bear Lincoln, "They've roughed up our elders and put guns to our children's heads."

Representatives from Round Valley went to the Mendocino County Board of Supervisors to seek relief from law-enforcement harassment. Their complaint acknowledged, a meeting was called to allow residents a forum in which to air their grievances—or so they were told. Instead, the meeting proved to be a grandstand for angry law-enforcement supporters.

In the end, reservation residents were convinced that "gross racism" had culminated in a cover-up of the deaths of Acorn Peters and Bob Davis that would never be penetrated.

. . .

Bear Lincoln became an icon for Indian rights. The gravity of the death penalty rallied indigenous people throughout America and supporters as far away as Europe. The tribal community was present every day in the courthouse, even through the 3,800 people polled during three long months of jury selection. And this wasn't easy for them. The Round Valley Reservation was a good 90 minutes away and transportation was scarce. Many people hitchhiked, standing out on the road well before dawn in order to attend the 8 a.m. lottery drawing for the few available seats in the tiny 35-seat courtroom. Some people camped out in Coyote Valley, an Indian encampment area 20 minutes away. When it rained, they came to court in their wet clothes. Most people were not afforded seating in the courtroom, but they came anyway. Elders leaning on canes limped up the two flights of stairs. Some showed up in wheelchairs. Entire families, including young children, arrived. Supporters were everywhere—out in the hallway, down the steps, and all the way out to the courthouse lawn. Drumming, rallies, and vigils accompanied this case from its inception to its end.

The courthouse had a huge painted mural that spanned two floors: the portrait of an Indian. I found it ironic that although the face of a Native is minted on some American coins, they remain among the poorest people in this rich country. The poverty of the *real* Indians in this courthouse was sickening, heartbreaking, in contrast to the honor and respect implied in the mural. Americans revere their idealization of the Native American, but disregard the reality.

A lunch table was set up every day outside the courthouse, paid for by the defense fund. It provided simple sandwich makings such as bread, peanut butter and jelly, along with cheese and crackers and soda.

The sacred deerskin vest was worn by Bear in court. Special prayers were sewn into the vest and at the end of each day of the trial, the vest was placed in the hands of the women. Every night, it was purified of the day's courtroom anxieties and refreshed with the energies of nature, the night, and the moon. Ribbon prayer shirts were hand-sewn by a relative to empower Bear throughout his courtroom ordeal. Every morning in court, Tony assisted Bear in slipping on the vest, arranging his long wavy black hair, followed by a reassuring pat on his back. It was a small silent gesture, but it confirmed the solidarity between Bear's tribe and his lawyer.

On the stand, Tony Serra questioned his client. He led Bear through the day, hearing about Gene Britton getting shot by Arlis Peters, walking in the dark up the road, shots ringing out, and Acorn Peters falling.

"What did you do then?" Serra asked in his direct examination.

"I chambered a round in my gun and I returned fire," Bear answered.

"What did you think then? What was in your mind?" Serra asked.

"Well, I thought it was the Brittons who were hiding up there and that they had ambushed Acorn and killed him."

"And when you said you returned fire, where did you shoot? At what did you shoot?"

"I just fired toward the intersection. I didn't have a target. I just fired."

"Did you see a police car? Did you fire at a police car?"

"No."

"Did you see two sheriffs there? Did you fire at a sheriff?"

"No, I didn't."

"Did you fire from a fixed position?"

"No, I ran toward the edge of the road; I was firing as I went."

"Firing at what while you moved?" Serra continued on direct.

"Just firing in the dark. I didn't have a target; I couldn't see anything," Bear replied.

"Hit anything?"

"I couldn't tell."

"Why'd you fire?"

"To make whoever was firing to stop, or ... I don't know ... a reaction."

"Seeing Acorn shot by a barrage of bullets in front of you, did you then believe that your life was in peril?"

"Yes!"

"Why?"

"Well, because there was a lot of bullets going off, and I was standing right there in the open, in the middle of the road, and I figured I was going to be shot next," Bear stated gravely. "I assumed that I was going to be killed, too."

"Why did you believe you'd be killed?"

"Well, because they shot him [Acorn] down for no reason, and I couldn't think of any reason why they would spare me ... and then hearing that the officer was killed, I just assumed that I was going to be killed, too."

"Did you ever tell them or anyone to this point that you had killed an officer?"

"No, I didn't."

"Did you believe then that you had killed an officer?" Serra asked.

"No, I didn't."

"Do you believe *now* that you killed an officer?"

"No, I don't."

"We call Lucille Lincoln to the stand," announced Tony Serra. As Bear Lincoln's mother rose to take the stand, the jury seemed taken aback by how small she was, how crippled by arthritis, as she limped to the witness stand with the aid of her cane. She bore a striking resemblance to her son Bear, the eldest of her seven children.

Lucille Lincoln answered each question directly and with simple modest dignity. She made no pretense about who she was or was not. Her straightforward guileless countenance clearly impacted the jury as she told of large officers behaving like vicious brutes in their treatment of her, a diminutive, elderly, arthritic woman. Lucille's description of the state troopers roughing her up sent a perceptible shudder through the courtroom.

. . .

On the day of closing arguments, people jammed the courthouse even earlier and in greater numbers than on any preceding day of the trial. The limited lottery tickets were all gone by 7:30 a.m.

District Attorney Aaron Williams was the first to give his closing argument. He mostly leveled sweeping condemnations of Bear Lincoln and his dignified mother. "Eugene Bear Lincoln is an evil liar who triggered a gun battle with sheriff's deputies, fled for cover, and then returned a few minutes later to kill one of them in cold blood," he said. Insisting that manslaughter was too light a verdict, an overconfident Williams gave the jury an ultimatum: Either find Bear Lincoln guilty of first-degree murder or return him, a free man, to the reservation.

Williams brashly minimized the task of the jury, stating, "There were two starkly different stories, and that makes it easy for you." The *Anderson Valley Advertiser* later commented, "There are more than two starkly different stories from the police side *alone*."

Next, Williams launched into a degrading attack on Lucille Lincoln's character. Freely misquoting her, he pushed things too far. The grandmother rose from her seat and boldly retaliated, "I never said that, Aaron!" She purposely called him by his first name in disrespect for his status in the courtroom. When the judge gave her the choice of sitting down and remaining silent or leaving the courtroom, she grabbed her cane and limped right out of the courtroom in tears, shouting over her shoulder as she left, "You're a big liar, Aaron!"

Little did this angry grandmother know that, by doing so, she was making history for her people. No other gesture could have made a more powerful refutation of Williams's falsehoods. She'd attended every day of her son's trial. She'd been present for every hearing over the two and a half years. And now, for closing arguments—the climax of it all—she stalked out of court in a tearful rage. For her to walk out of court and miss this moment was like spitting directly in Aaron Williams's face.

The jury felt it, the spectators felt it, Bear Lincoln felt it, and Tony Serra felt it.

After Lucille Lincoln's dramatic exit, Aaron Williams closed suddenly, abruptly, as if the wind had been knocked out of him. Forty-five minutes were left in the day's schedule.

Judge John Golden asked the jury for a show of hands of anyone who wanted to quit and go home at this time. No hands were raised. Jury members just sat there looking at one another. Then he asked for a show of hands indicating who wanted Serra to begin his closing argument for the remaining forty-five minutes. It was unanimous. Tony Serra would have the last word of the day.

As Aaron Williams had slogged through the litany of his closing argument, Tony Serra remained statue-still at the defense table, his silence punctuating the prosecutor's numerous bold-faced lies. Each one hit a nerve of rage in him, but the insult to Lucille Lincoln penetrated to his core. He could feel the lava starting to rise, its heat infusing his whole being. The blood pulsed powerfully in his veins. A lust for justice burned like fire inside him, burned like abandon, burned like a cleansing. He felt the clarity of divine wrath. He felt its force, and he contained it.

Everyone was weary and spent from the heat and the long intense afternoon. The air in the overcrowded room was stale and used up, like in an airplane cabin after a long flight. I wondered how on earth Tony could revitalize this wilted crowd with so little time left.

The courtroom fell silent as he rose and walked, without notes, to the podium in a slow deliberate stride, his head lowered in the posture of an angry bull about to toss the taunting matador onto its horns.

He began by acknowledging the judge and jurors, thanking the judge for a fair trial and the jurors for their patient attention. He had Bear stand up to face the jury at close range. Bear looked directly at the members of the jury and said simply, "Thank you." Then Tony Serra restated, "Every word Bear has testified is true."

Bear sat down and J. Tony Serra squared up for the first big strike against Aaron Williams's argument. His voice had the components of lightning. The first bolt struck the jury full force from close range. "All of this extravagant B.S. is just *falsity* about my client!" Serra raged.

Faces turned toward one another in expressions of disbelief that Serra would deign to allude to the District Attorney's argument as extravagant *bullshit.* Everyone felt the jolt. The room was his. He had plunged the silver stake into the heart of the prosecution's case. Now it was just a matter of watching the life drain out of it like sunlight on a vampire. Serra then proceeded to dismantle, limb by limb, fact by fact, beyond all doubt, the flimsy façade of the prosecution's argument.

At one point in his closing argument, he was grasping out with his hand to the jury to get his point across. I saw this gesture to be that of a bear clawing out a statement. I did an art piece of this vision that is part Serra, part bear, with the bear superimposed in the background in the same clawing gesture as Serra. Then I did another drawing of Serra enraged, his long arms outstretched in an elliptical shape, framing the faces of cunning and deceit that he portrayed in the officers. The arms and hands take on a form of an open trap. A stoic portrait of Bear Lincoln rises above the faces of deceit, dominating the picture. The expression on Bear's face is one of steadfastness, staring off into the distance, as if to hold the vision of his innocence. The *Willits News* gave this art a full half of its front page, a daring breakthrough for unconventional courtroom art.

Serra's rage was now erupting in clear and devastating accusations. "What you've been treated to here is a lot of speculation and supposition by a prosecutor. All of his rhetoric and all of his invective and all of his many ways of twisting the testimony you heard do not detract from the fact that my client took the stand ... and he told you the *truth.*"

The tone of Serra's voice was loud and penetrating. "Officer Miller has borne false witness to extricate himself from his involvement in an alleged police cover-up involving authorities in Mendocino and Sonoma counties, the California Highway Patrol, and the FBI." He then pointed his finger at Miller and stated accusingly, "Miller has lied to you. Miller has falsified. Knowing that he has been caught in a cover-up, in a lie, he says, 'Oh, my memory came back to me.'" Here Serra pantomimed Miller, shuffling his feet, cowering, covering his mouth, looking with an expression of crafty innocence, like a child caught in a whopper. "It wasn't a *recovered* memory, but a *changed* memory!"

Serra spoke about the mishandled crime scene, moving Acorn's body, repositioning his rifle. "That's fabricating!" Serra yelled. "That is conspiracy to fabricate! That is premeditated fabrication! That isn't wholesome and is not right!"

Then Serra went into the subject of a cover-up, referring to the cut tree. "That's what gives rise, ladies and gentlemen of the jury, to a defense accusation from the inception that there has been a cover-up. Doggone it, if a piece of tree had some kind of an impact on the evidence, they wouldn't have taken it unless there was a reason. I infer it had a bullet in it, or something of evidentiary significance. And then they don't present it. They don't discover it—you never see it again. That's more than incompetence; that's purposeful. That's designed to suppress, to exempt evidence from ultimate consideration by you, the triers of the fact and us."

Now Serra moved in close to the jury to implore them for justice. "And so, we cry out to you, ladies and gentlemen of the jury. We're crying out here for justice, for what's right, what's moral, what's good, what's true. You know, you have to believe that a jury trial is a truth-seeking process, and if the truth-seeking process is predicated ultimately on corrupt and inadequate uncertainties that have been built into the case by the incompetence of the officer assigned to the task, then you have to punish them for that. That's *reasonable doubt!*"

Tony Serra's five-and-a-half-hour closing summation ran over a period of two days and was carried live on local public radio. All that remained of Williams's case by the time Serra was through with it was a pile of lifeless words, like dry leaves after the fall.

"Tony Serra was like a tidal wave that washed away Aaron Williams's mound of bullshit," courtroom observer Karen Picket told the *Albion Monitor*. This was what great litigation was all about.

"'My god! He's spitting in my face! He's right in front of me!'" exclaimed one of the jurors later, about Serra's closing argument. "You could just see her wishing he would back off or tone it down," recounted juror Doreen Burdick in her interview for the *New Settler*. She went on to say, "And there were jokes. There was an older woman on the panel, an alternate, whose hearing was not too good, who would say, 'Maybe you could get Mr. Serra to speak up?' And the judge would blanch and go, 'Don't say that. We don't want to get him riled up again,' because he goes onto this long calm, almost like a snake toying with something. He gets into this hushed way of talking. It makes you listen more, because you wonder what he is building up to, when he is going to become un-glued again. I was enthralled. I was elated by him! Here is this guy who is so flamboyant and all over the place, who wants *feeling* from you, who wants to get something from you. At first, I thought *leave me alone*, but by the end, I was really teary and emotional throughout his whole clos-ing argument because it was such a release of *my* anger and frustration. He doesn't just say what you expect. He, like, lunges on these words and comes up with something inflammatory, but if you think about it, it's true. For me, it was exciting. He was so impassioned."

The jury, after two-and-a-half days of deliberation, announced that it had reached its verdict. When the two-hour advance notice that a ver-dict had been reached was announced, people swarmed the courthouse like metal filings to a magnet. The Ukiah sheriff's department, expecting a guilty verdict, encircled the courthouse with riot-gear-equipped SWAT teams to handle the anticipated mayhem. Groups of Native Americans mingled with mobs of officers heavily armed with guns and billy clubs and tear gas in what looked like a modern-day circling the wagons. An ambulance was parked nearby. A canine unit was stationed at the rear of the courthouse. Undercover officers with long riot sticks on their belts tried to act nonchalant as they entered via the back door. Other under-cover agents, too prim and perfectly attired, mingled in the crowd and lounged in storefronts bordering the courthouse, trying to blend in, but looking more like mannequins than ordinary folk.

I made my way through this war zone to re-enter the courtroom, filing through a high-security metal detector and a phalanx of armed deputies. Inside, the corridors of the courthouse were also thick with riot-ready SWAT officers. I wondered if the police misconduct around which this trial centered was now going to be re-enacted for us, *live*.

Tony Serra, commenting on this demonstration of excessive force at a news gathering said, "Why was their SWAT team surrounding the courthouse? What does the SWAT team do? The SWAT team swats! They normally swat with weapons. They normally shoot. Did any of the Indians come armed? Were there armed supporters parading around the court? Was there some indication there was going to be violence? Abso-lutely not! All of our supporters, all of them, were pledged to utter peaceful demonstration, to utter non-violence. There was never any threat whatsoever that there would be violence.

"Bear Lincoln said, 'They could open the transportation vehicle and I would stay there. They could take my handcuffs off and I would stay there. They could take my leg irons off and I would stay there.' He knew they wanted him to run, to seek some kind of escape, so they could shoot him in the back. And the SWAT team was at the ready, just like Miller and Davis were at the ready that night, so that if something happened, they could shoot and, in this instance, they would be shooting unarmed supporters.

"There was no necessity for the SWAT team, and it's just another manifestation of the overzealous law enforcement that caused this situation, that charged this situation, that covered up this situation. Ultimately, they wanted to throw more oil on the fire if verdicts resulted in any kind of a public demonstration."

The courtroom was filled beyond capacity. Officers of the court added folding chairs wherever possible to accommodate the extra media and reporters. For the first time since the trial began, Judge Golden allowed in a TV camera and still photographer. As the appointed hour approached, the tension was such that even whispers and throat clearings had ceased. The only audible sound was the rhythmic beat of the drum outside the courthouse.

Tony Serra and the defense team took their places next to Bear Lincoln. They stared intently at the jurors, who were filing solemnly to their seats, trying to read beyond the deadpan expressions on their faces.

"No emotional display will be tolerated in the courtroom," admonished Judge Golden. The uncomfortable tension tightened a notch. "Have you reached a verdict?" the judge asked.

"We have, Your Honor," replied the jury foreman.

The foreman handed a piece of folded paper to the bailiff, who passed it on to the judge. The judge opened the folded paper, frowned, twitched an eyebrow, refolded the paper, and returned it to the bailiff, who returned it to the foreman.

"What say ye?" the judge asked. Standing tall, head high, the foreman held out the paper at eye level and in a loud clear voice read the verdict: "Not guilty!"

Tony Serra and Bear Lincoln and the defense team looked at one another with a flood of radiance on their faces that said it all.

The "not guilty" verdict echoed seven times for the first seven counts of the indictment.

On the eighth indictment, the manslaughter charge, the jury hung, ten to two, in favor of not guilty. (It would be another six months for the manslaughter charge to be dropped, thus freeing Bear of all charges.) By the last call, the supporters of Bear Lincoln were already choking in tears.

"SILENCE!" bellowed Judge John Golden, as mass relief and a spontaneous outpour of jubilation threatened to disrupt the pristine order of his court. This was to be his last trial before his retirement. It was a landmark case with a verdict that made history and he didn't want any rogue behavior to ruin the propriety of his ordered domain in its final moment.

In the midst of muzzled joy, we had to sit through another legal ambush that threatened Bear's immediate release. Members of the defense team scrambled to meet the large bond required to keep him from further imprisonment, since manslaughter was still hanging over his head. The defense team presumed that the sheriff's department was vindictively running interference in order to keep Bear locked up one more night—feared by some to be a plot on the part of the embittered deputies in order for Bear to encounter an unfortunate "accident."

Finally, Serra's defense team was successful in raising the bond and the judge released everyone, with the admonition that the gag order remained in effect until the matter of bail reduction and the manslaughter charges were resolved.

We couldn't wait to get out of that courtroom. The need to shout out loud for joy and hug one another was overwhelming. The cheers that erupted outside the courthouse bore no anger. The SWAT team stood its ground, still frowning, all dressed up at the ready with nothing to do.

Bounding down the front steps of the courthouse with a smile that covered his entire face, Tony Serra raised his upturned thumb on high to the cheers of the awaiting crowd below. The honking of car horns added to the joyous clamor.

Asked how he felt, Serra replied, "Somewhere between gagged and ecstatic!" Bear Lincoln, garbed in his prayer shirt, exited the courthouse slowly, relishing this moment, as if his feet were experiencing freedom one step at a time. He walked in his proud but humble manner halfway down the long fan of steps, pausing briefly to address the assemblage. He was completely at ease—composed, open, and direct in thought and in speech. His main attribute was his innocence; it manifested both at trial and in the thoughts he shared with his audience.

In so many words, Bear said, "We abhor violence. We want peace. We praise the justice this system has finally given us."

Cora Lee, a spokeswoman for the Round Valley Reservation, opened a press conference at a later date saying, "Gone are the days when a dollar would pay for an Indian scalp; gone are the days when our babies were put on a post beside the fire and hung until they were dead; gone are the days, Pete Wilson [then governor of California]: Your $100,000 reward has been no good. We have proven that we can work together, we can love together, we can make change together. We did it all, you people—look at the colors of multi-racial supporters, how beautiful! We can make the change!"

Tony Serra said, "The death penalty was sought purely as revenge and retribution by law enforcement. The officers on duty couldn't find Bear to kill him that fateful night of April 14, 1995, so they took a second opportunity to get him by imposing the death penalty in the trial. They hoped that the overwhelming white population of the small town of Ukiah would join in their vindictive lust for vengeance.

"This was a case where the legal team, including the defendant, had been 'gagged' by court order," Serra continued. "We let the drums do our speaking. We were silent, but the voices of the drums were large."

Bear Lincoln loomed over us throughout the trial. He was like a Buddha. His strength was in his bearing, his dignity, his candor, in the directness of his manner, the sanctity of his carriage. He came out a shining knight.

"This was an Indian-cause case replete with prayer, vigil, drum beating, white-smoke purification ceremonies, fasting, and Indian children with their innocent glowing eyes fixed on the courthouse," Tony Serra said. "I softly cried inside whenever the drums began to beat. The sound permeated the entire courthouse. It reached into the courthouse jail cell where Bear was being held. It went deep into the conscience of the jury."

After the trial was over, several of the jurors joined hands with our prayer gathering, along with dozens of whites, dozens of trial watchers, dozens of civil libertarians, dozens of journalists. The circle was huge. The drum beat in the center of the circle in front of the courthouse steps. Amidst tears of joy and tremendous applause, Bear Lincoln stepped down off the last of the courthouse steps and, as a free man, rejoined his people.

. . .

Repercussions of the case included Aaron Williams's resignation as District Attorney for Mendocino County. District Attorney Susan Massini, who had vowed to retry the Lincoln case, was voted out of office. Sheriff James Tuso, who went on the offensive after having a deputy killed for the first time in nearly 50 years, didn't run for reelection. His successor Tony Craver, it was reported, opened a dialogue to repair relations with residents of the Round Valley Reservation. Cora Lee Simmons of Round Valley Indians for Justice told *Mother Jones* magazine, "We're being treated by police a little bit better. And the elders say that we've made history."

Mother Jones also reported that Leota Card, tribal historian on the Round Valley Reservation, said, "Bear's acquittal gave the community something that has been missing since the last of the tribes was forced into this beautiful cruel valley. It gave a lot of people hope."

Juror Ron Norfolk told *Mother Jones*, "My whole attitude, from the beginning, totally turned around." The 50-year-old disabled logger and self-described hermit had been ready to hang Bear Lincoln himself if he was guilty. "You sit there and you watch this story unfold. And you want to believe that a cop is the guy to put your trust in. But they started changing their stories to fit the circumstances, and then they just started lying! I think they just assumed that everybody would believe their story simply because they're cops and the Indians don't matter anyway. When Bear Lincoln took the stand in his own defense, he made a convincing witness. Lincoln didn't try to pretend he *couldn't* have shot Davis. He admitted firing back in self-defense. He wasn't nervous. And he believed in his heart that, white or not, we would find the truth." Norfolk eventually came to feel that even if Lincoln did shoot Bob Davis, he did so in self-defense, believing he was under attack by the Brittons. Further, he'd run from the police because everything in his personal experience and that of his people told him that to surrender was to commit suicide.

Juror Dorene Burdick later described the impact of Lucille Lincoln's testimony on the jury: They were all outraged. "Every time they went through the abusive way [Mrs. Lincoln's arrest] was handled, we all fell apart." Though the prosecution attempted to defend the police tactics—believing Arlis might be in the vehicle, armed, justified the use of force—Burdick explained how this only increased the jury's skepticism, since the deputies had already testified they thought they had shot Arlis dead. Moreover, once the officers saw they were dealing with a small elderly woman, Burdick questioned why they didn't relent and soften their handling of her. "Did they have to drag this little woman in her sixties out onto the ground?" Burdick demanded, noting with wry humor that it was precisely because of their foul cursing and rough handling that Lucille Lincoln realized she was being assaulted by sheriffs. As Burdick commented, "Who else would talk like that? That's how the sheriffs act."

"The beauty of the Bear Lincoln case," Tony Serra concluded at the time, "was the dream of the Native American fulfilled. The dream of justice that's not administered on the basis of race or color or religion, but that comes from fair and universally applied law, reason and impartiality. This has been the craving of the Native American from the earliest days: Just to be treated *fairly* by the dominant white population. This was the dream of Bear Lincoln, this was the dream of his mother Lucille, this was the defense lawyer's dream, and of the defense team. And the all-white jury came through. The not-guilty verdict was, for members of the reservation, a mandate from the spiritual side of their existence. It was their ancestors speaking through them to the white population, once again asking for the justice that historically has eluded them."

Several years later, Serra had a far more somber—and saddened—view of the Bear Lincoln trial. "The joy of victory was short-lived for me. The longer-term outcome was that instead of good feelings and happy postcards of remembrance ever after, my phone never stopped ringing for the plight of Native Americans. Indians charged with serious cases wanted me to work my magic for *them*. Some were horrible cases, with no political or social redemption. I was filled with a terrible sadness of the inevitable plight of Native Americans in the white culture. I saw that so many people were perishing out there, unable to make the transition from Native to urban life, caught in the web of frustration, despair, and crime. They pleaded for my *pro bono* magic. And I felt the ultimate despair of inadequacy, of not being able to give them what they needed, of not being able to take on their dire burden, of not being able to reach that far. So instead of the victory of the Bear Lincoln case filling me with strength, it weakened me. I felt like I had stepped into quicksand. The ultimate outcome was greater pain and suffering.

"Still, the case cast new hope for Native Americans charged with crimes targeted by racism. Native Americans never trusted the white-man's legal system, and this victory for the Indian helped open that door, to some degree. Indians always believed that justice meant 'just us,' in favor of the white race only. They believed that if the police didn't kill you with bullets, that the courts would kill you by imprisoning you for life. They viewed white-man's court like 'it was a good day to die.' Now there was a spark of hope. The outcome of the Bear Lincoln trial was that it helped to heal the breach between Native Americans and the law."

Chapter 2

A True Believer

"I order you to divulge the names of the people involved in this crime!" the judge commanded. "If you don't tell the court their names, I will sentence you to prison."

The defendant was a young woman, being crushed under the wheels of the justice system and a crime syndicate.

"If I rat," she sputtered, crying uncontrollably, "they'll kill me. I'll get out of prison sooner than I'll get out of the grave."

This is great stuff, I thought, as my pen raced over the pad of 11-by-14-inch paper on my knees to capture the moment in art. It was my first trial as a courtroom artist and just by dumb luck, I'd landed a good case. My senses were heightened. I was possessed with an urgency and alertness I'd never before associated with art. These moments were few and far between and when they happened, the artist had to be ready. The drawing had to tell the story at a glance: the defendant, the judge, the lawyers, indications of the jury, the American flag, the seal of the state on the wall, the microphones, and any other pertinent detail, such as evidence or images on a screen, or the pitcher of water for the judge, or the architecture of the room. Observers had to feel that they were present at that moment.

I'd never done art like this before. I'd never had to meet the time crunch of TV deadlines twice a day. Courtroom art was a form of life drawing, but the models were fully clothed and in constant motion. I had to develop the ability to freeze-stop the image in my mind and hold it long enough to translate it onto the page on my lap. The suits had to be the right color, the hair had to correspond with the subject in question, an ability for portraiture was essential.

Courtroom artists working for the media are expected to have three pieces of camera-ready art twice a day for the noon and evening news. It's extremely demanding. Artists don't have time for coffee breaks, for lunch, not even for the bathroom. They just paint as fast as they can. The courtroom artist is like being a simultaneous translator, except with visuals, in color, and sometimes in multiple courtrooms in one day. It's a special kind of discipline involving single-mindedness and speed.

In 1991, I was a rookie courtroom artist. I didn't know one lawyer from another and didn't even know I wanted to tell them apart. I was looking for drama and it didn't matter who delivered it.

On this, my first case, I mentioned my quest for excitement and grandiloquence to a lawyer who told me, "The man you want to draw is J. Tony Serra. There's no one like him. He's brilliant, perceptive, masterful, hard-hitting, and outrageous. He wears funky old clothes from the thrift. He speaks without notes. He's the law and drama at their very best."

It took me a year to hone my skills to the extent that I was confident of taking on the likes of Tony Serra.

When I caught up with him a year later, I was electrified by what I saw. I was expecting an unreconstructed hippie lawyer strutting around in ill-fitting clothes spouting pomposities. I was not expecting a magnificently eloquent, earthy, passionate lion in a Mickey Mouse tie whose roar in the courtroom was archetypal energy itself. I asked myself, who is this wizard behind all that thunder and smoke, whose magic is to create a new order out of chaos and confusion?

I asked myself, how could my drawings possibly convey that?

I stalked him out of the courtroom and into a phone booth. He was placing a call to his secretary about a big heroin bust in Hawaii. When he was done, I blocked his escape and introduced myself.

Standing right in front of him, I was taken aback by his size. Everything about him seemed huge, or was it that his presence diminished everyone else? His stature, his arms, his hands, the size of his head, his voice, his ego—his force-field was heady. He bent down to shake my hand. The deafening pounding of my heart signaled to me that this was a now-or-never moment. The sea of possibilities had momentarily parted and the waves were arched in expectancy. I didn't hesitate to exercise boldness. I told him I was a courtroom artist and, referring to the Hawaii bust, I blurted out, "Take me with you."

Time stood still for an instant as we exchanged hard eye-contact. Then, with a condescending smile that flashed his gold front tooth, he shook my hand and blew me off.

It was a cruel beginning, but I refused to be vanished like an object in a magic trick. Serra grossly underestimated me. My determination to be his artist had taken seed. Courtroom artists are many, but in my opinion, none had done him justice. I needed to come up with a style that nailed his energy in court. My art had to have the same magnetism that he projected with his voice. It had to draw the viewer in. What took him hours to project to a jury in words, I had to convey to the viewer in an instant. I had to sense his energy as though it were my own. What did it feel like to rage like that? Where was his center of focus? In order to make him more than one-dimensional, I needed to know my subject.

I questioned why a man gifted with such a brilliant mind would limit himself to the criminal element? Was he like some mythological creature that fed off criminal acts to purge society of its dregs? Or was this a lifestyle that fueled his own rebel spirit?

I also questioned, certainly, my motives. Why was I, with my cultured background and refined education, attracted to this realm of the dark side?

In answering my own question, I came to recognize that my life had always been in keeping with what was considered "socially acceptable." It'd been lived in avoidance of the raw, the ugly, the brutal. But if I were to get down to the essence in a man as complex and paradoxical as J. Tony Serra, I had to explore the underbelly, the underworld, the depths, the daring, and the muck of the human condition. Serra and his clients would be my guide into this world that was completely foreign to me.

And so I started down the path of capturing the paradoxical energy of J. Tony Serra and putting it into concrete form on paper, both in words and illustrations.

My career as a courtroom artist has taken me into many courtrooms with many lawyers, all the way to the U.S. Supreme Court. But, as I was told on that very first day, no one can hold a candle to Serra. He's the law and drama at its best.

As my notebook filled with sketches of Serra in action, I realized that it wasn't just a matter of drawing what my eyes saw; I had to draw what my extra senses perceived. I had to translate the visceral into the visual. I knew that one image of Serra would never do, because he was so kinetic. The art had to show him in action; it had to emit his intensity. It had to convey his eloquence, his passion and compassion, his soul. The drawings had to voice his outcry. It had to scream his fury. The courtroom art I'd seen was static in its form. I studied Daumier's art for expressiveness and drama; I pored over comic-book art for movement and perspective. Eventually, the artistic style represented by the images in this book came into being. It's as unique to courtroom art as Serra's lawyering is unique to the law.

．　．　．

This book began as my naïve, simple, and whole-hearted attempt to describe an eccentric radical lawyer who caught my artist's eye.

I began like a hound with my nose to the ground, baying on the scent of something big and indefinable. The closer I got to the essence of Tony Serra, the more I became enmeshed in the tangle of complexities and contradictions that comprise human nature itself. His character qualities extend from the most laudable to the most infuriating and banal. It is precisely his range—like a great singer whose voice touches the highest and the lowest spectrum of notes on the scale—that makes him such an intriguing character and makes his law so far-reaching.

We finally met for coffee in a courtroom cafeteria, one on one. When we first had real eye contact—as opposed to all the hit-and-run glances of passing in hallways—I perceived the great depth of his soul. In the quality of largeness that surrounds him I experienced a new sense of dimension, similar to standing on a power spot. His force field went right to my head and my heart. I felt an immediate familiarity with him.

I couldn't determine his age. His exuberance was youthful, but his wisdom and long white hair were as timeless as Zeus. His wide face, with the high Slavic cheekbones and finely chiseled aquiline nose, was a strangely handsome combination. His eyes had the piercing intensity of a jungle cat, the cognac warmth of a Mediterranean smile, and the ferocity of a Cossack in battle. He looked like someone from everywhere.

His immediate easy presence was totally disarming. The wink of his gold front tooth was a sign that he understood the theater of the absurd, and that laughter—at his own stories—was soon to follow. He seemed to be carried away by the fascination of his own cascading energy that assumed a life of its own as soon as he had an audience. His expressive voice and silver-tongued use of language switched with the facility of a fiddler's bow from highbrow to lowbrow, from legalese to prison jargon, from street talk and hip talk to just plain joy-of-language talk. He was a bard, a poet, a gangster, a bit of every man. His gestures said as much as his words. I don't recall a word of the conversation, only that Serra did all the talking and that I was totally spellbound in the comfort of his presence.

He surely had me pegged, but I didn't care. My courage was moth-like; I was too mesmerized to notice my wings singeing at the edge of his flame. I was one on one with a legend who moved mountains in court, who captivated jurors around the country. Native Americans identified with his earthiness, people of foreign cultures related to his worldliness, hippies shared his philosophy, intellectuals admired his intelligence, street people felt his compassion. Criminals considered him a soul brother.

I wondered what kind of person inhabited this cloak of charisma. Who was this magnet to whom so many metal filings were attracted and, certainly, repelled? Who was this lawyer who harbored such disdain for lawyers, but engendered respect from judges, his co-workers, and opponents alike? Did his outrage in court extend beyond the bar into his personal life? I was totaly spellbound as his audience of one.

· · ·

37

In those beginning years, my determination to know more about Serra was an irritation for everyone concerned. His secretarial staff flicked me off at every opportunity and Tony himself didn't take me seriously. I was treated like a meddlesome mosquito that keeps circling. My persistence was more real to him than I was. After a year of weekly phone calls to the office, it was impossible to ignore me. This mosquito didn't go away, so finally Tony invited me to accompany him on a trip to Fresno for a hearing. The long drive would give us an opportunity to have some time to know each other.

We drove with Christina Dalton, Serra's co-counsel in his Benevito case. I had been laid up sick with the flu. The night before the trip I had run a fever, but I was determined to heal by dawn to make the trip. It was mind over virus. Sure enough, by the time the alarm went off at 5 a.m., my symptoms were gone and I was heading down the long coastal drive to Serra's office, some 50 miles away. The drive to his office was an hour. The drive to the court south of Fresno was another four hours. Round trip, that totaled a lot of road and a long day. Once we were under way, Tony put on some Grateful Dead music full volume and disappeared into his own reverie, his head bobbing to the rhythms in an invisible snake dance that he was experiencing internally. I didn't know how to break into this deafening beat to begin conversation with this mythological man in the seat in front of me. I felt I was being tested at every level and I didn't want to come away with a bad grade. It wasn't until he had played out all his Dead cassettes and we had entered that forsaken stretch of land that is barren of beauty that conversation began.

· · ·

What gene pool creates such a character? Tony Serra is the descendant of minorities all the way from Russia to the Balearic Islands to Australia to the USA. His birth on December 30, 1934, in the depth of winter and the cusp of a new year, in and of itself symbolizes the dark time of the year, reaching toward renewal and the light. He is the sign of Capricorn, the surefooted mountain goat that scales the rocky heights of formidable peaks. It is the frame and the metaphor for his life's work.

His taproot feeds from a mixture of the peasant stock of four continents. His father, Anthony Serra, for whom Tony is named, was born in February 1911. He was a first-generation immigrant from Palma, located on Mallorca in the Balearic Islands; he was a Spanish Moor. The Serra lineage from Mallorca included the sainted Father Junipero Serra, known to Californians as the founder of nearly two dozen Franciscan missions from San Diego to California in the late 1700s. Tony Serra is not proud of this distant relative, since the true history of Junipero Serra in America is that of the conquering, colonizing, and bloodshed of indigenous people, no less vicious or villainous than the Spanish conquistadores he accompanied.

Tony Serra's mother, Gitl "Gladys" Fineburg, was two years older than her husband, born in August 1909. She was a Russian-Jew kickback, born in this country. Around the turn of the century, his maternal grandmother's lineage migrated from Russia to Australia, where his grandmother was born, then from there to the United States. Serra's mother was an American citizen, but his father was not. Though his parents' education did not exceed the fourth grade, this cross-cultural pollination brought with it a richness of background that was an education unto itself.

According to Tony, his mother was highly emotional, introspective, moody. Depending on one's perspective, she was either crazy or brilliant, but always ferociously and unconditionally loving. He says, "I could have committed triple murder, and still she would have supported me. She was a screamer; she was a brooder. She was a natural poet and artist." She had an artistic temperament, which she poured into her sons. All of her creative energies went into raising her family on precious little money, married to a man from a culture vastly different from her own.

His mother's Russian dramatics undoubtedly excited and repelled Tony. To safeguard himself from being consumed by the same tempests that ruled her life, Tony became a Platonist. He relegated emotions to the cerebral realm where they could chill out, while he tidied them up in his mental rationale. This explains a lot of his behavior, which often seems a cold cop-out. He only cuts the furies loose in court, where he can experience their power through the vicarious heat of the passion of his clients.

In contrast to his mother's dramatic temperament, his father was a simple man: hardworking, salt-of-the-earth, stable, strong, loyal, honest, and loving, with no excesses in his character. Even though his education never went beyond elementary school, he had a sharp focus and an innate understanding of mechanical things. He could draw the motor of a washing machine without ever seeing it. He began as a shipyard laborer and later worked his way up to become the foreman of a jellybean factory. Mother was the force of lightning; father was the grounding rod.

. . .

J. Tony Serra (the initial J. stands for Joseph) was born and raised in the outer Sunset District of San Francisco; the Serras lived between 33rd Avenue and Taraval, a blue-collar area on the fringe of the city not far from Ocean Beach on Great Highway, known as "outside lands."

Tony is the oldest; he has two younger brothers, Richard and Rudy.

Their mother lived for her sons. Though lacking material wealth, Serra family life was rich in the passion and attention that fortify and fulfill the spirit and that imbued all three sons with an overwhelming sense of self. Rather than focusing on the material things they couldn't afford, Tony's mother instilled in her sons an appreciation of who they were as individuals. She taught the three boys to value what most people take for granted: experiences, knowledge, excellence, aesthetics, sports, fairness, ideas, and a love of color.

In some respects, Tony had a permissive childhood: He started smoking marijuana when he was 12 years old. Along with other people, he grew his own among the dunes along the ocean. His mother actually watered his plants for him. She didn't see anything wrong with growing or smoking pot.

She lived for her three sons, pouring her creative spirit into them. Richard Serra graduated Yale and has achieved world class recognition as a sculptor. Rudy graduated from UC Berkeley and is a distinguished sculptor in his own right who's taught art and sculpture at the University of Vermont, Rutgers, and Bennington.

When her sons were grown and gone, Gladys Serra's vessel was empty. Tony senior was a loving husband, but that wasn't enough for her. She felt she had nothing to live for once her sons left the nest. One day in February 1977—the same month as her husband's birthday—she took a city bus to the end of the line at the beach, as she had done with her family so often before. It was the same beach where she used to yell at her boys, "Come back! You're out too far!" She walked into the swirling fog, into the cascading water, into the ruckus of the waves, taking each one head-on as it came. She just walked into a horizon of waves and she never came back. Was it a metaphor of her life, which had surely been an ongoing struggle against the forces of big challenges? As a person of Russian temperament, did she feel estranged? Her husband was of a different culture and temperament. This woman, the mother of giants, a solitary figure, challenged herself one last time to shoulder up to the metaphorical and physical waves, walking into the deep, over her head and beyond, resolute, no longer afraid. Tony's father died of cancer two years after his wife in 1979.

The suicide had strong repercussions in the Serra family. Their tree of life was gone. Richard said that when something of this magnitude happens, you have to stop and reread the pages of the book. He went into therapy for many years. Tony turned the page and moved on. He didn't attend the funeral of either his mother or his father. This caused a breach between Richard and Tony that still continues. They respect each other's achievements, but are not on speaking terms.

Tony claims not to know why his mother committed suicide. "Probably she was depressed," he shrugs. He doesn't know how old she was when she died. He doesn't know how old his father was when he died. Apparently, he doesn't want to know. These are pains that are stored in the darkness of closed inner chambers. Does his issue around death stem from the fact that it so often awaits the fate of his clients? Death is his chess game of winner takes all.

Tony has a thing about illness and death. "The thought of getting cancer terrifies me," he says. "I'm in complete denial about disease. I never go to doctors or dentists. When my hips went out on me, I refused to believe it. I exercised harder than ever, determined to make them strong again. It was probably the worst thing I could have done. I never even looked at the stitches or at the scars."

Tony had double hip-replacement surgery, both hips at the same time. He refused all visitors at that time, even those close to him, even his office staff. He went into his cave and licked his wounds in his own style until he was fully healed. He didn't want people to see him "like that." He healed in record time; his doctors were astounded at his strength for a man his age. Before his allotted "time off" had ended, he was back in his office, climbing the two steep flights of stairs, and back in court, lunging and jumping with passion in his closing arguments. His doctors declared it a "perfect recovery."

. . .

Tony always stood out as being different in school. When other kids were eating peanut-butter-and-jelly sandwiches on sliced Wonder bread from their lunch boxes, he was chewing on a baguette with salami. His teachers noticed his intelligence, frequently calling him to the blackboard to perform and solve equations for his classmates and even to assist more advanced classes. Not only didn't it bother him, he seemed to enjoy being singled out. As he grew older, this calling to perform and help others developed into a lifestyle. This was the portent of a larger stage that awaited him. Indeed, just as his mother schlepped Richard to museums and introduced him as "my son the artist," she predicted that Tony would become a lawyer. It goes to show the powerful imprint of a Jewish mother.

While attending Lincoln High School in San Francisco, Serra earned straight A's and won a scholastic scholarship to Stanford, where he majored in philosophy with a minor in English poetry. While maintaining high grades and working as a waiter on campus, he also played football, baseball, basketball, and soccer, and ran track and boxed light-heavyweight. In a slug-out in the ring, he lost one of his front teeth; it was replaced with a gold tooth that to this day winks in the light when he smiles. He was probably the only member of the philosophy department who had a broken nose from football and boxing. Among the most prized accomplishments of his life is a 410-foot home run over center field fence at Stanford's Sunken Diamond ballpark. Surely never before or since has Stanford had a six-sport jock who majored in epistemological philosophy with a minor in nineteenth-century English poetry.

Serra's fellow students either loved him or were put off by him.

Many thought he was just plain crazy. At Stanford, in the Fiji fraternity house, he painted his room black, from floor to ceiling, and placed a huge boulder in the center of it. It just seemed like the thing to do, no matter how weird, at the time.

During Serra's undergrad years, he pieced together the philosophies of great minds to form a solid picture of a meaningful universe and man's place in it. His intellect joined forces with his athletic abilities in an epiphany that awakened him to the wholeness of mind and body. He likened it to kicking a perfect spiral punt that arched high overhead—not a victory, *per se*, but the perfect unity of mind, body, and object.

Serra's love of poetry and literature inspired a post-graduation bohemian pilgrimage to North Africa, following in the footsteps of Ernest Hemingway, William Burroughs, and Alan Ginsberg. In Morocco's fabled hashish parlors (and later in an opium den in Iran), he had a vision of living the life of a Beat poet, becoming an expatriate, writing bad verse, dying, and being discovered posthumously. The idealist in him fancied becoming a rugged sandal-wearing writer with a beard in exotic lands, but he soon learned that his romanticized expat writers seemed content to waste their lives sloshed on alcohol or hammered on heroin.

Serra was too much of an athlete to go down that road. He was the guy who never smoked cigarettes or drank to excess. He did push-ups and ran laps. He certainly didn't want to turn into a junkie. He had no compulsion to destroy his athlete's body or his scholar's mind. So after a short test-drive of the Hemingway lifestyle abroad, he realized he had an excess of creative energy and suddenly nowhere to put it. Finally, he said to himself, "Fuck it; I'll become a lawyer," thereby fulfilling his Jewish mother's prophesy.

Serra turned down a contract as a professional baseball player to study law at Boalt Hall at the University of California–Berkeley. In his first year at law school, Serra ranked number 11 in his class of more than 300 students; two students who didn't pass the first year committed suicide. It was so highly competitive that the law students' grade-point averages after each semester were posted on a public wall. After receiving the highest grade on the contracts exam, he graded the contracts question on the California bar exam. He made law review and graduated in the top ten of his class in 1961.

This was around the beginning of the free-speech movement at Berkeley, with its social-protest demonstrations on the university campus, its fiery speeches, political chants and slogans, and emergence of Eastern consciousness that began filtering through the incipient hippie movement.

The law, as it turned out, was the perfect calling for all of Serra's intellectual and competitive hallmarks: the suit-and-tie equivalent of bumping off opponents and running the distance in football, delivering the knock-out punch in boxing, and hitting the home run in baseball. In addition, it gave him the platform to transform sterile legalese into philosophy, drama, spirituality, and poetry.

. . .

After graduating law school, Tony Serra went to work as an assistant D.A. at the Alameda County (east Bay Area) District Attorney's office, with a specialty in search-and-seizure cases. He was good at it, but he couldn't reconcile morally with the great goal of prosecution: putting people in cages. He quickly had his fill.

While at the D.A.'s office, he took a trip to South America. When he returned, he brought with him a woolly monkey, considered to be one of the most precocious of all mammals. Its mother had been killed by poachers and Tony adopted it. The young and rambunctious monkey and the young and rambunctious lawyer bonded so deeply that they went everywhere together, the monkey hanging from Serra's neck with its prehensile tail, like an animated ornament. After eleven months as a prosecutor, Serra announced that he was quitting and going into private practice, wherein the woolly would write the briefs, while he would handle the arguments. And with that, Serra turned heel; he and the monkey took their leave from the District Attorney's office and the prosecution side of the law for all time.

Serra immediately hung out his shingle for his own private practice as a criminal-defense trial lawyer in San Francisco, specializing in appellate work. He took on the appeals of indigent prisoners, charging $10 an hour. To solicit clients, he went to Bay Area prisons, visited with convicts and their families, and heard their grievances. He pursued their cases with a passion, but at the appellate level, he was lucky to win one out of 50.

By that time, the Beat scene, centered on the poet Lawrence Ferlinghetti's City Lights bookstore, was evolving into the hippie counterculture. Serra, who'd already been smoking marijuana for more than 10 years, plunged in head first, without fear or doubt. He did all the drugs of the day, became a Deadhead, danced naked in Golden Gate Park at night, while arguing cases by day. Soaking in the hot springs of Esalen at Big Sur, under the night canopy alive with stars, he journeyed to the edge of time. Although he turned on and tuned in every chance he could get, he never dropped out, and never burned out. In fact, his drug use seemed to enhance his law, to give him the perceptual edge of oversight and insight other lawyers didn't, and still don't, have. His extensive use of drugs has made him an expert in drug law.

His quintessential drug experience was the time when, as a young idealistic lawyer, he tripped on LSD in the Baja desert. With the sun directly overhead, the convection-oven heat creating undulating veils of rippling light, he strapped himself to a cactus and ingested 300 micrograms of pure lysergic acid. As the drug took effect in the blinding sunlight, he witnessed the meltdown of the scene before him: Reality, as he knew it, dissolved into a pulsating phantasmagoria. Light patterns blended with thought patterns, all moving in a paisley swirl in harmony with his vision, his breath, and his very vibrations. He was not only witnessing pure energy, he was an oscillating, resonating, integral part of it. In this critical awareness, he willed himself to align his body, mind, and soul with the highest calling of the law: the cause of justice. When he experienced the alignment, he willfully ended the cactus ritual, drank gallons of water, and got the hell out of the sun before he did serious damage to his body and brain.

In the culmination of the ritual, Serra vowed never to make money the purpose of his practice, adding to that a personal promise of poverty, of never buying anything new, a vow that he staunchly upholds nearly 50 years later.

Robustly self-confident and of a mind that he'd rather be in his own little rowboat, plotting his own course, than on someone else's cruise ship, Serra began by representing the people in the commune where he lived, as well as friends and other hippies who'd been brought up on various charges relating to a counterculture lifestyle. His victories soon catapulted him into the role of legal mouthpiece for high-ranking rebels.

During this era—this opalescent window into an incipient and evolved consciousness that emanated from right where Tony Serra lived and worked—he melded his individual spirit with the spirit of change, of awakening, of rebellion. He discarded past paradigms and made up his own equation. His consciousness shifted from the pages of law in books to the reality of law on the streets and the law of human rights and the heart. And in the process, he turned into the lawyer he remains today: a brilliant and uncompromising legal crusader of freedom for the people, a social healer, a legal shaman.

Chapter 3

The Golden Age of Law

During Tony Serra's formative years as a defense attorney, the 1960s, the nation was experiencing a social awakening precipitated by the Boomer generation. It was a time of great turmoil, challenge, and change. Illicit drugs altered consciousness and raised awareness forever. The youth of the country were in a state of rebellion, protesting publicly against the Vietnam War and disconnecting privately from the establishment values of their parent's generation. Racial tensions erupted in the streets and strong proponents of the cause of civil rights stepped forward. Some espoused idealism and nonviolence. Others advocated violence as a necessary means to a just end.

This era of upheaval, this epoch of changing values, was Tony Serra's "Golden Age of Law." He surfed its wave, balancing precariously on its board, pushing the boundaries of propriety with a notoriety so strong that you could only stop and stare. No one had ever seen the likes of him in court. He was a young, astoundingly eccentric, political-cause lawyer with frightening insight, lightning-quick reflexes, and theatrical aplomb, who won cases by day and danced his ass off at night. He was the cutting edge of the law on the cutting edge of society.

It wasn't long before Serra's counterculture victories put him in the spotlight and the great radical leaders of the time were calling for his legal services. They could see that Serra understood the language of the streets, of minorities, of drugs, and the courts. The cases he won in this era are some of the greatest of his career. They laid the cornerstones of his philosophy, which have never changed over the subsequent 45 plus years and counting.

Tony Serra recalls the Golden Age of Law fondly. There was no police state. There was no war on drugs. The judges were all liberal. The juries were all liberal. They threw out cases on constitutional grounds. Defense attorneys won motions to suppress. Juries acquitted drug cases. Rather than the gang violence over drug turf in ghettos seen today, the images were of proud Panthers, Black and White, working for the benefit of their communities. Their causes were tailor-made for an idealistic young lawyer to build a practice around social and political issues.

· · ·

Perhaps the most famous of his counterculture clients was Huey Newton.

Huey Percy Newton was born on February 17, 1942, in Monroe, Louisiana; his family moved to Oakland when he was three. Though he managed to graduate from Oakland Technical High School, he was functionally illiterate. Newton taught himself to read before attending Merritt College, where he met Bobby Seale, and the San Francisco School of Law, which he attended, he claimed, to become a better burglar.

In 1966 Newton and Seale formed the Black Panther Party in response to incidents of racism on the streets of Oakland. The party's original purpose was to patrol ghettos and protect residents from acts of police brutality. The Panthers eventually developed into a Marxist revolutionary group that called for the arming of all African Americans, their exemption from the draft and from all sanctions of so-called "white America," their release from all jails and prisons throughout the country, and the payment of compensation for centuries of exploitation. At its peak in the late '60s, Panther membership exceeded 2,000 and the organization operated chapters in several major cities.

In 1967 Huey Newton was convicted of voluntary manslaughter in the death of a police officer, but his conviction was overturned 22 months later and he was released from prison. In 1971 he announced that the party would adopt a nonviolent manifesto and dedicate itself to providing social services to the African American community. In 1974 he was accused of another murder, this time of a 17-year-old streetwalker named Kathleen Smith.

The incident occurred at three or four in the morning at one of the more infamous prostitute areas in Oakland, where as many as 20 prostitutes congregate at one intersection—young black women, a few transvestites, lots of pimps, lots of drug dealers—all working the area until the wee hours.

Allegedly, a large yellow car, belonging to the Panthers and Huey Newton at the time, pulled up to the intersection. The driver got out and summoned one of the young prostitutes, Kathleen Smith, who held a short conversation through the car window with someone in the back seat. The back door of the car opened and the passenger got out, aimed a gun point-blank at Kathleen, and shot her dead. The car sped off.

The police quickly ascertained that the vehicle was the alleged Huey Newton mobile, the symbol of the Black Panther party. The car was found, still warm, in Huey's parking lot. But Huey wasn't around. And when word went out that the Oakland police were attempting to pin this rap on him, he fled to Cuba.

He remained in Cuba for three years. During this time, people close to him were requesting as much of his federal dossier as possible, under the Freedom of Information Act that had been signed into law by Lyndon Johnson eight or so years earlier. Thousands and thousands of pages of documents covered federal law-enforcement efforts to plant evidence, informants, and provocateurs within the Black Panther Party. These people weren't only framing the radicals, they were also instigating crime. In terms of dirty tricks, much had been done to implicate Newton, who was wise to flee.

Indeed, during the Oakland police investigation, word got around that any prostitute, pimp, or drug dealer who would identify Huey Newton as the shooter would, in essence, be given a free pass to operate on that corner.

49

Three years later, after a shift in the political winds indicated that Newton might have a better chance at a fair trial, he returned to the Bay Area to face the charge. When the case came up, Serra and his defense team checked the records of all the witnesses who ultimately ID'd Huey Newton as the man who shot Kathleen Smith and noticed a distinct moratorium on prostitution charges in that part of Oakland following the Smith murder; all the so-called witnesses were given immunity from prostitution arrests.

Serra presented a chart, like a big cartoon, that displayed the testimony of all the witnesses. One witness described the shooter as wearing a black hat, a brown shirt, and sandals. Another claimed he was wearing boots and no hat. Altogether, Serra compiled 24 completely different descriptions.

The prosecution's most important witness was a prostitute who'd claimed to be closest to the yellow car and seemingly had the best vantage point from which to identify Newton as the shooter. However, when Serra checked her whereabouts on the night of the shooting, it turned out that she was in jail. This was the pillar of the prosecution's case.

In this way, it was revealed that the police had completely contrived the case. Huey Newton didn't shoot Kathleen Smith. The Black Panthers knew who shot her, but they weren't giving him up. Serra was defending an innocent man whom the government was trying to railroad back into prison.

"When I was in it, I was numb. I was in shock. It was just so big," Serra recalls. "And it was so obviously a vacuous case, a police contrivance, a joke. For our part, we had a super packed court, an innocent defendant, a trumped-up charge, good press. We didn't even put Huey on the stand.

"The blacks were so beautiful. I'd be speaking and there's a cadence to the language that's instinctual. I don't even realize that as it comes out of my mouth. But *they* caught it. I'd be arguing or doing some kind of summation, and I'd become aware of this rhythm of murmuring, of humming, in the background. It was like a church scene, like a call from the preacher and a response from the congregation. It was *fabulous*. Just simple, tear-jerking, sentimental, romantic, pristine, glorious theater.

"We won, of course. We won big. The truth was, Huey Newton was innocent.

"I got to know him for a limited time. He was easy to get close to and I chummed with him a bit. He was brilliant and physically very strong. When he went to jail, all he did was push weights. He got so strong, so perfect. He was a true champion of his people. He's *still* a true champion. He regarded all black people as *his* people. It was the only time in my life when I felt I was touching a real leader, in the Old Testament sense, a King David.

"In fact, he was well versed in the Old Testament. His father was a religious teacher in the South, so Huey was brought up with it in his vocabulary from the beginning. He considered himself a black Jew. He was Ethiopian by origin.

"We had a little verbal scuffle with Judge Karresh, an ex-rabbi. Every time Karresh would say something about the Old Testament, Huey said something else, until there they were, arguing like two rabbis.

"Everything he did, he did with a purity as though he would *die* for it at that time, and those around him would die for *him*. To see that, to touch that, to be a part of that was a real privilege for me. It was a privilege just to know him."

Huey Newton received a Ph.D. in social philosophy from the University of California at Santa Cruz in 1980. His dissertation, "War Against the Panthers," was subtitled, "A Study of Repression in America." Succumbing to factionalism and pressure from government agencies, the Black Panther Party disbanded in 1982. In March 1989, Newton was sentenced to a six-month jail term for misappropriating public funds intended for a Panther-founded Oakland school; it's believed he did so to support his drug addiction. In August of that year he was shot dead in Oakland by a drug dealer who was sentenced to 32 years in prison for the murder.

· · ·

From the Black Panthers, Tony Serra defended one of the leaders of the Bay Area branch of the White Panthers, a group originated in

Detroit by John Sinclair and Lawrence Plamondon that sought to inject revolutionary politics into rock concerts and youth culture. They believed in dope, rock 'n' roll, sex in the streets, and freeing political prisoners; some counterculture historians claim they were simply a fan club for the Detroit rock band the MC5 and the "members" were no more than friends living together, student-style, in old houses, getting stoned, playing music, putting out free newsletters, and occasionally fighting drug charges in court. From the Motor City, chapters spread to Ann Arbor, Portland, and San Francisco.

Tom Stevens served as an Army private in Vietnam from 1966 to 1967. Afterward, he joined the White Panthers, an offshoot of the Black Panther Party, where he became a leader. He was charged with marijuana possession in the early 1970s.

Tony Serra puts it this way. "The White Panthers were pure perfection to a fault. They were so committed, disciplined, loyal, altruistic, so self-sacrificial that they became counterproductive to their own objective, at least from a wider perspective. That is, being too consistent, too tautological, too methodical ultimately repels allegiances and coalition."

In the early '70s, he and Jack McClellen, a defense attorney from Bolinas, represented Tom Stevens in the White Panthers' highest-profile case.

The White Panthers lived in a house near Haight Street in the Haight-Ashbury district in San Francisco. It was communally occupied by people of all ages and backgrounds, including lots of children, and dogs and cats. Many people in the community respected and honored them. They ran all kinds of food programs; they fixed cars. But because they were strong and dedicated, they were considered suspect. They attracted derision and persecution from law enforcement.

In this instance, the police believed that stolen property was being kept in the White Panthers' house. But that, it turned out, was just an excuse to bust in. Just as the police were about to enter the house, Tom Stevens was standing at the top of the stairs with a gun. His colleague, Terry, was right there next to him. The officers charged in and shots were fired from both directions. The officers retreated and called in the tactical squad, who surrounded the house, then started shooting in hard. They knew there were babies and children, pregnant women and dogs in this dwelling; nonetheless, they lobbed in firebombs and burned the house almost all the way down to the ground.

In the aftermath, everyone believed that they'd find the charred remains of men, women, children, and animals. However, unbeknownst to police, through the wisdom of the conspiratorially oriented, the White Panthers had tunnels. They'd all escaped.

Then Tom or Terry went on television and said, "Those motherfuckers burned us down. They had no probable cause to enter our house. They rushed us and we have a right to defend ourselves, to resist excessive force." Even if there's reasonable cause to arrest, if it's done with excessive force you can resist the excessive force. So the White Panthers had every right to shoot.

By appearing on television, Tom and Terry were identified, then arrested.

Jim La Sartre was the prosecutor assigned to the case. He was good, and he was wild. He graduated from the University of San Francisco, an ex-Marine, an experienced trial lawyer, a tough adversary. But in every case Tony Serra ever contested against him, he'd always offered the moon for a plea bargain.

True to form, before the White Panther trial began, La Sartre tried to negotiate Tom and Terry to plead guilty to a misdemeanor. They were charged with assault with intent to commit murder and conspiracy to commit murder, attempted murder—all heavy charges. And here the prosecutor was offering a 243, simple assault on a police officer, with a maximum penalty of probation.

Serra picked up the case. "What happened was part wisdom and part martyrdom. It was wise insofar as a movement was building around this. There was plenty of support from a variety of groups around a case where police officers tried to burn down their house, and occupants were just defending themselves, and had it not been for an escape hatch, they would have all burned to death.

"They said, 'Fuck it! We're not taking misdemeanors. We were right and they were wrong. The law is the law. And we'll go to trial. We'll tell our story to the *people.*'

"And that's why Tom is so beautiful and why, in my heart, I'll always have this softness and this sense of inadequacy when I think of him.

You know, *no* sacrifice, *no* compromise. All the way, every time. *All* or *nothing.*

"At trial, things got down to small points. The officers were charging up the stairs. Tom and Terry were at the top of the stairs, armed with guns. The issue was whether or not a warning shot was fired as the officers came up the stairs. Bullets were found on the stairway wall and our intent was to show that the officers had barely begun their ascent when the shots were fired. If you shoot over someone's head, then the bullets aren't being aimed at them. You're just trying to scare them. That was the gist of it and I figured we had the case won. All Tom and Terry had to say was, 'Yes. The officers were coming up the stairs. We shot over their heads, then they turned and fled.' End of story. Just a warning shot. Not guilty of attempted anything. The jury was primed to accept that.

"Now the harder—and maybe technically more correct—position, if we were submitting the case to a robot instead of a jury, would be that the defendants were justified in firing at the police, because they were charging up the stairs, having shown no proof of probable cause to be in this house, and they were armed. But that's a real hard position to defend, and that's not the way lawyers like it. Lawyers are compromisers. Lawyers try to mediate between two positions. By nature lawyers are fence-straddlers, always looking to the right and the left, always talking out of their mouths two ways at the same time. That's the nature of the *disease.*

"So we, the defense lawyers, said to Tom and Terry, 'Just say you shot over his head. That'll be the end of the trial and you'll walk right out of here."

"So now Tom's on the stand. I ask him, 'Did you have a weapon?' and he says, 'Yes.'

"'Did you draw the weapon?'

"'Yes.'

"'Were the officers coming up the stairs?'

"'Yes.'

"'And did you *aim* the shot?'

"'Yes!'

"'And *where* did you aim it?'

"Here, I hold my breath. The whole case rests on his answer. And he says, without hesitation, 'I aimed it right at his *fucking head!*'

"Tom refused to lie! He wanted to win the hard way. That's the way his whole life was. Well, they were convicted and went to prison for about four years. When they came out, they just went right back to the street, pamphleteering and creating righteous anti-Establishment propaganda.

"Wherever Tom is right now, he's *fighting*. Beside this moral strength, I'm still a child. My gig is puny and self-gratifying, full of conceit and arrogance and lots of bullshit rewards, while Tom is, right now, somewhere *hard* on the streets, doing something pure and perfect, and he doesn't give a shit if he's going to prison for another four years. He'll tell the *truth*. The truth is freedom for him."

• • •

The New World Liberation Front (NWLF) was one of hundreds of groups formed during the '60s' anti-government movement. It was a loosely organized group of Berkeley student radicals and African American ex-cons, formed in 1971. Throughout the 1970s, though most of what they did was suppressed by the media, the NWLF conducted a campaign of successfully exploding more anti-establishment bombs than most of the other radical organizations of the time combined. They sent bombs in candy boxes to members of the San Francisco Board of Supervisors. They bombed Pacific Gas & Electric, a Bank of America branch, courthouses, cars, bank presidents' and board of directors' homes. According to Tony Serra, they didn't bomb to maim or kill; they never *intentionally* injured anyone. They bombed to scare and, therefore, to effectuate change.

Jacques Rogiers had been a member since the early days of the movement. He owned a printing press and printed NWLF literature; he was a courier who delivered public communiqués to the media and private messages to other members. In the late 1970s, Rogiers was charged with aiding and abetting the NWLF in their bombing campaign and Tony Serra defended him against 12 counts of serious criminal activity.

Serra remembers being in awe of Jacques Rogiers. In many ways he was "larger" than anyone else he met during that era. Serra cites

Rogiers being subpoenaed by the feds, before he was prosecuted locally, to appear before a grand jury. The authorities wanted him to snitch, to describe the NWLF communiqués, how he got them, where they came from, who was connected to them, and everything else he knew about them. That put him in a quandary. He wasn't about to turn and testify against the NWLF. And he couldn't invoke the Fifth Amendment, because in a grand-jury proceeding, you can only refuse to testify against yourself, not anyone else. But if you don't testify, you risk a contempt-of-court charge and you can be held indefinitely; a number of journalists have rotted in jail protecting their deep-throat sources against zealous prosecutors, for whom the grand jury is a cherished tool.

So what did Rogiers do? He took a vow of silence, a religious renunciation of speaking altogether. He spoke to no one, including the grand jury. He was thrown into jail anyway, where he sat for six months, refusing to speak. He was finally let go and that was that, until formal charges of aiding and abetting were brought against him.

This was a notorious case at the time and right in the middle of it, the district attorney's vehicle was exploded in front of his house. A big picture of the DA's car, upside down in his driveway, appeared on the front page of the *San Francisco Chronicle*. The NWLF had bombed his car to protest Jacques's prosecution.

All the overground members of the NWLF filed into the courtroom and sat in the back row as Serra defended Jacques Rogiers on First Amendment grounds. He and his team vociferously denied any conspiracy with the NWLF bombers. "This man runs a printing press. He uncovers the truth, he reveals the truth, and he prints the truth, as is his right under the First Amendment to the United States Constitution."

Serra remembers this case as one of the wildest in his long wild career. For one, he had to squat to talk to his client. Jacques had done time for a variety of things in the state penitentiary, where convicts squat on their haunches, face to face and very close, for privacy. The prison guards walk around them, but they can't hear what's being said, and that constitutes privacy for an inmate. And that's the way Jacques communicated with his lawyer.

He also insisted that his lawyer get stoned after lunch. Early in the trial, Jacques, Tony, and the NWLF supporters sat down on the floor of

City Hall for the lunch break. Jacques asked Tony, "If we start smoking grass, what will they do?"

Tony thought about it, then said, 'Well, they could arrest us, but they won't. The publicity's too heavy and it would be too chickenshit."

"Fine!" Jacques exclaimed. "Then let's all light up!"

After that, every day, right in the middle of the San Francisco City Hall during the long trial, Jacques Rogiers, his NWLF cadre, and his defense attorney got ripped and filed back into the courtroom for the afternoon session, flying high.

A fondness for the memory is evident as Serra recalls the experience. "Jacques had several different kinds of grass. The kind we smoked after lunch was for working; it was less potent than his after-dinner grass, which was for talking to God. Still, his working pot was heavy-duty shit.

"You know, when a lawyer's in trial on a major case, it's twenty hours a day. You have to absorb huge amounts of data *the night before*. There's so much data that, if you did it all, say, the *month* before you go to trial, you won't remember it. You've also got to know every little detail and your recall has to be instant. You need a photographic memory, at least for twenty-four hours, and after a while you get that way. I'm like that now. That's what I do.

"Sharks smell blood a hundred miles away. Hawks see things as if they're looking through a microscope. I carry paragraphs in my head, so that when I cross-examine, I can really *see* page twenty-four. I see like the third line down where it says, 'At nine a.m., so and so went into the theater.' Then, when the witness says, 'Well, I went into the theater about eleven a.m.,' I check the third line in paragraph nine and retort, 'You didn't go at eleven, you went at *nine* a.m.' And they all look at me as if I have the transcript in my hand.

"That's my game, but the point is it's twenty-hour days and with Jacques, I had to be stoned about half the time. Now, I've been smoking dope a long time and I enjoy a joint every day after work to unwind. But it never was and never has been my practice to conduct my *cases* stoned. Sometimes after the lunch smoke with Jacques—when I was at the counsel table—I'd raise my foot to cross my leg and it felt like it was *floating*, and I wondered if people were noticing I was in the *air* in the courtroom."

Finally, the trial ended, the jury deliberated, and the verdict came in: not guilty on all twelve counts. After the verdicts were announced, the jury was polled to make it all official.

"Mrs. Jones, with respect to count one, what was your verdict?"

"Not guilty."

"Mr. Smith, with respect to count one, what was your verdict?"

"Not guilty."

Normally, with one or two counts, the verdict is recited 24 times. But this was 12 counts, so Serra had the euphoric experience of listening to what he called *"freedom bells"* in court: "not guilty" 144 times. The whole poll took 45 minutes.

Afterward, the defense team, Jacques, and the whole overground NWLF had a huge party to celebrate the victory. The jurors got drunk and were kissing the defendants, who were dancing, and everyone was happy about the First Amendment.

Right afterwards, Jacques vanished without a trace. He went underground. In the context of his religious silence, Jacques "went to the mountain." He disappeared into a monastery somewhere in the world. Serra has talked to some of his close friends, his ex-girlfriends, asking each one, "Where's Jacques?"

All they say is, "He's gone. He's a monk now."

"Jacques taught me more just by watching him, by feeling him, by osmosis, just by sucking up his spirit, than any professor ever could," Serra remembers. "He taught us how to occupy territory over the line. That is, you don't just stop at whatever's legal, you *take* a little. Into whatever zone divides legal from illegal, Jacques would be leading the charge. That's the only way to evolve. Myself, I'm good at dancing over the line, but then dancing back; working that line is my path. But not Jacques. Jacques was *always* on the other side, scrambling for a little enemy territory, whatever it might be: printing up an NWLF demand or smoking marijuana right in City Hall.

"Wherever he is, in the realm of aura, when you can feel the presence of a wise man within ten miles, that's Jacques. He's a beacon flashing. He'll flash for the rest of his life. He has some kind of ineffable potency and it was a privilege to be where he was for a while. I don't think anyone's ever said anything negative about Jacques. Many other sixties' radical leaders were subjected to too much media and got compromised by ego-tripping. But everyone knows Jacques is perfect. He was one beautiful dude."

. . .

Mary Jane Rathbun, also known as "Brownie Mary," mixed up more than marijuana in her cannabis brownies for AIDS patients. She stirred up a social and political hullabaloo that the California authorities did not know how to deal with.

Mary baked batches of strong marijuana-laced brownies for AIDS patients occupying a ward in San Francisco General Hospital. Under the auspices of the San Francisco Medical Society and the Mayor Board of Supervisors of San Francisco, Mary administered them to the terminally ill. The brownies alleviated their pain and increased their appetites; from the perspectives of the patients, medicine, and society, it was a highly worthwhile endeavor. Brownie Mary was acclaimed Volunteer of the Year in 1986, receiving a big award in City Hall from the San Francisco Board of Supervisors for her activities.

In 1992, she was baking her special brownies in Sonoma County. Someone alerted the authorities, who sent narcotics officers to arrest her red-handed and charge her with possession of marijuana for distribution, a felony, which could have landed her a long sentence in the state penitentiary.

Her pre-trial hearing was held in Santa Rosa, California, in October 1992. It was such a big event that when I asked Tony Serra for directions to the courthouse and the name of the judge, he replied, "Just follow the crowds."

The second-floor hallway leading to the small courtroom in Santa Rosa was jammed with hippies, media, AIDS patients and other supporters, and, of course, law-enforcement officers ready to use their weapons if necessary. It took some aggressive elbowing to advance myself to the front of this dense crowd, where I was shocked to see a wizened old woman in her seventies at the center of a circle of bailiffs.

Brownie Mary didn't look threatening enough to stir up such a fuss. She was small of stature, frail, and clearly scared about her impending fate. She was dressed in pastel polyester slacks with a blouse and a black sweater vest pinned with numerous cause buttons: "Free Brownie Mary," "Medical Marijuana," and "Weed, not Bush." (It was an election year.) These Brownie Mary buttons became the envy of everyone in the hallways. Intense trading went on to acquire them. I was amused to see one of the officers aggressively trading for a button. He assured me he only wanted it for a souvenir—not to wear, of course!

Her small stick figure showed through her loose-fitting garments. Thick bifocals covered a third of her face, giving her eyes a magnified and warped appearance, distorting the rest of her features. This was a face that showed its mileage; it was at once strong, frightened, and stubborn. It reflected the determination of one who's old and has nothing to lose.

Tony Serra, her lawyer, towered protectively over her. The court bailiffs, too, seemed especially massive next to Brownie Mary. They were like pistol-flanking rhinos posturing their might before an aged sparrow, cornered in court, whose only crime was compassion, and producing loaded brownies to alleviate the suffering of AIDS victims. It all seemed so grotesque, so disproportionate, such a waste of time, money, and life's precious resources in the name of the drug war and the law.

It was impossible to discern, among this mob of shaggy long-haired freaks, who was the snitch. He blended in so perfectly with the tie-dyed patterns of the crowd that one would never have suspected that there was a Judas in the flock.

The legalization of marijuana for medical uses was such a hot issue on the California ballot at this time that the courtroom was filled beyond capacity, with overflow crowds jamming the hallways while the hearing was in session. There was an impending sense that the repercussions could not be contained within the courtroom's walls.

The whole spectacle so overwhelmed the judge that he offered Brownie Mary a judicial slap on the wrist and a fine of $10,000 to call it quits. But here Brownie Mary showed her mettle. She thanked the judge kindly, but refused to be bought off. She insisted on a full-blown jury trial. The judge paled at the imagined specter of his courtroom filled with AIDS and chemotherapy victims in the later stages of their diseases, testifying to the medical benefits of marijuana, the ensuing headlines and media attention, and all the accompanying implications that would arise.

It was later announced that the case had been dismissed. But it laid the cornerstone for the legalization of medical marijuana that passed in the California elections of 1996.

Tony Serra was in his element representing Brownie Mary. He was especially striking at the hearing, thanks to his bright yellow tie with its vertical lineup of hand-painted green marijuana leaves. The marijuana tie was as eye-catching as a blinking exclamation point; it could not be ignored. The legalization of marijuana is one of Serra's pet causes and he was a walking advertisement.

"Brownie Mary was providing marijuana brownies to terminally ill AIDS patients in San Francisco General Hospital, so it was an act of mercy," Tony Serra recalls. "Only her humanitarian conscience guided her. She never made a penny on it and she exposed herself to the full fury of the law. She couldn't have lasted long in the state penitentiary. So she was very brave.

"In Brownie Mary's defense, we argued the doctrine of necessity [described in Chapter 7: Jury Nullification]. We brought out the arsenal for the medical usage of marijuana: motions relating to constitutional rights; psychiatrists and doctors and marijuana activists all submitting affidavits. We marched to court. The radio and television stations all covered it. The court and the halls were filled with everyone from flower children to medical specialists. We so overwhelmed the judiciary that the case was dismissed after the preliminary hearing. It was a milestone experience that led the way to the de facto legalization of medical-marijuana usage by people who are afflicted with AIDS. Brownie Mary is a heroine in the eyes of many; she won herself a place in history. It was just good karma to be involved in that case."

Serra comments on the art piece I did of him and Mary. "This is almost a caricature of me and Brownie Mary. What I'm doing here is expressing how aghast I am that society would indict such a woman who, while she was being prosecuted in Sonoma County for possession of marijuana, was simultaneously being acclaimed by the Board of Supervisors in San Francisco as Volunteer of the Year for her selfless gift to AIDS patients of marijuana brownies. It just shows how two subcultures can be so different. So in this drawing I'm aghast, I'm frenzied, I'm angry, I'm pained. I'm tortured that society would do this to her. How primitive. How backward. What a Dark Ages mentality. It was a passionate presentation. I felt it even more deeply because of my own marijuana activism."

. . .

On January 10, 1974, Russell Little and Joe Remiro were booked into the Concord city jail, charged with the murder of Marcus Foster, superintendent of the Oakland, California, school district. They were identified by police as soldiers of the Symbionese Liberation Army, forever infamous for the kidnapping of Patty Hearst.

Marcus Foster, the first black superintendent of Oakland schools, was respected and revered by the community. But the SLA believed that he was trying to institute an identification system with ghetto blacks in primary schools; they also objected to police officers in Oakland schools. (According to Foster's Wikipedia entry, he opposed cops in schools and the ID cards and "had worked to water down the plan.") Foster was shot eight times with cyanide-tipped bullets. His assistant, Robert Blackburn, was also shot, but he survived.

A number of alleged eyewitnesses to the killing contended that they saw two males, one black-haired and Latin-looking, the other with long blond hair and a fair complexion. The two defendants were tried separately. Joe Remiro was convicted after three or four days of jury deliberation; he was sentenced to life imprisonment.

In Russell Little's trial, the jury deliberated for 10 days before the judge, fearing a hung jury, delivered the "Allen charge." Tony Serra explains. "This instruction to the jury goes something like this. 'You're the smartest jury to ever hear this case. It's productive to the resources of the state that every case culminate in a verdict. The court wants the minority to re-examine their views, to better consider the views of the majority.' This instruction essentially pressures the minority into giving up their position. It worked in this case. The judge issued the Allen charge on the eleventh day. On the eleventh day, the jury convicted Russell Little."

The Allen charge provided one basis for appeal. It's still used in federal courts, but the California Supreme Court threw it out while deliberating on the Little appeal, ruling it coercive and unconstitutional. After serving seven or eight years of a life sentence, Russell Little was granted a retrial, where Tony Serra defended him.

Because they'd been convicted of killing a black leader, Little and Remiro's lives were in jeopardy in San Quentin. They tried to escape and in the process a guard was stabbed through the ear with a pencil. Serra recalls one incident that captures the tone of what imprisonment was like for Russell Little. "The guards invaded his cell in the middle of the night, telling him they were taking him to the gas chamber. They stuck the hood over his head, like "dead men walking" wear, and put him into the death cell, pretending they were going to execute him. Then they all started laughing, like it was just a big joke, ha ha ha, and returned him to his cell."

The second trial was held in Salinas, California, roughly 100 miles south of Oakland.

Russell Little was a philosophy major and a straight A student at the University of California, Berkeley. Serra remembers him as one of the most brilliant people he ever met. "He dealt the case out to us. We were like scribes, carrying our pencils and paper to capture where he was at; we took all of our cues from him."

The case against Little was circumstantial; the eyewitnesses had a general make on Remiro and Little, but nothing specific. The prosecution had a general description of the two shooters, plus some incriminating documentary evidence, and a shoot-out with the police on a different occasion. But that was all. Serra and his team had little trouble establishing reasonable doubt at the retrial and Russell Little was free. He married his investigator, a woman who'd been devoted to him for seven years, and moved to Florida.

"The goodness and strength of Russell Little were his intelligence, his perseverance, the richness of his knowledge. In that sense, he was the symbolic head of the sixties movement. Others were the body, the theater, the brutality. Russell Little was the intellectual piston of the action. A movement without intellect, that's raw with hate, that's *only* emotional, spawned only from privation and deprivation, need, hostility—that kind of a movement cannot endure. It can't fulfill itself. It can't flower. It needs the mind, the overall vision. And for me, in my naive eclectic lawyeristic way, Russell Little embodied that: another dream, another beautiful man, another sixties flower in my imagination."

. . .

Chol Soo Lee was a young Korean immigrant who came to the U.S. in 1964 at the tender age of twelve. Escaping a harsh life in Korea, he expected to be welcomed to a better one in America, the land of milk and money, where everyone spoke Korean. Just the opposite happened. He barely spoke English. He had neither a father nor an education. Times were hard and he always felt like an outsider forced to live by his wits on San Francisco streets rife with gangs. He quickly fell afoul of the law, with lots of detentions for burglary, robbery, and minor drug sales.

Then, in June 1973 at age 21, his life changed forever.

It was a balmy summer evening in Chinatown on Sunday June 3, with the rich smells of exotic food, voices in all languages punctuated by the ringing of wind chimes, and not a hint of violence in the air. A Wah Ching gang member, Yip Yee Tak, was walking along Grand Avenue when a "young Asian guy" in a suit approached him, shot him once in the chest, then shot him again in the back of the head as he went down. The assassin took off running. He ditched the snub-nose .38 revolver in nearby Beckett Alley and disappeared.

Nearly a hundred people witnessed the murder at the intersection of Grand and Pacific. But because it was a gang killing, no Asians came forward to offer information. The police did manage to interview three Caucasian tourists from Los Angeles who claimed to have seen the shooter from across the street.

At the time, Chinatown gangs were out of control and crime was affecting tourism. There had been 13 unsolved gang murders in China town in the past three years, so the police were under intense pressure to "get somebody, anybody, Asian." And this shooting was drawing nationwide publicity.

The recovered gun was traced back to Chol Soo Lee through a previous incident. Even though the ballistics test didn't match up with Chol's gun, he was put in a line-up.

The killer's identity was no secret among the Asian community; he was a young Chinese gang member by the name of Danny Choi. This was his first hit and he couldn't resist boasting of it. Prior to the shooting, he'd gone by the nickname Trout, but after the murder he was known as Killer. Choi was around five-nine. Chol, meanwhile, was the sole short Korean man, measuring only five-two, in the line-up of tall Chinese men.

The three eyewitnesses knew nothing about Orientals; they couldn't distinguish any differences among Chinese, Japanese, or Korean. Thus, it was unlikely that three tourists could positively identify a Korean among a mob of Chinese in the scant few seconds that the shooting occurred, especially at that distance. Yet they ID'd Chol, who stood trial for the murder.

The prosecution alleged that Chol had been hired by a rival Chinese gang to commit a daring daylight assassination at the height of tourist season. He was originally defended by court-appointed attorneys who failed to produce a single witness of their own. In fact, only 10 hours of investigation had been undertaken by the defense and one of the public defenders suffered a heart attack in the process.

Thus, the testimony of the three witnesses convicted Chol Soo Lee. He was sentenced to life in prison for murder in the first degree.

While in prison, Chol associated with a Mexican prison gang. Believed to be a hit man for a Chinese gang, he was highly prized and touted as a ruthless Korean assassin.

In order to prove his worth, the Mexicans arranged for him to fight—to the death—Morris Needham, a member of the Aryan Brotherhood. Chol's opponent stood over six feet tall and had teardrop tattoos beneath his eyes, signifying previous killings for which he was revered in his circle. He was armed with a single prison-made knife. Chol had two short prison-made knives taped to each hand so he couldn't drop them or throw them away.

They fought in the prison yard.

As the guards stood by pretending not to watch, Needham grabbed Chol and Chol went at him with such swift precision that no one could even see his arms; they were like whirling propeller blades. By the time his hands became visible, the Aryan Brotherhood contender lay dead on the ground. Chol was never touched. He didn't deny the killing, though he insisted it was in self-defense. The charge, first-degree murder with "special circumstances," carried the death penalty. Chol was immediately transferred from Deuel Vocational Institution, a state prison in Tracy, CA, to San Quentin Prison where his cell on death row was near the gas chamber. He remained there, awaiting trial, for four years.

Ironically, it was this prison murder that rallied the support of the Korean community and got the attention of the media. Koreans raised money for a top-of-the-line legal defense. Leonard Weinglass, renowned for his work in the cases of the Chicago Seven and the Pentagon Papers, was retained. Weinglass hired a local private investigator, Josiah "Tink" Thompson, with whom he had worked on an AIM (American Indian Movement) case. Thompson joined forces with Raul Ramirez, a Cuban reporter for the *San Francisco Examiner* with an expertise on Chinatown.

Thompson describes, in his book *Gumshoe,* one of the many ironies of the case. Weinglass comments at a breakfast meeting, "It's crazy, isn't it? You get put away for life for a killing you didn't do, and the only time anybody pays any attention to you is when you kill someone in prison and the state of California starts cranking up the little green room."

Thompson goes on to describe the gas chamber. "I had seen it once on a visit to San Quentin years earlier. [The Green Room] wasn't really green, but a sickly pale shade of cyan. The prisoner is strapped into a metal chair painted the same color as the room. He can look out through the windows of his space capsule at the witnesses in the adjoining room as the final arrangements are made. The warden of San Quentin then gives a nod, the executioner pulls a lever, and the hockey puck of cyanide drops into the acid. There hadn't been an execution in California since 1967, but a recent court decision had prompted the San Quentin authorities to refurbish the chamber. Apparently, they'd tested it by strapping a pig into the chair and timing how long it squealed after the pellet hit the acid. Somewhere in the back of my mind I knew how cyanide worked: It blocked cells' capacity to absorb oxygen. You died after convulsions."

. . .

Even though five years had elapsed since the Chinatown killing, investigator Thompson found that the trial was a real mess. First, he managed to produce a key eyewitness, Steve Morris, who was only 10 feet from the shooting. Morris had reported in to the police the day after the shooting and was called, twice, by homicide inspector Frank Falzon, but his information, which contradicted prosecution witnesses, didn't fit into law-enforcement's scheme of things, so his existence was never revealed to the defense. Next, Chol came out clean after two days on a polygraph machine. Then there was the matter of the negative match of the murder weapon based on ballistics that was never presented in trial.

An appeals judge believed Steve Morris's story had been suppressed and Chol Soo Lee was granted a second trial. Still, five years had elapsed since the murder and Morris was having a hard time recalling specific details. Investigator Thompson had read that hypnosis was remarkable in clarifying recall, so he brought Morris to a San Francisco hypnotherapist, Dr. George Karalis. Thompson tape recorded the session. At one point, Morris broke into a sweat as he revisited the murder scene. Thompson wrote, "The words were gushing out of Morris's mouth in a mixture of surprise and terror."

Describing the moment of the shooting, Morris said, "Everyone is pushing to get out of the way. We're in some doorway. There are more bangs and people are screaming. He's looking right over at us now, swinging his gun in front of him. He swings it in a circle, and no one says anything or does anything. He's looking at me with those dark mean eyes and I'm scared ... I look away, because I think he'll shoot. But he doesn't. I look back and he's gone."

"What does he look like?" Dr. Karalis asked.

"About five-foot-nine, dark hair to his shoulders. His eyes are dark and he has this mole under his eye."

"Which eye?"

"Right eye. He's facing me and it's ... Yeah, it's under his right eye, sort of close to his nose."

At the hearing, Chol's hair had been cut and he no longer wore a mustache. Nor did he have a mole on his face. As Thompson wrote in *Gumshoe*, "He looked tiny but strong after years of weight lifting in prison. He looked extremely handsome and clean cut." When Thompson asked Morris "Was he the man?" Morris replied, "Not possible. Lee's tiny. The man I saw was about average height, maybe five-nine or so. And the face is completely different. Lee's good-looking. The man I saw was mean, you might even say ugly."

Len Weinglass dropped out after the appeals hearing and Thompson brought in local lawyers J. Tony Serra and Stuart Hanlon. Thompson and Hanlon did all the pretrial work; Serra stepped in at the last minute to score the final goal in court. It was precision teamwork.

. . .

After a long investigation, Thompson managed to locate and contact the killer's girlfriend, but she too refused to risk her life by testifying. So Thompson set it up for Raul Ramirez to meet with her for a late-night dinner at a non-disclosed location where she told him everything, including the mole under the right eye, but it wasn't on tape. Thompson passed on the information to Serra, who said it wasn't worth a thing if it wasn't on tape.

Thompson said, "No way!" He couldn't risk a repeat interview with the woman, who carried a gun, just to get her story on tape.

But Serra insisted. "You gotta get it on tape or the information's useless."

So Thompson called Raul and the two of them set up another meeting with the girlfriend in a basement restaurant at the Fairmont. Thompson figured she wouldn't shoot them in the Fairmont Hotel. It worked. The defense had its hard evidence.

. . .

Chol was in San Quentin on death row when Serra met him. "He'd already grown from what he was," Serra said, "a smack-shooting Korean immigrant with a reputation for fierceness in and out of prison. He thought the state was going to execute him, but he had an aura, a glow, around him. It was like being in the presence of some kind of Oriental master. His head was shaved. Strong, stable, a man of few words, he had a noticeable directness and candor. I knew when I saw him that he would be a fine witness. A type of natural charisma emanated from him."

Serra never doubted that Chol was innocent of the first murder. Not only was the real assassin known to the Chinese gangs, they actually initiated the claim that an act of judicial racism had occurred in Chol Soo Lee's conviction for the Chinatown killing. It started at street level and made its way up into the higher echelons of the entire Asian community.

The media saw the case as charged with political and racial tensions and much public attention was focused on the retrial, which took place in San Francisco superior court in a "secured" courtroom on the third floor. Everyone had to pass through a metal detector to get into the courtroom; inside a large bulletproof-glass partition separated spectators from the lawyers' section and more bulletproof glass separated the judge and the witness box. It was equipped to protect against an armed attack by spectators. (In Marin County, California, such an attack had occurred shortly before this trial, in which a superior court judge had been abducted from the courtroom and ultimately murdered.)

. . .

An Asian "cause case" of national prominence, the court was packed every day of the trial. Korean immigrants in their native dress attended the trial, as did the Korean ambassador. They brought home-cooked traditional food, which Serra, his team, and the supporters ate during recesses in the hallways. "The pickled vegetables burned my mouth and made my oratory fiery and spiced," he says.

Because it was a death-penalty case, Chol's lawyers prepared an elaborate defense. They presented in court a scale model of the murder scene in Chinatown, aiming to create uncertainty on the part of the three eyewitnesses whose testimony again formed the basis of the prosecution's case. They questioned whether or not any of the prosecution witnesses had the time or ability to identify the killer.

Defense investigator Tink Thompson combed crime-scene photographs for possible Asian witnesses. They identified an Asian American named Steven Lo, who said he saw the killer as he tossed his gun into an alley and it wasn't Chol Soo Lee. In fact, five possible suspects had been picked out of a mug-shot book by witnesses just after the shooting, but when the police line-up was held, only one, Chol, was shown to the witnesses.

Next, defense attorneys discovered that one of the prosecution witnesses, David Lennon, had worked at San Francisco's juvenile hall and had encountered Chol as an inmate four years prior to the Chinatown murder. It was clear that Lennon had identified Chol on the basis of a four-year-old encounter.

In the retrial, the prosecution's key witness was a prison mate of Chol, Arthur Serrato, who claimed Chol had confessed to the killing in a conversation. Serrato, however, had committed three murders, disfiguring one of his victims with a screwdriver before killing him with a shotgun blast to the head. Serrato became a snitch for the prosecution when prosecutor James Lassart offered to appear on Serrato's behalf before the parole board. So the prosecution was offering to aid a man who had acknowledged to committing multiple murders to convict a man whose guilt was in doubt. The jury couldn't help but conclude that if the prosecution had to make a deal with someone like Serrato, they don't have a case.

All of it—the overflow crowds, the attention from Asians and civil libertarians from around the country and the world, the pro-defense pronouncements in the press, and especially the essential weakness of the cross-racial identification—contributed to Chol Soo Lee's acquittal by the retrial jury.

When the verdict came in, the courtroom was filled with Koreans. The judge warned that any commotion would force him to clear the courtroom. Chol, Tony Serra, Tink Thompson, and Stuart Hanlon were at the defense table. When the verdict was read, all they heard was "NOT ..." It was like a pressure wave had entered and purged the courtroom. Chol Soo Lee was acquitted of the crime of the Chinatown murder of Yip Yee Tak for which he was always innocent.

Chol asked permission from the judge to address the court. It was the first time he had spoken in the course of the entire trial. "Your Honor, may I thank my people?" he asked. The judge allowed it. Then Chol took the bit in his teeth and said, "There will be no justice in the criminal-justice system so long as there are prosecutors like *that*," and he pointed his finger at them. With his fist clenched, he announced in a loud and accusatory voice that the prosecutor knew all along that he was innocent, that it was a trumped-up charge, that the whole first trial was a farce.

In the judge's chambers afterwards, defense attorney Stuart Hanlon went to shake homicide investigator Frank Falzon's hand, but Falzon wouldn't take it.

. . .

Chol Soo Lee was vindicated, but he'd already spent 10 years in prison. He'd killed in prison as the result of being incarcerated for a crime he didn't commit. He was ultimately changed by the experience. He represented for Asians in prison someone strong and courageous in a world that was peopled mostly by Aryans, African Americans, and Chicanos. The retrial turned his life around.

Despite the victory, Chol remained in San Quentin, on death row, for the prison killing of Morris Needham.

A candlelight vigil was staged in Sacramento in late 1982, where demonstrators demanded that outgoing Governor Jerry Brown issue a pardon for Chol. But neither Brown nor his successor, George Deukmejian, responded to the pardon demands, waiting for the courts to act. The courts did act. An appeals judge overturned Chol's second murder conviction and ordered a retrial in that case. Finally, eligible for bail, Chol walked out of San Quentin on March 28, 1983, on a quarter-million-dollar bail raised by his defense committee.

The murder of the Aryan Brotherhood member was reduced by the appellate court to second-degree. Chol was given time served and immediately paroled. When he hit the streets, he became a Korean activist. He traveled from Asian community to Asian community around the United States, where he made civil-rights speeches, organized Asians for various political causes, and became a spokesperson for Asian political objectives.

"Normally, in order to acquire society's endearments, one must carve a niche of some sort on the ladder of success," Serra says. "Chol carved his niche by being 'not guilty.' It was almost metaphysical, because he *wasn't* guilty, but he'd been judged so. He had a universal appeal among minority groups. Like Bear Lincoln, he symbolized their experience of mistreatment by the police and judicial process. Chol was a champion and endures in my memory with great fondness."

The Chol Soo Lee case was to become the first of three of Serra's triumphant acquittals of prisoners condemned to death. The other two are Eugene Bear Lincoln and Patrick Hooty Croy.

The many dimensions and colorful images of this case attracted Columbia Pictures, which used it as the inspiration for its 1989 film *True Believer*. It was a major production and commercially very successful.

James Woods played the character based on Serra; he researched his role and subject during an Oakland murder trial in which Serra represented the defendant, who was convicted. His performance was described by writer Michael Checchio as "scenery-chewing."

"I like James Woods," Serra told Checchio. "His face is full of fury and passion. Those things don't come artificially. Woods is confrontational, passionate, loud, aggressive, antagonistic. He speaks on his feet and is full of emotion. When I'm good, that's what I'm like."

However, because the moviemakers couldn't risk libel litigation from the San Francisco authorities, the facts of the Chol Soo Lee case were rearranged, along with the setting (New York) and the Serra character (a burned-out defense attorney who despises his clients). The long and painstaking work of private investigator Josiah "Tink" Thompson was portrayed by a woman who appeared to have nothing much to do.

"Nonetheless," Serra adds, "the case portrayed by Hollywood was of an innocent man who'd been convicted for politically ulterior motives by the district attorney's office. Therefore, I was satisfied with the theme of the movie, which in fact was accurate, even though much of the alleged factual data and circumstances had been meddled with in Hollywood fashion.

"The film industry treated me well; my children were allowed to meet the actors and we watched the shooting of the court scenes, which were done in local courts, even using one judge who presided locally."

Serra was supposed to receive $100,000 for the rights to his story, but perpetually in trouble with the federal tax authorities (a tax protestor since Vietnam days), the IRS grabbed the money before it even left Hollywood.

Serra's comment on that? *"C'ést la vie."*

. . .

"When I was a child, I was riding in a car driving through the Broadway tunnel in San Francisco," Tony says. "In front of us was a member of the Hell's Angels on a Harley. The engine roared and the tires squealed in my ears. Then, to my astonishment, the Hell's Angel somewhat acrobatically dangled one leg so that the metal heeltap on his boot scraped along the pavement. From the impact, sparks flew like the Fourth of July. It was a fabulous image, forever etched in my immature imagination. At that moment, I wanted to be a Hell's Angel when I grew up. In my more innocent moments, I still revere the sound and sight of a Harley Davidson roaring through a tunnel with sparks flying from the foot of its driver."

This, no doubt, is a moment similar to the first time Tony Serra got high on marijuana as a 12-year-old. Who knows? He might have been high when he saw the Hell's Angel Harley. Perhaps the image watered the seed of speed and freedom, already planted in him, that flowered into his destiny as a defender of outlaws.

Hell's Angels, he believes, are poetry on two wheels, a symbol of the fight and freedom of the American West. They are, to the 20th century, what the cowboys were to the 19th. Hell's Angels' freedoms represent our own freedoms. Serra respects their self-respect. He also respects their impulse and commitment to confront the image of overzealous, overreaching, and harassing law enforcement.

He's defended Hell's Angels members off and on in minor and major cases for 25 years. The bike club, after all, has a history of violence. The phrase "hell on wheels" originates from a reference to members of the Hell's Angels.

During one of Serra's Hell's Angels' trials, the judge allowed the defense lawyers rare leeway in court. At one point during cross-examination, Tony badgered FBI Special Agent Tim McKinley about what Serra called an "outrageous memo" McKinley had supposedly penned. The FBI agent was confused. He hadn't written the memo, he told the court, yet there was Serra waving it in his face. McKinley finally figured out that the document had been cut and pasted from three original memos by the prosecution to create a damning, but fictitious, document. It made McKinley look ridiculous.

Serra then called the prosecutor who presented the memo into evidence a "lying dog." The prosecutor objected, to which Serra explained, "Well, Your Honor, what I meant was supine canine." Tony got away with it.

Serra's most memorable Hell's Angels' case, however, was a federal trial conducted over several months in San Francisco in the late '70s. Dozens of Hell's Angels were charged with racketeering. The FBI had seized their motorcycles, their clubhouse accoutrements, their emblems, even their colors, all under the authority of what was called an "indicia warrant," which the defense considered a flagrant violation of the First Amendment.

"The racketeering charge against them was politically and spitefully motivated," Tony recounts. "It was a contest, really, for a basic freedom of association and the Hell's Angels, under the tutelage of their brilliant-minded leader Sonny Barger, well-recognized the historical significance of the contest. Best of all, it was a litigation spectacle without rival."

Hell's Angels chapters from all over the world helped fund the trial. Motorcycle clubs routinely attended the trial flamboyantly wearing similar colors to the ones that had been confiscated. On any given day, up to 100 bikers arrived together at Tony Serra's office, in San Francisco's starched-collar designer district, creating an unequalled sound and fury. They parked all the motorcycles parallel on the sidewalk, and they congregated in a large circle, joined in heated discussion on various aspects of the trial. The literal largeness of the men and the figurative largeness of their presence were overwhelming nonverbal factors in the trial and all that surrounded it.

Serra represented Kenny "K.O." Owen. Most people believed his nickname, K.O., stemmed from his ability to knock you out with one punch. But his friends said that the name was given to him when, in fact, he was KOed during an altercation with a rival gang.

The government, according to Serra, was trying to frame K.O. as a member of a criminal-racketeering organization. "The truth, however, is that he was the most improvident, the most nonmaterialistic, and the most humble of all the Hell's Angels I ever met. In my opening statement, I showed a huge mounted blow-up of him, probably four-by-six-feet, to the jury. He was perched on top of his motorcycle along a highway in Nevada, sunning himself in the desert glare. He was bearded, his clothes were dirty, the motorcycle looked abused. It was the quintessential image of 'man and his machine' against the backdrop of a baked-dry geography. The most poignant part of the photo was the somewhat beatific smile on his face as he contemplated his metaphysical existential being. It was an overwhelming symbol, almost religious in connotation.

"'Is this the man they claim is a racketeer?' I said to the jury. 'He doesn't even possess the proverbial pot to piss in, or even to cook his daily stew. This photo symbolizes the strength and the unity of all Hell's Angels. They *are* their motorcycles; their motorcycles are *them*. There's a unity between man and machine, an aesthetic balance point where man and machine unify. Therefore, no Hell's Angel—as a true Hell's Angel—can ever be a racketeer. The Hell's Angel is the melody and rhythm of metal and motor and movement. That is their singular strength. That is their singular poetry.'"

In the trial, the witnesses ranged from drug-addict snitches to undercover cops; their misidentifications and failures of recollection ran rampant. The government's widespread search warrants had netted a little methamphetamine, which was the central stage of the prosecution. The murders referred to during the course of the trial had, it was later revealed, been committed by the government's own informants.

No one was convicted. All the seized indicia of the Hell's Angels organization were returned. It was a paramount victory for First Amendment rights and, for at least a decade, served as an impediment to government attempts to secure racketeering convictions against motorcycle organizations.

"I still have that photo in my office and each day I send a silent smile to K.O.," Serra says. "He's doing life in federal prison in California now, convicted in the mid-eighties of possession and sale of methamphetamine. He became a victim of a vicious prosecution and an unfeeling federal judge. May he be at peace with himself."

Chapter 4

The Monk, the Family Man, the Warrior-Lawyer

He seemed to be charged by a bolt of lightning. Not run-of-the-mill lightning, either, but an errant bolt, charged by the gods with something extra, which made him seem more than merely radiant and electric. When he walked into a room, for example, hairs stood on end. Electromagnetic currents rearranged themselves to accommodate his presence. Wherever he went, *that* was the place to be. That was the central vortex around which everything else swirled.

As his secretary, Penelope Rose, once told me, "He's the white tornado. When he enters a room, everything changes."

Though his life was mostly in the public eye, he wasn't one to mingle in the usual sense of the word. He was more like an ambulatory stage around which others gathered. He was the lit match in the grand tinderbox of life.

At first I watched in awe. I kept my distance, like a raven scoping out the scene from a safe branch neither too near, nor too far. Later, I joined into stride with his other devotees, spellbound, carried along by the pull of his tide.

That was when I began to learn about J. Tony Serra, the man, the lawyer, the myth. I watched and listened and sensed and mulled. I heard about him in his own words and in the words of others. I read about him in newspaper accounts of his trials and feature stories about his life. And in his orbit, eventually, I started recording impressions of him in words of my own.

.   .   .

One of the first aspects of Tony Serra that fascinated me was his vow of poverty. Exactly when is lost to the mists of history, but long ago, Tony Serra decided never to buy anything new. Certainly, he wasn't imbued by his parents with an acquisitive nature; he was never taught that true worth was found in material things. Placing no value in consumerism, he's free to live life like a gladiator, like a samurai, like a warrior who prizes the battle more than the booty. He practices law like Robin Hood. He takes half his cases on a pro bono basis and he pays the court costs out of his own pocket. He rarely has more than $100 on him. Unlike the vast majority of his colleagues, he's not a materialist. He's not a capitalist. He's proud of it.

Serra conducts his life without any of the normal securities. He has no checking account, no savings account, no credit cards, no insurance policies, no real property, no possessions of any consequence. He doesn't wear a watch. His clothes are from the thrift shop, the Salvation Army, or various free-boxes around the country. A good romp through a Goodwill store in some podunk town piques his excitement like a kid in a candy store. When you have nothing, he says, everything is something.

One of his passions is junk cars. At any given time, two or three of them can be found squatting in his yard with flat tires. His criteria? It has to run and the brakes have to work. Anything beyond that is gravy. Then he relaxes. His philosophy is you can do practically anything you please while driving a disposable vehicle; the cops are looking for the fancy sporty models. When it breaks down, he abandons it, often painting "Please Tow!" on it for a quick pickup. (He once abandoned a burning Lincoln on his way to court when its transmission spontaneously combusted.) He never grows attached to a disposable car; when it's no longer drivable, he simply lets go.

In keeping with carving out his own singular image of non-conformity, Serra's courtroom attire is a mockery of the high-priced designer wear of his peers. He thrills at spending four dollars to buy a suit for court. The clothes rarely fit, usually a size too small, the fabric straining to accommodate the muscular outline of his athletic body. He wears shirts with the cuffs stapled shut and pants torn at the knee and mended from the inside with colored duct tape. His prized possessions are offbeat ties and a mountainous soap collection from the motels in cities where he's tried cases. The ties hang from crisscrossed lines in his rent-controlled apartment like prayer flags. The soap collection has become so large that it occupies prime space—like a valued objet d'art—in the entryway of his small North Beach apartment, which he's rented for over 40 years for $411 a month. It has no telephone or TV. A potted marijuana plant lives and thrives on the stove, which serves no other purpose.

He insists, "It's not what you wear that counts. It's who you are."

Serra generates just enough money to pay his share of office expenses and cover his simple lifestyle. He conducts his life on an all-cash basis: no receipts, no deductible expenses, no paper trail. In the '70s he was sent to federal prison camp at Lompoc for four months for his refusal to pay income taxes. Shortly after check-in, he applied to set up a free legal service for inmates. "All I need is a room and a typewriter," he said. He was assigned to garbage detail instead.

The IRS is still waiting for him to open a bank account, so they can seize it. "The IRS comes after me every minute of my life. But I don't have anything. I'm not felonious, I don't deceive, I don't cheat. I just don't pay."

Still, despite his commitment to remain in poverty, Serra's mentality is the personification of abundance. Wherever he goes, a richness of spirit accompanies him. He gives generously of his time, his most precious commodity. It's not uncommon for Serra to take time out from a trial to give a speech to a law-school class or a small community gathering. Grateful clients say to him, "Stay in my condo in Hawaii." "Use my apartment in Paris."

As I got to know him, I began to understand that at some level, Tony Serra is spiritually tapped into life's deep well whence all things flow.

. . .

Outside the courtroom, Serra is a contented homebody. He's an earthy man, hands-on in every aspect of his personal life. When in Bolinas, he chops his own firewood, takes pride in the status of his home-grown tomatoes and marijuana, tends to the laundry, and tidies up the kitchen. He can frequently be seen lying under the chassis of one of his old cars, wrench in hand, doing the repairs himself. He's savvy with the breeds and needs of plants and a friend to animals. His coffee cup runneth over, and the bird feeder is always full.

The history of Serra's domestic relationships includes a short marriage to Judith Kuster in his footloose days after college. They ventured off to South America together on a motorcycle. By the time they returned, the partnership was over and so was Serra's belief in marriage contracts.

Serra fathered five children with his second partner, Mary Edna Dinneen. He helped home-deliver all of his own children with Mary Edna in their funky house in the hippie town of Bolinas, California, on the wild and somewhat remote coast of Marin County. A friend says the Serra family lived in a house that looked as if it grew out of a tree, out of the earth, out of the flowers, spilling over with children and animals. His partnership with Mary Edna lost out to the demands of the law, and after they broke up, as rumor has it, she said, "The problem is, after Tony, there's no one."

Mary Edna's painted portrait continued to occupy a central position on one wall of Tony Serra's Pier 5 office on the Embarcadero long after their breakup. While I was photographing the office, I asked him if there was anything in particular he didn't want me to miss. He looked around and grumbled, as if nothing mattered. Then, on reconsideration, his eyes settled upon the portrait, titled *Mary Edna of Bolinas,* and he pointed to it, saying, "This is the mother of my children."

The eldest of his children are twin boys, Shelter and Ivory, born in 1973. Two years younger is Serra's third son, Chime Day, then two girls: Wonder Fortune is two years younger than Chime, and Lilac Bright is three years younger than Wonder. His children adore their father. Serra is as emphatic about the importance of education as he is about his disdain for consumerism and TV. He told his kids they could rob banks if they wanted, but that they were not allowed to watch TV. Beyond that, he claims not to have imposed his expectations on his children. "Your kids should start on your horizon," he says. "They should pick up where you left off. If you understand your kids, the species is not advancing."

His dominating personality pervaded family life, but so, too, did his ferocious love of his children and his respect and support of their individuality. He speaks with regret about having been absent for so many of their formative years. Serra lived in his North Beach apartment during the week, visiting his family in Bolinas on the weekends. Even so, the bond between the father and his children has remained a close one. Certainly, they must have inherited and received enough of the right stuff for they each possess an immediate personable quality and are creatively endowed, confident, successful, and productive.

Even though they were born and raised in west Marin County and never had a television, they're in no way provincial. Serra always encouraged them to enlarge their horizons out into the world and then, like many parents who encourage independence in their children, he bemoaned the fact when they all flew the coop. They attended colleges in California and around the East Coast. Richard Serra, Tony's brother who has no children of his own, paid their tuition.

Each chose a profession in the arts. Shelter, the older twin, is a painter, Ivory a photographer. Both reside in New York. Chime is in theater-production design in Los Angeles. Wonder is in the film industry. Lilac is a jewelry designer. Whenever time allows, they return home to Bolinas, home to their roots, to the wind and fog of the small seashore town of their birth.

Their father is happy that none aspires to be a lawyer. "The practice of law," he says, "as an advocate, as a trial lawyer, is a hard life. It's mostly what I call a martial life. You're at war. You're constantly going from battle to battle. I don't wish that upon my children."

Serra co-parented the son of his current partner, Vicki Day. Though they're not married, he considers Vicki's son Eric his stepson. Ironically, it's Eric who has become the lawyer in the family.

· · ·

The same interpersonal dynamic of family closeness can't be said about Tony Serra's relationship to his younger brother Richard, whose colossal sculptures of steel torqued and tipped have garnered him world-class acclaim. It's as though the genes of genius find the same expression in different media.

The *New York Times* has called Richard Serra the most significant sculptor of his generation. Tony Serra has been acclaimed one of the greatest criminal-defense lawyers of the century. Nearly every notable museum in the world owns a Richard Serra sculpture. Tony boasts he has adjudicated every type of crime.

I find it fascinating that these two brothers, these two titans, are polar opposites, achieving exactly the same result at opposite ends of the country, Richard in the arts bending massive tonnages of steel, Tony in the law, bending the iron-locked mind-set of jurors. But they didn't get it by comparing notes. They're not even on speaking terms with each other.

Richard's rivalry with his older brother finally came to a head with the death of their mother. Word has it that Richard never forgave Tony for not attending her funeral. Maybe it stems from a deeper place. Maybe it has to do with the fact that Richard always had to struggle for everything he got, whereas life came easy to Tony, the older brother whom Richard looked up to. Though both brothers were born with a fierce determination and brawn and both were and are brilliant, Tony was tall, good-looking, and charismatic. Richard was short and scrappy, and coarse-featured like his peasant ancestry. Tony was a football champion. Richard played football, but broke his back. Richard's bowlegged loping gait suggests someone who has had a back injury. Tony's loping gait suggests someone who has hip problems.

Richard traces his first epiphany regarding perception back to the age of four when he noticed that his footprints in the sand on the beach were different in one direction than in another, leading the little boy to conclude that direction and perception are interconnected. The probe into the nature of perception and direction and its effect on the mind has been a major part of Richard's life's work. Richard does it consciously. Tony does it unconsciously.

"To compete with my older brother for my parents' affections, I would draw all the time," Richard says. "After about the third grade, my mother started taking me to museums and introducing me as her son the artist. She also told my older brother he was going to become an attorney. And he became an attorney. The strength of a Jewish mother."

Tony was such a bright light in his mother's eye that Richard lived in his shadow. But there was enough maternal Jewish pride to pitch them both over the top. Still, their standoff is so great that on Charlie Rose's two-part interview with Richard Serra prior to his 40-year retrospective at the New York Museum of Modern Art in 2007, Richard referred to his brother as "the lawyer," never by name.

Tony says of Richard and Rudy, "We're the Brothers Karamazov, definitely fratricidal. We have the Achilles tendon of vanity, all three of us." He goes on to characterize Richard. "I'm the oldest, but with Richard and me, the roles are reversed; he's always been like the judgmental grandfather, profoundly disapproving. At all levels I admire him, except the interpersonal. On the other hand, he's been very good to my kids." It's an amazing irony that even the normal financial destinies have been switched in their case. Tony says, "I'm the poor lawyer and he's the rich artist."

Yet both Richard and Tony have turned their art forms into something that has never been done before. There is an uncanny similarity in their work at its deepest level. They've both mastered the art of altering perception to align itself with their desired result.

. . .

Tony Serra's lust for life has always manifested a worldliness acquired from extensive travel.

"Anyone who wants to practice law on a meaningful level must travel, must experience the sociological diversities of life, must journey externally, meaning geographically, and internally, meaning psychologically," he insists.

In the days prior to psychedelics, Serra traveled hobo-style through Central America, South America, Asia, the Middle East, and Australia.

On one such adventure, he and Mary Edna, with their newborn twins in tow, were traveling through the Ethiopian desert on unpaved roads in a rented car. The area was known to be dangerous, subject to gangs of desert thieves. Tourists were cautioned to hire an armed escort, but Serra took the risk of going it alone. After their vehicle overheated and stalled, with the five-week-old twins asleep in the back seat, a gang of all-white camels mounted by thieves surrounded the car. Having nothing else to offer the bandits, Serra reached back and produced the two naked infants, one in each hand like squirming footballs, and held them out as an offering. The bandits were so disarmed by this absurd gesture that they just laughed and went on their way. A short time later, two French tourists weren't so lucky. They were robbed and killed in the same area.

. . .

In the '70s, Serra campaigned to become mayor of his native San Francisco on the Platypus Party ticket. His campaign slogan was, "Make the streets safe for dancing." His platform included a stand for decriminalizing victimless crime, which he believed would create *de facto* legalization of a lot of so-called criminal activity. Most victimless crimes, especially drug use, fall more in the medical and social realms. Although Serra lost his bid for mayor, he came in first among the alternative candidates. He is still fighting the battle for the decriminalization of victimless crimes, which includes the legalization of marijuana.

"The last battlefield for constitutional rights is being waged over drugs," he declared back in the '90s. He was one of the first Californians to receive a medical-marijuana card, which allows him to smoke anywhere, anytime. He touts that it is because of his forty-year history of smoking pot that he has been able to sustain the balance of sanity that it takes to survive as a criminal-defense trial lawyer for so many decades.

Indeed, the medical reason for his marijuana card is exactly that. "My doctor recommended it, because of stress. Most of the great criminal-defense lawyers were alcoholics and I have escaped that. I don't have high blood pressure. I don't have migraines. I don't have any of that shit, and I think it's because of grass. My doctor agrees. He agrees that criminal law is a high-stress occupation and that stress is a condition that can be alleviated by marijuana."

. . .

In the decades since he began his career, Serra has experienced the full swing of the pendulum. He considers his dauntless perseverance to be his greatest attribute, comparable to the fact that he played football without a helmet. In fact, when I asked him what he considered to be his greatest accomplishment, he responded, "Forty-five years of back-to-back jury trials." Traditionally, a semantic warrior can last a decade or so. The all-or-nothing intensity required to be a true believer, to fight to the death, only lasts that long. In the field of criminal-defense law, attorneys seem to burn out fast, falling prey to a variety of infirmities, not the least of which are workaholism, alcoholism, and drug abuse. But through some fortuity, Serra has a stronger constitution, or a stronger will, or both. Thus, he's prevailed in this realm because he's lasted.

"The narrow focus of my expertise," he says, "is fighting overzealous police in court. How small, how trivial that is. I'm like one foot-soldier fighting another in a huge battle. I'm not the war theorist. I'm not the general. But it turns out that foot soldier, he's been fighting these other foot soldiers for more than forty years and he's still fighting.

"Most criminal-defense attorneys, after ten years or so, start to like butterflies, children, music, the sound of the sea. They become romanced with life. They're no longer one hundred percent disciplined. They're no longer made of iron. One symptom of the decaying warrior's mind is extending compassion to the enemy. I've got to guard against transcending the conflict and seeing both sides of it. I've got to see both sides of it to win, but I can't give credence to the other side. Old soldiers begin to lose the acute sense of the kill, the ability to always go for the jugular. Because I'm an aging warrior, I sometimes find myself having sympathy for a young district attorney who's crude in his arts of deception. It's tempting to smile and forgive instead of crush."

. . .

Which brings us to the courtroom, where trial lawyers practice their powers, their magic, and their skill to crush. It is in the courtroom that Tony Serra reigns supreme. The courtroom is his birthright and his *rai-*

son d' être. This is where all of his life experiences come together: the years of excelling in combative sports, the hobo travels, the street life, the love of classic literature, the fine tuning of higher education, the psychedelic insight, the rhythm and cadence of dance, his rage against injustice, and his lust for conflict.

To trials he brings an artistry that is unparalleled. When Serra is good, there's no one like him. His cross-examinations of snitches and his closing arguments attract lawyers and law students from all over the country.

In court Serra is drama at its best. But the performance is *real*, spontaneously improvised, passionately executed, and frequently a matter of life and death. It's no accident that Tony Serra has achieved some of the most important and unlikely trial successes of his time. At his best, his nexus with juries is uncanny; lawyers from all over the country spectate at his trials to witness and learn from his courtroom histrionics, savage cross-examinations, and erudite and impassioned closing arguments. Serra doesn't hold back. He acts out all the roles: now the victim, now the assailant, now the cop, now the snitch, now the narc, in a one-man moral passion play. His commanding voice, massive hands, powerful body, and agile mind are his only instruments, and he employs them to the fullest.

Serra considers himself a "semantic warrior." He keeps his warrior spirit disciplined and honed for battle by way of obsessive focus on his work, physical exercise, medical marijuana, and a passion for truth and justice. Part of this discipline is to be unencumbered with material baggage; he hasn't sold out his integrity for the price of material well-being. He fits the warrior image much better than he fits the lawyer image. He has never surrendered to the conformity of the court system. Rather, he brings to the system a vision of compassion for the human predicament in an imperfect world.

True to his own rebellious nature, Serra is the champion of outlaws. He is the mouthpiece of the oppressed, protector of the underprivileged, legal spokesman for leaders of radical political causes, heroic lone wolves, and social rebels. He gives them a voice by articulating their plight. He ennobles their social status by dignifying their humanity. Serra's commitment to the cause of justice for the maligned is so unwavering that if the tables of power were to turn, if law-enforcement agents were the ones being persecuted, Serra would gird his loins for battle and rush to represent *them*, trumpeting his battle-cry: "It's not their fault. They've been conditioned by sociopolitical forces beyond their control!"

It is here that Serra becomes the alchemist, transforming base elements into gold. He internalizes the qualities of his client; he "shoots up" the outrages perpetrated on them by the unjust socio-political circumstances of an unfair society. Then he elevates it to new levels of conscious expression, hitting the jury hard in their humanity, so that the person accused of criminal acts is not a taint on society, but rather a fellow human being who, but for the grace of God ...

The law, Serra is convinced, does not reach out and extend an egalitarian beneficence to the citizenry at large. Law is a bulwark the ruling class erects to protect its power and prosperity. The law is for the preservation of the status quo, the establishment. The law sustains and enriches the corporate, military, and political elite. Like the American Indian declares: "Justice is 'just us': the white mans law is for the white man only."

The underbelly of each culture, he says, except in rare historical moments, is too suppressed to revolt. So the most courageous, intelligent, and aggressive of the socio-politically and economically vanquished class engage in so-called criminal activity. This is a form of class struggle, he says. This is covert rebellion. The vast majority of criminal acts are declarations of estrangement from the establishment and quests for psychological and economic independence. Most crime arises from deprivation and privation: social, economic, political, and psychological.

"No," Serra rails in the voice of the people he defends. "I will not be your lackey. I will not be your wage slave. I will not be the bricks and mortar of your resplendent edifices."

Prisons are not populated, he firmly believes, with the vicious and the incompetent. Rather, they're filled with the bold and the free-willed.

"I will not work for MacDonald's," Serra continues. "Instead, I will steal from MacDonalds. I will not sell your TVs. Instead, I will sell my dope. I will not be your consumer credit-card victim. Instead, I will be your identity thief."

Where did Serra's anti-authority attitude originate, I wondered.

"It's a prenatal thing," he responds. "It's in your nature. Then it gets curried and developed. Anti-authority anti-social people are the ones who get into fights. They go to jail. I could have gone that route. I just happened to get good grades, so I got funneled into the law, which is a great place to be anti-establishment.

"I have a built-in tenet, a deep belief that if you divest society from its constraints, its oppression, its exploitation, its imbalance, its self-destruction, if you can be just a *part* of that process, with a blind trust in the forces of evolution, then of necessity society will get better. In that sense, you either impede or facilitate the flow. If you think you can facilitate the flow toward goodness, then you fight the battle with the glimmer of some idealistic image you have high in your thought process that trusts it all."

Still, as one who shoulders so much of the world's pain and sorrow, Serra is not immune to the impact of his own despair. Over the course of time, this semantic warrior has certainly incurred his share of battle wounds. The passion and deep feelings for which he is famous turn inward with his losses. He takes each blow to the heart. His torrential energy hurls him into a seeming abyss of darkness where he battles with his own inner forces.

But somewhere in this dark and heaving sea, he plumbs that special place within himself where he taps his source of regeneration. His moods are consuming, but he doesn't impose them on others. What Serra has going for him is that while he is in his personal underworld, he never loses touch with the overview. While part of him is fully locked in the experience, another part of him observes the poignancy of it all.

Chapter 5

What Others Say

Houghton case
J. Tony Serra   1-31-94   © Paulette Frankl

Not everyone is swayed by Serra's theatrics. His cases involve alleged drug dealers, murderers, subversives, organized-crime figures, and the like, some of whom leave a scum on one's teeth. "Talk Left: the Politics of Crime," an Internet forum, contains this blurb about Serra. "Tony will tell you that he has to achieve total empathy with a client before he can defend him. He has to convince *himself*. He loses objectivity. He wills himself to. Tony won't ask a client what really happened. He'll just listen to his version of the events and he'll help create a scenario within ethical limits that would stand up to cross-examination. He goes through a process, much like an actor will, until he becomes a man who believes in his client, or even becomes the client himself."

Furthering that line of thinking, Gary Delanges, president of the San Francisco Police Officers Association, told journalist Burr Snider in a November 2006 *San Francisco Magazine* piece on Serra, "As far as I'm concerned, he's just another classic-liberal whacked-out San Francisco defense attorney. I'm always fascinated by these guys, how when ninety-nine percent of their clients are guilty, they can rationalize defending them." Then he adds, "I was in narcotics for fifteen years and was cross-examined by him on several occasions, and I have to say, he's no cheap-shot artist. I kind of respect guys that believe their own bullshit, and Tony, God bless him, believes his."

In that same article, Burr Snider wrote that Jeff Adachi, Public De-fender for the City and County of San Francisco, "routinely encourages his young lawyers to experience Serra in courtroom action. He not only does meticulous preparation and has a tremendous command of detail, he has that rare ability to grab a jury and bring them into his reality. When they look at him, they don't see a slick defense lawyer trying to argue a technicality; they see a smart down-to-earth guy with all this integrity."

I found this to be a common sentiment. In spite of Serra's blatant re-fusal to conform to courtroom decorum, he's highly respected by judges, jurors, even adversaries.

George Vinson, Agent in Charge of the FBI's Fresno office, said of Serra, "He's fantastic. I certainly wouldn't want anyone in the govern-ment to ever underestimate him."

U.S. Attorney James Lassart says of his adversary, "It's a pleasure to be an opponent to the best, because it brings out the best in you. He's tough and he's strong and he has a tremendous presence in the court-room." In spite of their opposing viewpoints, Lassart goes on to say, "He has integrity. If he represents that he's going to do something, he does it. I trust him." Lassart adds, "The key to Serra's success is his discipline and his commitment to ideology. If he didn't believe, he'd lose his verve. Tony only has two positions, stop and go, and if he ever got disillusioned, he couldn't go anymore."

Santa Clara County Superior Judge Lawrence Terry says, "He's a trial judge's dream. He follows the rules and regulations, he's not rude, he's always on time, and he's always prepared. He fights vigorously, but if you rule against him, he accepts it and goes back to work."

A fellow lawyer remarked, "He's a lawyer's lawyer. His style and his cross-examinations are seamless. He's the Joe Montana of lawyers."

"It's not just theatrics," says Frank Fernandez, a San Francisco dep-uty public defender who attended the Patrick "Hooty" Croy trial as often as he could. "He's extremely well-prepared and quick on his feet. He can catch a witness in a contradiction before the words are all out of the person's mouth. I come to just watch and learn."

Aaron Williams, prosecutor for the Bear Lincoln case, stated, "He has great presence and he's a master of the English language."

One witness for the prosecution said after a grueling goring on the witness stand by Serra, "If I ever get into trouble, get me *that* lawyer!"

Internet columnist "Mike" of CrimeandFederalism.com had this to say about Serra. "I've met him and many of the lawyers at his law firm. He is brilliant, creative, and studied in local court practice and procedure. If I needed legal representation, I'd hire him. I would take out a credit card if that's what it took. He is that good. If I lived in San Francisco, I would want to work for him. In fact, he's probably the only lawyer I am really interested in studying under. Not too many people know about him, because he's low-key. He drives a crappy car and smokes medical marijuana every day. He'll tell you everything I'm telling you. I'd put money up that he is about 20 IQ points above any of his critics. The lawyers he works with at his law firm are similarly intelligent, creative, and tough."

National and international recognition of his work includes his ranking by *American Lawyer* magazine in December 1982 as the second-best criminal defense attorney in the country for his handling of both the Chol Soo Lee trial and, that same year, the Faez Boukaran case. Boukaran was a Lebanese merchant charged with being one of the world's largest smugglers of hashish. Serra's brutal cross-examination of the government's main witness, James Hoffman, discredited the entire case. (James Hoffman was discredited a second time when he testified against John DeLorean in DeLorean's infamous cocaine trial.) Serra was also selected as one of the ten top criminal defense attorneys of the century by *California Lawyer* magazine.

In 1992, Serra received the National Reformer's Award from the National Drug Policy Foundation in Washington, D.C., for his contribution to drug reform. His Brownie Mary case in 1992 led to the passage of California's medical-marijuana law and his Clean Needle Exchange case, also in 1992, prompted legal reforms that have assisted in curbing the AIDS epidemic.

In 1997, the American Civil Liberties Union presented Serra with the Benjamin Dreyfus Civil Liberties Award. The television programs

"60 Minutes" and "20/20" have featured segments on Serra; "20/20" did a documentary of his Chol Soo Lee case. He's also appeared on "Larry King Live." And due to his mastery of the law and his devotion to humanitarian justice, Cambodia invited Serra to help restructure its judicial system.

Scott McKay said that he and his partner David Nevin, reputed to be Idaho's most famous defense lawyer who worked on the case of Khalid Sheik Mohammed (Guantanamo Bay's most infamous detainee), drove to the courthouse listening to motivational tapes by Tony Serra. "It would get us fired up," McKay said. "His whole thing is the criminal-defense attorney is a warrior—not a fence-mender, not a pacifier, not a negotiator. A warrior!"

.   .   .

Serra's world is a paradigm of paradox.

Certainly, according to his peers, colleagues, and adversaries, he's a lawyer's lawyer. Yet Serra considers himself an "anti-lawyer lawyer." He refers to most lawyers as "carrion-eaters who prey on the undisciplined acts of human behavior. Lawyers don't contribute directly in their profession to the prosperity of the country. They are parasites who aid and abet the status quo. They're birds of prey who don't even make their own kills. They're waiting for a mishap, a misdeed, a negligence, a breach of contract, a death or probate, a dissolution of marriage, a child-support issue, a crime. They prey like buzzards feeding off of despair, pain, conflict, and defeat."

Also, and much to my surprise, I found Serra to be a remarkably gentle soul outside of court. His killer instincts, generally, retract like a lion's claws. The lion, is in fact, a vegetarian! Even more astounding was that in all the years that I was in his presence, I never heard him so much as raise his thunder roll to those who worked for him, even though there were plenty of times when life's imperfections warranted a bona fide rage.

Serra himself goes into deeper detail about his paradoxes and flaws in Chapters 17 and 18. But his character flaws can't be judged in normal terms. He's all heart, grandiosely generous and caring, at the same time that he's inconsiderate, self-absorbed, stubborn, and unapologetically infuriating. He's a package deal, but he's worth it. Everyone who comes into contact with him is bigger for the experience. He walks with the great ones, puffing on his joint instead of a Briar. He brings light to places in the darkness where others fear to tread.

After seeing the film *True Believer,* I expected Serra's office to be a stark no-nonsense smoke-filled cell in a life-threatening part of the city, comparable to a newspaper press room, with people shouting, paper everywhere, and a pervading sense of unnerving frenzy. So much for Hollywood.

The Pier 5 Law Offices have occupied three different locations in the course of this book (and I have moved to two different states). When I first began this project, the office was located on Jackson Street in San Francisco's colorful designer district on the third floor of a converted whiskey warehouse. From there, it moved to Pier 5 on the Embarcadero waterfront, and now the new address is 506 Broadway, at the intersection of Broadway and Kearny, across from a porn shop—right in the heart of North Beach—in what used to be Finocchios, the best transvestite cabaret in town. The address was also renowned for Enrico's restaurant. Each change of address brings with it a change of architecture, size, and layout, but what hasn't changed is the psychedelic decor and retro-ambience of the '60s. Whatever the address, I always think of Serra's law office as a trip into another era, where a certain gentle hospitality welcomes the desperate cross-cultural lives of criminals from everywhere.

Noteworthy on the office website is the figure of Lady Justice, sitting on her throne, with her scales of justice in one hand and the sword of truth in the other. Her cheeks are inordinately flushed, perhaps because she's surrounded by a resplendent growth of marijuana plants. A wavy banner reads: "Marijuana Defense." And below the image is a statement, "We have successfully defended more medical-marijuana cases than any other group of lawyers in the State of California for over 40 years."

Outside, a black marquee, frosted with the white splattering of pigeon droppings, reads in large letters, JUSTICE FOR ALL. Open the door and follow the sign: Honest Lawyer One Flight Up.

Steep stairs lead the visitor into another world. Two small dogs announce the arrival of a stranger in piercing yaps. The scene is colorful, homey, spiritual, and gamey; it's punctuated with humor and grim reminders of reality. Red-painted Chinese dragons face off with each other head to head on the air duct overhead, while the beneficent face of the Dalai Lama on a poster smiles compassionately upon the secretaries who transcribe the briefs. A nearly life-sized painting, depicting a prison scene with two hooded guards dressed in black leading a handcuffed inmate in orange prison issue between a line of cells with an American flag behind the bars, dominates the entire wall behind the conference table.

Elsewhere in the office, Eastern art blends with Native American and courtroom art, along with plants, photos, and a totem pole. A large black throw rug underfoot displays the yellow outline of a corpse, like a crime scene.

In a 1989 profile of Serra in the *San Francisco Recorder*, writer Michael Checchio described one of the more colorful artifacts in the office: "In a box beneath the lawyer's desk lie the cremated remains of one of Serra's best friends, murdered drug dealer and former client Sammy Gee."

A team of high-energy hip lawyers, dogs, and assorted staff members all call this place home, claiming, "There's nowhere else we'd rather be." In the 6/13/07 *San Francisco Chronicle,* a blurb in Leah Garchk's column announced, "Tony Serra, honest ex-con, labels this piece of information 'potentially interesting': 'I have unofficially ascertained that our office holds the record for law-office canine-to-personnel ratio: We have six daily present dogs and eighteen daily present persons. The dogs range from Chihuahua to Chow; the people range from barkers to biters.'"

Once, years ago, one of San Francisco's wild parakeets flew in the window and made the law office its home-of-choice. It lived out its life, caged but cheerful, chirping its song of freedom beside the window.

Unlike most legal offices, which are bereft of intimacy and smack of other people's money, Serra's office is personal, a lair of "treasures," memorabilia, and rubble. In place of certificates of consequence, the walls seem to be growing memory like moss in a dense forest. Each photo, each piece of art, each sculpture, totem, hookah, gargoyle, skull, hide, beaded necklace, hat, urn of ashes of deceased clients, pin, poem, feather, endearment, each item is a page of history in the life of Tony Serra. He only has to focus on any object for its story to unfold in its entirety with all its energy intact.

The painted pattern on his office floor differs from location to location. In the last office it was a bright psychedelic mandala handpainted by two of his close friends. The current office offers a strewing of painted flowers underfoot, a sharp contrast to the dire nature of his cases.

Simple wooden chairs encircle a round table, upon which rests a clay sculpture with struggling bodies and fused heads done by his son, Shelter. These mementos and symbols comprise the pow-wow area where Serra convenes in private with his clients.

Plants and children's toys are also a part of Serra's mondo. On his desk is always a mostly empty cup of coffee and a fuzzy toy seal used as a paperweight for piles of court papers that spill over onto the floor.

The greater partnership law office is a vortex of creative energy. True to the now politically incorrect phrase, "behind every great man is a great woman," this office is a citadel for great women. Serra's devoted secretary of nearly 30 years, Penelope Rose, is also an acclaimed fashion designer and organizer par excellence of extraordinary office events. Stephanie Brown, Serra's "right arm" and personal secretary, was once a superb cabaret singer.

Diana Samuelson is a top-notch death-penalty lawyer, who frequently co-counsels Tony's cases. When Diana's daughter Ella was a toddler, Diana frequently brought her to work instead of to day care. The cheerful child enjoyed the affection of everyone in the office and brought her own exuberance to the work place.

Serra shares cases with a dozen or more lawyers in the office, half of whom are women. At any given time, Serra carries 20-something cases as his pending caseload. His associates and assistants are critical and dear to him.

The office is run on the principle that all the lawyers in the firm share the operating expenses. But beyond that, all fees earned are their own.

The spirit of the law office is almost tribal. It's more than a job. It's a belonging. It's a working team of like-minded people, composed of tried-and-true long-timers and brilliant young lawyers learning firsthand from Serra, a domineering, though caring, leader and teacher. His purpose is to share his knowledge and to empower others. The experience is one of rare democracy.

Serra maintains a grueling calendar of back-to-back jury trials. The eager young lawyers do all his pretrial preparation. He relies entirely on his team—whom he trusts implicitly—to provide him with the vital information. A fanatic about detail, he insists that every move, no matter how minor, be scripted in advance. "If it's not on the page, it's not on the stage" is Serra's motto. Every stone must be turned over twice, so that when Serra walks on hot coals in front of a judge and jury, there are no surprises, no pitfalls.

Building a case is a long and involved process that takes on a life of its own. But on the night prior to opening statements, Serra hunkers down and commits his colleagues' massive findings to his photographic memory. His ability to absorb the intricacies of a case in so little time never ceases to flabbergast those who know him. But it's just this terrifying improvisation that gives his style of litigation its electrifying vitality.

. . .

And then, late in the afternoon just before the office closes, Tony Serra returns from court. More often than not, he's drained and spent, his face ashen, careworn and weary, having taken on the pains of his clients. He retreats into his office, where papers are stacked high on his desk with the urgencies of other clients, awaiting his immediate attention.

But first, he settles into his big chair and smokes a joint. He stares out the window for a spell, then returns to his paperwork, renewed, centered, at peace, ready for a long night's work ahead.

Though Serra admits quite readily that he's a pot addict, it seems to me that his real addiction isn't the weed, it's the work. Over the decades, thus, Serra has created a system of checks and balances whereby one addiction zeroes out the other. Workaholism is time-consuming, whereas the addiction of marijuana is time-restoring. It slows and elongates time. Marijuana changes the pace of his inner metronome.

Tony is living proof that long-term use of marijuana doesn't necessarily dull the brain or collapse the memory and that it's not such a bad thing to be conscious on many levels at once. When the multi-levels of awareness are in sync with one another, it's personal power in alignment. Marijuana mends and recoups the fractures of his day and makes him whole again.

"My significance lies in being the best hippie-radical criminal-defense trial lawyer in the U.S.A," Serra proudly proclaims, adding, "I've taken more LSD than any peer colleague!"

As for retirement, Serra says, "I won't. I'll die on the podium. I'll have a heart attack making a final argument. There's nothing else out there I want to do."

Chapter 6

The Last of
a Dying Breed

Tony Serra
7/31/95   P. Frankel

J. Tony Serra considers himself the last of a dying breed. He has carried the torch of the tradition from the last century of the old-fashioned lawyer, whose arguments in court attracted people for the sheer experience of being in the same room as great oratory. In those days before television, before radio, before motion pictures, spectators turned out dressed in their finest apparel, comparable to dressing in honor of great theater. Such occasions made everyone feel a little taller, a little larger for having experienced the giants of the justice system at close range.

Clarence Darrow was such a lawyer. Darrow was best known for representing the well-to-do teenage thrill killers Leopold and Loeb at their sentencing hearing, after they confessed to murdering 14-year-old Bobby Franks in 1924; in his 12-hour closing argument, Darrow convinced the judge that Leopold and Loeb were mentally deranged and shouldn't be put to death. A year later, Darrow defended John T. Scopes in the so-called Scopes "Monkey" Trial. For most of his career, Darrow was a leading member of the American Civil Liberties Union.

William Kunstler was another of the Darrow breed of attorney. A board member of the ACLU and a celebrated civil-rights lawyer, Kunstler was known far and wide for successfully defending the Chicago Seven, who were charged with conspiracy and inciting to riot after demonstrations in Chicago outside the 1968 Democratic National Convention. He also represented members of the Black Panther Party, the Weather Underground, the Attica Prison rioters, and the American Indian Movement.

Percy Sutton was, perhaps, the most radical African American defense attorney. Early in his career, he defended Malcolm X. Johnny Cochran followed in his footsteps, pulling off the almost-impossible stunt of successfully defending O.J. Simpson in his murder trial.

Atticus Finch was a fictional attorney in the same mold. The small-town lawyer in the novel *To Kill a Mockingbird*, Finch defended a black man wrongly accused of raping a white woman.

The halls of justice resonate still with the voices of these great men.

For his part, J. Tony Serra is among this breed, though, for sheer endurance, he might outshine them all. When I began work as a courtroom artist in 1991, I didn't know that within 10 years, Tony Serra would be acclaimed as one of the top-ten criminal defense lawyers of the century.

Serra is an anachronism, who has managed to withstand the battering of change while remaining rooted in his values. Indeed, he considers the very fact that he has values to be anachronistic. Most lawyers consider their profession not a calling, but rather a good way to get rich off the calamities of others.

The radical lawyer, instead, builds his or her practice on a foundation of fundamental principles. For example, Serra quotes the Declaration of Independence. "We hold these truths to be self-evident, that all men are created equal, that they are endowed by their creator with certain unalienable rights, that among these are life, liberty and the pursuit of happiness. In other words, "Give liberty!" He continues, "These words are the highest calling of the criminal-defense attorney. They are the guiding force behind our work as radical lawyers."

"Give liberty" is why his first priority, the first calls he returns from his long list of daily messages, is from people who are already in jail or prison. This is a critical piece of the puzzle of understanding Tony Serra, the priorities that often come under attack from those near to him whose needs get pushed aside as lower on his list. People in jail or prison, of course, occupy a very long line, but they always come first; they're always priority number one. Second are people who are potentially going to jail or prison. Only after those two long lines of people are attended to does Serra see to his eating, sleeping, family, social life, events, and so forth. Everything on the third tier, however, fades into a haze when someone needs to be released from jail or to be kept out of jail. "If I don't honor and dignify the concept of bestowing liberty," he insists, "then from the perspective of a trial lawyer, all the rest is bullshit."

This is his first love, his main challenge, his reason for being. There has always been, and there will always be, this challenge: to obtain the dream of America with respect to freedom and liberty, with respect to equality, with respect to the dignity that is to be accorded every human being who stands before the court of law.

What else distinguishes him from other lawyers? He's a force-field. He says, "I unleash primitive emotions—fury and anger and pain—in the unlikely, sedate, and sterile setting of the courtroom."

He describes himself as a shaman and a peasant. "I have the countenance of a Stone Age savage. I have rage, defiance, protest. I'm the potency of presence."

This raw energy in a formal setting is startling, unpredictable, and unexpected. This sense that he is a gladiator risking his own life in defense of his client each time he enters into battle against forces both staid and malevolent—the prosecution, informants, and the unfair system of justice itself—sets him in a league apart from his colleagues, who appear guarded, one-dimensional, by comparison.

He masters the facts of the case and he knows the law. "But that's just the substratum. That's a given," he says. "It's the inspirational school of talk rather than perspirational school of oratory. I have in my mind only a rough sketch of an outline. Then I get up there and look the jurors and alternates in the face and do it in a way that's almost spontaneous combustion."

In addition, his unequivocal belief in his own arguments resonates with juries like the voice of truth.

"The most vital human force on the face of the Earth," he says, "is the true believer. It's naive. It's simple. It's non-intellectual. It's a whole-hearted commitment to a cause. It's what everyone's afraid of. That's what I bring into the courtroom."

· · ·

Serra's insistence on swimming against the current on occasion, however, doesn't translate outside the courtroom, even right outside the door. Considering himself the last of a dying breed, a sociological throwback, often results in estrangement. Wherever he goes, he admits, he feels estranged.

"Existentialism 101," he says. "Disgorge yourself of everything, and redefine yourself, and ultimately the first level you reach is estrangement. The first level you feel is your alienation. I've never overcome that."

One example of this played itself out when he was in trial in the town of Riverside, California. At the door of the courtroom, the bailiff said to Serra, "Show me your bar card and picture identification."

Serra replied, "Hey, man, I'm a lawyer. I've got a case on the calendar."

"I don't care who you are," the bailiff insisted. "You don't get into my courtroom until you show me your bar card and identification."

In all the cases he'd tried over nearly 40 years, this had never happened before. He thought, "Oh well, this is a small town. Maybe that's the way they do things here in Riverside."

He gave the bailiff the bar card, but he didn't have any photo identification. He burned his driver's license decades ago to protest the Vietnam War. So he had to go through a big hassle with the bailiff, until he convinced him of who he was; he was finally admitted into the courtroom and sat up front with the other lawyers. But all the while, he thought, "There *is* something different about me. I'm alien. I'm estranged. I always feel a little odd."

Later that day, Serra approaches the front desk of the hotel where his room has been reserved and paid for. The front desk clerk tells him, "Yes, you're registered. You have a room here. But you've got to put up a credit card."

Serra says, "I don't have a credit card. I don't believe in credit cards," again feeling strange.

"That's all right," the clerk says. "You can write us a check."

"I don't have checks either," he says, thinking, even if I did have checks, there wouldn't be any money in the account, since the IRS would have it all. "I don't believe in them. I gave that all up in 1968. I'm here as a kind of representative of the sixties, the hippie culture." Thinking: No photo ID, no driver's license, no credit cards, no checks, barely any money on me at all.

The clerk looks at him long and hard.

Serra says, "Look, my room's paid for. I was invited here. I'm the guest speaker."

But the front desk clerk doesn't care. He doesn't know J. Tony Serra. J. Tony Serra is a stranger. And he's strange.

Finally, the clerk consults with his boss in the back room, then returns and hands him a key. "But, again," he says, "it's that alienation, like I'm a visitor from another era, like I don't belong in this one."

Serra's law, therefore, doesn't draw from the same source material, books, as that of other lawyers. It is a creative conglomeration of the mental and the physical that had its inception when he was a student of philosophy at Stanford. When the 1960s arrived with mind-altering drugs, Serra discarded past paradigms and formulated his own equation, based on diverse life experiences, the rules of the court, and the dictates of the heart.

Serra believes that the old-fashioned, outspoken, maverick, radical lawyer, the idealist who championed the rights of people, who fought nobly and selflessly for the balance of power in this country, has been crushed. The judiciary has squashed this kind of lawyer in every way. Few defense attorneys aspire to become judges. Judges mostly come up through, and continue to identify with, the prosecution. They silence defense attorneys, especially the most vocal ones like Serra, with court orders, known as the "gag rule." They threaten them with contempt of court. They call their cases first, then make them sit there until the end of the calendar. Whatever their means, they're getting rid of the opposition, the voice of dissent, the defiant cry of people who are oppressed by government. But everything Serra does still embodies that old-fashioned kind of legal standard, that dying legal ideal.

When he looks around, he doesn't see too many young lawyers who aspire to follow in his radical footsteps, who want to be targeted as the voice of opposition. The popular image of the lawyer, especially today, is questionable at best anyway. Lawyer jokes are all the rage: "First, we kill all the lawyers," as Shakespeare said. The media focuses on tricky lawyers, sneaky lawyers, dishonest, incompetent, unethical, greedy lawyers. So the cadre of highly principled defense attorneys is going fast, by attrition. Most lawyers don't want that kind of burden to bear. They want to win. They want money. They want respect. They don't want to feel like some kind of tainted professional. And criminal defense is now a tainted profession. Those lawyers don't get any respect. They get no money to speak of. They no longer have the mainstream support behind them.

The radical lawyer is a gadfly. He's the canary in the coal mine; he sacrifices himself to alert others. He's the Paul Revere who, whether he shows up with one lantern or two, is warning about the imminent arrival of the shock troops. Serra believes the end of America as a free society is marked by the end of the old-fashioned lawyer, whose rhetoric has opposed government, authority, and tyranny since the days of Patrick Henry. "Give liberty!" That voice against the oppressors is being undermined and strangled today.

. . .

Serra started out hopeful and idealistic. He had a deep-seated love for humanity and he wanted to channel all of his life energies into it. On Saturdays, when he might have taken time off and relaxed at home, he spent his day in jails or prisons. He recalls going to see clients and potential clients in San Quentin, the maximum-security California-state prison on a wind-swept little peninsula in Marin County across the Golden Gate Bridge. It's a hellhole now, but in the sixties, it was even more so, a bastion of gang-related violence and prison brutalities. He entered the prison and saw lines of people waiting. A prisoner's loved ones have to stand in long lines to get very limited contact during visiting hours. However, prisons always have a separate line for lawyers, busy professionals who can get in more quickly than families. Serra, being Serra, couldn't stand in the lawyer line. He wanted to be close to the people, to feel the mood, to empathize with the throngs who visit the prison regularly. So he waited in the people's long long line.

He quickly noted that about 80% of the people were black and Hispanic. He remembers feeling like he was standing in a sea of poor Third World people. Waiting in those endless lines, he saw that the system wasn't balanced, that it was fundamentally flawed. Ironically, this was his first inkling that the justice system isn't only rotten, but also, in some small respect, workable; later, after decades of picking juries and adjudicating jury trials, he learned that the great majority of Americans actually admit that they're biased. Some say straight out: "I'm *racist*. I'm biased against minority defendants." Some say that they equate crime in the country with blacks, Native Americans, Hispanics, Asians, and all foreigners. They say, candidly, that they can't be fair.

Yes, Serra learned quickly, there *is* racism in the courts. People of color don't get a fair shot with all or mostly white juries. These juries will not give minority defendants the benefit of the doubt. They won't presume innocence. They won't treat them as equal, the same way they would a white defendant. He came to recognize it as a simple fact of life. It made him sad. And it made him angry.

"When first you come into court, when you're young, you know something entirely unwholesome is occurring," he says. "The forces of the prosecution are overwhelming and you stand up, as you should stand up, and you object! To the radical lawyer, the law is a class struggle, a relationship between oppressor and oppressed. The law has always been a struggle by poor people against the status quo, and too often it has been for them an impediment. It doesn't facilitate change. It doesn't promote prosperity and equality. In fact, it impedes them all."

As he spoke, I had visions of Daumier's art of lawyers done in 1845. The image that came to mind was of an impoverished parent in court, garbed in rags and tatters, teeth missing, hair entangled, holding one waif in his arms, while another bedraggled child clings to his side. This pitiful trio stands before a judge who is snoozing in his robed authority, while a pompous lawyer struts his own image of wealth and arrogance. Neither lawyer nor judge show any concern for the plight of this specter of poverty before them in court. It's been happening for centuries.

"Thus," Serra continues, "the radical lawyer pledges him or herself to fight that injustice wherever it appears. The radical lawyer isn't interested in obtaining judgments for money or litigating for rules that result in property or disputed funds being dispersed. No. The radical lawyer is only interested in obtaining liberty and freedom for oppressed people. The radical lawyer will always be on the side of the underdog, will always oppose the status quo. That's what allows for change and reform. That's what facilitates evolution. That's what redistributes wealth. That's what ultimately allows for equality under law."

The radical lawyer, according to one of the greatest radical lawyers in history, must be an angry semantic fist in the face of the establishment. He or she must not be materialistic; the pursuit must be freedom, rather than prosperity, and always defending the minority position. He or she must fight in the street, on the steps of the courthouse, outside the court system, inside the court system.

. . .

The radical lawyer always opposes, as a first principle, racism wherever it's prevalent: in the judicial system, the jury system, the District Attorney's office, the Public Defender's office, the political and business arenas; the racism battlefield is manifold.

The next area the radical lawyer inevitably confronts is the death penalty. The death penalty falls, Serra believes, unevenly on minorities, Native Americans, African Americans, Hispanics, and poor people whatever their race or class.

In an article he wrote for the January 1997 issue of *California Lawyer* magazine, he describes the awful moment when a jury delivers their sentence on a death-penalty charge.

"The courtroom is packed. The jury is returning. They're issuing out of the side door from the jury room. They have reached a verdict. It is a death-penalty case. I thought there would be hushed silence, but the background sound in my head is a mighty roar that fails to still the voracious bird trying to claw its way out of my chest. My outside—austere, passive, introspective; my inside—wild, rushing, splashing, collapsing, a waterfall of disintegrating thought.

"The moment of truth in a death-penalty case is a revisiting of all the political, sociological, philosophical, and religious truths that sustain the criminal-defense attorney in all his or her legal battles. Mental imagery floods kaleidoscopically, and each moment, as the jury files in, is an infinity."

"When one addresses the question of the death penalty, one has to probe one's core belief system," Serra explains. "In order to oppose the death penalty and be truly consistent, you have to think about killing and homicide in general. For example, is killing justified in war? Is killing justified in self-defense? Can police be excused from killing if it's to save their own or others' lives? What about killings without premeditation and deliberation? Do we honor theories like heat of passion or psychotic-oriented killings to justify or excuse or explain or mitigate the taking of another's life?

"With my background in philosophy and criminal-defense law, I've examined all the different varieties of society's inhumanity toward itself. Ideologically, I oppose homicide. I don't justify it when it's done in wartime. I don't excuse it when police do it. And I oppose it when it's accompanied by any intent to kill. But that's a philosophic doctrine and obviously I've defended people charged with homicide with all of the applicable defenses.

"The reason the death penalty specifically is noxious to a developed society is that it's the coldest and most premeditated form of first-degree murder. You see, people kill in the heat of passion. People kill because they're intoxicated, they're confronted with dangerous situations, they're temporarily insane. People kill due to jealousy and greed. There are all sorts of reasons why people kill and you can look into the backgrounds of the people and locate the causative factors. But when society's allegedly wise representatives of the legislature, judiciary, and prosecution sit down and hammer out a death-penalty law, and prosecutors ask for the death penalty, and jurors mete out the death penalty, and judges impose the death penalty, when all that occurs, it's tantamount to deliberation, the ultimate intent in cold abstract legalese. It's a societal decree of first-degree premeditated murder! Therefore, it should be the most obnoxious form of killing."

Tony Serra rejects the death penalty absolutely. He does not and cannot empathize with it at all. To him, it's a form of premeditated murder that has no socially redeemable features. The most advanced cultures, he argues, do not have it.

Serra believes that in the United States, those who suffer the death penalty, as a rule, are in one of three categories: minority, impoverished, or mentally impaired. Rich people in general aren't subjected to the death penalty even after they've committed heinous murders. Rather, it's the blacks, the Native Americans, the marginally retarded, and always the poor, people from the ghetto, people who've been exposed to dysfunctional behavior from their environment, from their families, from their relationships.

When the death penalty is delivered discriminately, when the elite and the wealthy are exempt from the death penalty, that's class warfare. It's unconscionable, Serra insists, and it cannot be allowed.

Furthermore, the prosecution swells with resources. The government allocates fortunes to the prosecution of death-penalty cases. Yet, in the "death zones" of this country, such as the South, the defense is lucky if it's given $5,000 per death-penalty case. So there's a built-in unfairness: The government denies due process when it won't allocate enough funds for defense experts and witnesses, and travel, and teams of lawyers and research, and the assimilation of all of the discovery material, like the D.A.s have. Defense lawyers work on a shoestring.

"The death-penalty defense practitioners, from my perspective, are holy men and women. They're the most sacred of our profession."

Another reason Serra opposes the death penalty is that it's unequivocally not a deterrent. It's easy for politicians and the public to believe that if society puts to death murderers, other murderers will think twice about committing a killing. The rationalization is that we're saving lives by killing people. The problem is, it's not true. According to Serra, all the testing, all the statistics, all the articles written by law professors conclude that the death penalty does not deter. The reason is that people caught in a situation where rage consumes their behavior are not in a state of mind to reflect on ultimate punishment. It doesn't enter their minds.

"It's Vietnam all over again," he says. "The idea that we had to destroy the village to save it doesn't work for the death-penalty issue any more than it worked for those ruthlessly massacred villages."

The only rationalization for the death penalty is, Serra says, revenge. However, we're 2,000 years down the line from what's known as *lex taliones*, the pre-Christian notion of an eye for an eye, a tooth for a tooth. Supposedly, we've transcended this barbaric mentality by trying to understand and address the causes of criminal behavior, rather than just decapitating the person who manifests the behavior. The death penalty in this country is especially barbaric and hypocritical, given that the United States claims to be on the forefront of civility and moral superiority.

. . .

Another of J. Tony Serra's judicial foes is the grand jury. "The grand jury," he says, "is nothing more than a tool of a totalitarian state that prosecutes in secret."

The grand jury is hidden. The defendant does not participate. His attorney does not participate. There are no constitutional guarantees. There is no discovery. There is no cross-examination. The grand jury is a group of people who know nothing about the case; they are manipulated with predigested material delivered to them by the prosecutor, in a secret chamber with no witnesses, with no checks and balances, in order to arrive at an unfair indictment.

It is highly effective. America's perfect example of the power of the grand jury is Guantanamo Prison. Most of the inmates at Guantanamo ended up there with no legal representation, no trial, not even a notice of their whereabouts. America's black sites and secret renditions are also extreme examples of how this system has been put into force. The radical lawyer fights against grand juries on every occasion.

The radical lawyer also opposes another cancer that has infiltrated the judicial system: mandatory sentencing, also known as three-strike laws, mandatory minimums, mandatory 10-to-life and 20-to-life, and mandatory life. Serra insists that this system undermines the balance of powers in this country. It usurps the function of the judge and juries and allows legislators and prosecutors to determine sentencing. Without an empowered judicial system, he believes, we have the beginnings of a totalitarian state. The delivery of punishment is locked into a closed system devoid of opposition and, often, reason and compassion. Serra had one of the first of these cases (see Chapter 14).

Another taint visited upon the judicial system, to Tony, is preventative detention. This is a euphemism that means that in the federal system (and it is now creeping into the state system), bail is no longer a right. For hundreds of years, in every case except capital cases, the accused has had a right to reasonable bail. This right was ultimately predicated on the presumption of innocence. When there's no right to bail, an accused is presumed to be a flight risk, a danger to the community. Therefore, he waits in jail. He might wait a month; he might wait years for a trial.

"We're losing a precious presumption, the presumption of innocence, that should attend the pretrial and extend into the granting of bail. This is epidemic; it's catastrophic. The radical lawyer favors presumption of innocence, always argues for bail, and fights in every fashion against preventative detention."

· · ·

Atop the belief in and commitment to the radical-lawyer philosophy are the tools of Tony Serra's trade as a trial lawyer. He uses every form of empowerment possible to fight the system and free his client from its injustices.

A good trial lawyer, in addition to employing a semantic-warrior's logic and language, passion and emotion, also uses a form of nonverbal communication that flows from the aura of the lawyer to the aura of the jury. Many levels emanate from a lawyer's aura, but one of Serra's most important tools is magic.

"Any trial lawyer who doesn't believe in magic is a fool!" he exclaims. "Trial lawyers, I believe, have always been a type of medicine man in a ritualistic ceremony. We are the Western witch doctors of the judicial system. Our rattles and screeches, our words and expressions, hopefully cure society's ills in these symbolic contests that we call jury trials."

Serra found his own magic when he recognized that materialism's claim on one's energy ultimately deprives one of personal and true magical powers. So he made the trade: He determined never to make the practice of law a business or a merchandising process. His informal vow of poverty dictated that he'd never take profit from the practice of law, that he wouldn't buy anything new, that he'd recycle everything, that he'd own no properties, no stocks or bonds, no images or vestiges of prosperity. To this day, he drives a junker car, he barely makes the rent each month, he's accumulated nothing by way of savings, and he lives from hand to mouth. In addition, while in the battle of a jury trial, he eschews almost all forms of debasement. He doesn't drink alcohol, he doesn't stay out late, he avoids sensationalism of all kinds at all costs. According to his way of thinking, this purification process prepares him to enter into the zone of magic, to prepare his karma for the ordeal of court. It's the shaman's way.

Other forms of magic that Tony Serra has involved himself in are more concrete. He is aware that his long white hair and intense eyes have an effect on jurors. He explains, "I use my hair as an artist uses his brushes. I walk into court with it in a tight bun. The next day I may wear it completely open, going to my waist in the back. The next day it might be a ponytail. The next day, braided Indian fashion over my shoulders. The next day with ribbons. I give a full array, but always with a premeditated, disciplined, conscious objective in mind."

His old suits, old ties, and thread-bare shirts also imprint an impression on jurors. He derives personal power from certain 20- to 30-year-old suits, which he chooses for opening statements, cross-examination of major witnesses, and closing arguments. He has ties that are friendly, diverting, compelling. He sometimes wears bracelets. He sometimes carries lucky stones.

He chants silent mantras as he sits at the counsel table. He uses non-empirical, mind-to-mind, thought-to-thought communication. He closes his eyes and visualizes the faces, one by one, of the jurors. He brings them deep into his silent consciousness and enters their minds. Some he can't pull in all the way; they resist and he loses his sway over them. But he calls to them; through their images, he engulfs them.

He puts the hex on enemy witnesses. Many times, he obtains photos or signatures of such witnesses and sends arrows and spears and darts to their hearts, always silently, without even physically directing attention toward them. This is without doubt the shaman's magic. Good trial lawyers have this level of communication, whether they know it or not.

In the selection of jurors, he's consulted with astrologers, handwriting interpreters, numerologists, black-magic and white-magic magicians. Their insights are from another level of the brain and cannot be emulated by the paltry lawyer who deals only in cerebral word signs and means.

In court, Serra captures his space. Like Carlos Casteneda's Don Juan, he finds his power spot. He finds his own spot from which he speaks, from which he emotes. (This is when the judge doesn't confine him to the unbearable restraint of the podium.) It can't be where the prosecutor stands. He finds a place from which his unspoken strength emanates most potently, and he never varies his spot from witness to witness.

The importance of the lawyer's "place" in court is incalculable. It's like the Buddha who sits under the tree of enlightenment; it must be the center of his or her universe during the trial. Perhaps this isn't magic; maybe it's just common sense. But if one invests a site with special power, the power seems to flow from it thereafter.

Before a closing argument, he's eaten raw ginger root, or chewed on ginseng root, or taken psychedelic mushrooms or LSD, with the intended purpose of deepening his perception and gaining a greater overview. He's traveled to kiss the Blarney Stone for the gift of tongues. All of this is to intensify the shaking of the fist, the anger, the love, the compassion that must attend the lawyer's role at trial. All of this is to affect the jurors in an extrasensory or nonverbal fashion. All of this is a form of magic, preparing the higher mind for the broader focus of all aspects of a trial.

A good trial magician must consult with the specific source from which he or she obtains inspiration. Sitting high on a bluff overlooking the ocean, walking by the sea, screaming at the waves; sitting obscured in the tall grasses of a meadow, lying back on the earth in a redwood grove, sitting with one's back to an ancient eucalyptus tree: This is how Serra obtains inspiration from magical and potent places, from geographic areas that effuse a certain form of power.

I remember catching sight of Serra on the beach in Bolinas: a solitary figure walking into the wind with his long white hair blowing like a mane. He passed me in silence, lost in his thoughts. Then I lost sight of him as he blurred into the smudges of fog amidst the roar of the waves pounding and hissing foaming white water that raked back the stones of the shore. I wondered if he felt the surge of the sea in his courtroom arguments as he raked back the evidence like a wave gathering force to thrust it forward again for the judgment of the jury.

A trial lawyer's magic changes with the times and from one case to the next, but there are certain connecting metaphors. For example, for approximately 15 years, Serra had an old brown clay marble, about a half-inch in diameter, that he had each defendant clasp in a closed hand while testifying. That marble was held by 100 different people over a decade and a half. He told each one of them that the marble linked them to the success and the courage of the previous clients; each one was made to believe that it held magic and it gave each the strength of knowing that he or she had some kind of secret hidden power. It linked each to him and to one another. He still feels that he stands in the middle of a large circle of them.

A good trial lawyer uses every shred of magic available. Some are obvious and some are completely subliminal. In the Patrick "Hooty" Croy case (see Chapter 8), a Native American was accused of killing a white police officer in a death-penalty case. Serra's defense team was allowed, by First Amendment principles, to put Indian religious items on the counsel table. These consisted of bits of bark, stones, deer antler, feathers, and fragrant vegetation, all wrapped in deerskin. They were unfolded each day in a ceremonial fashion, only by an Indian, in front of the jury.

This was after Tony, his two co-counsels, and Hooty Croy were all smudged. Smudging is a purification ritual in which dried sage leaves, juniper and cedar along with bits of herbs and bark, are burned in a crucible. As the smoke billows out, it's wafted into the person's aura, usually directed by the use of an eagle feather. The four of them walked into the courtroom freshly smudged, the scent of sage on their clothes, and sat down facing the items on the table. It was religious, but it was also magic.

"Magic is everywhere," Tony Serra insists. "It's in the reclusive pristine spots of nature; it's in the thick of an urban jungle. It's in the sea, in the air, on the earth. It's inside the courthouse and outside the courthouse. All one has to do is feel it and harness it and it will be the trial lawyer's best ally."

The radical lawyer is a trial lawyer with the most powerful magic.

Chapter 7

Jury Nullification:
A Call to Conscience

According to the Fully Informed Jury Association (FIJA), "The high-est and best function of the jury is not, as many think, to dispense punishment to fellow citizens guilty of breaking the law, but rather to *protect* fellow citizens from tyrannical prosecutions and bad laws imposed by a power-hungry government.

"Jurors have a duty and responsibility to render a just verdict. They must take into account the facts of the case, mitigating circumstances, the merits of the law, and the fairness of its application in each case."

In other words, as opposed to the way most judges instruct juries, jurors have not only the right, but the duty, to return a verdict exactly as they see fit, without any encouragement or prompting or urging or instructing by anyone. More simply put in the TV program "Shark," James Woods states, "Jury trials are not about the law. They're about what twelve people think is right."

"The recognition of the authority and right of jurors to weigh the merits of the law and to render a verdict based on conscience dates from before the writing of our Constitution, in cases such as those of William Penn and Peter Zenger," FIJA states. "Should this right ever be suppressed, the people will retain the right to resist, having an unalienable right to veto or nullify bad and oppressive laws, and in fact then would be morally compelled to do so."

Again, this means that juries, by refusing to convict defendants of certain crimes that are prosecuted by the government, can in fact, nullify laws. In the John Peter Zenger trial of 1735, an American jury refused to convict Zenger, a printer and publisher, of libel for criticizing the British-appointed governor of New York, even though such criticism violated sedition laws. Clearly, Zenger was guilty of breaking the law, but the jury accepted the argument of Alexander Hamilton that all the criticism was based on fact. Thus, the Zenger jury nullified the British sedition laws in the American colonies.

In the William Penn trial, Penn was accused of violating the "common law" when he preached nonconformist religious views at a public meeting in London. The prosecution could not produce the specific law that Penn was accused of breaking, so the jury found him not guilty. The judge, personally insulted and outraged, fined and jailed the jurors for voting their conscience in direct disobeyal of his orders.

Northern juries in the mid-1800s refused to convict so many people who harbored fugitive slaves along the Underground Railroad that the government had to cease prosecuting such cases. So many California juries have refused to convict possessors of marijuana since the 1960s that they effectively nullified the cannabis part of the controlled-substance laws.

"Jurors, as the representatives of the people, hold no personal agenda during any trial and most certainly not the government's agenda," FIJA writes. "Let us not forget that the prosecutors, judges, arresting officers and the forensic investigators in most cases are all a part of and receive their paychecks from government, with personal power bases to build and personal careers to protect through the productivity of successful prosecutions resulting in convictions. Jurors have no such stake in the outcome, and are, in fact, the only truly objective individuals in the courtroom.

"The role of our jurors is to protect private citizens from dangerous government laws and actions. Many existing laws erode and deny the rights of the people. Jurors protect against tyranny by refusing to convict harmless people. Our country's founders planned and expected that we, the people, would exercise this power and authority to judge the law as well as the facts every time we serve as jurors. Juries are the last peaceful defense of our civil liberties."

Nullification as a legal concept isn't taught in law school and Tony Serra claims he's never seen it treated as an academic subject. He once had someone pull all the law-review articles, which he scanned, only to find that according to the law, there is no such thing as nullification. The fact that a jury, manifesting the conscience of the community, can nullify—negate, sidestep, abandon the mandate of—the law and vote for an acquittal, even though the letter of the law requires a guilty verdict, doesn't appear to exist. And God help the criminal-defense attorney who dares to utter the word, or refer to the concept, in court.

In short, the jury has the *power* to nullify, but it doesn't, in the eyes of the law, have the *right*. And since it doesn't have the right, defense attorneys cannot argue for it and judges, no matter where their personal sympathies lie in a case, can never instruct the jury about it. But since they do have the power to nullify laws, then they most certainly have the right. It's up to jurors to exercise that right. And it's up to radical lawyers, such as Tony Serra, to do everything they can, short of risking a contempt charge, to ensure jurors do so.

. . .

Tony Serra, indeed, loves nullification cases. Like his use of magic, he's raised their use to a fine art form.

The heart of nullification, in his experience, is a morality play. It's simplistic and direct. Its impact is sub-cerebral; he's not addressing the minds of the juries. Instead, he's engaging their consciences, their ethics, their morals.

Taking this tack calls on the eloquence, the finesse, of the lawyer. The lawyer, after all, is leading the jury across this invisible line of the law. It isn't the facts. It isn't the evidence so much. It isn't even the law that's allegedly been broken. It's the jury's emotions, their gut feelings, below-the-belt hits to their very belief systems.

Picture him, launching into his opening argument. He knows he's going for a nullification defense. He's going all the way. He's close to the jury, giving them intense eye contact. His brow is sweating from the heat of passion he feels. His arms are outstretched. The twelve are looking at him like a volcano that's about to blow. He proclaims, "Pity this busy monster man unkind not! Progress is a comfortable disease!"

He pauses, stares back at them wild-eyed, and repeats, "Pity this busy monster man unkind not! Progress is a comfortable disease!"

The jury is looking at him and he knows what they're thinking. "He's lost it!" "He went crazy on the way to court!" "He's jumped off the edge!" "This guy's stoned!"

But he's got them right where he wants them. Returning his voice to normal decibels, he says, "E. E. Cummings went mad, and at least one reason he went mad was because of oppressive government. And this was the first refrain of a poem he wrote. It attests to the feeling and the impact of man's inhumanity toward man. And ladies and gentlemen of the jury, that's what this case is about. The evidence you'll hear in this case will ultimately show man's inhumanity to man."

Serra spouts Shakespeare. He quotes scripture. He recites poetry. He calls on the higher awareness of the jury. He turns the whole trial into a morality play—good versus bad, right versus wrong.

"First, you'll hear the testimony of an informant, a snitch, a perjurer!" Then returning to his rant he explodes, "Ladies and gentlemen of the jury! Something that is unwholesome, something that is fraudulent, something that is perjurious, something that is corrupt can *never* be legal!"

He's used that concept many times. He never says the word "nullification," but he's striving for it. It's very basic: He's convincing the jurors to hate some facet of the prosecution's case and, at the same time, to feel compassion, or at least sympathy, for his client. It's unsophisticated, nonacademic, direct. It's poignant. It has to hit. It has to make them cry. Serra believes that if he can't make at least three jurors cry, his case is sunk.

"The best moment of all," he says, "is when the jury members come out at the end of a trial and surround my client and me, and say, 'Mr. Serra, we know your client's guilty, but we want to give him another chance.' Fabulous fucking words! This is what I call de facto nullification."

. . .

Defense lawyers use nullification tactics in most federal drug cases, because nine out of ten cases are based on informants. Serra says he's taken on a client assuming it's a two-snitch case. He plots his strategy: He'll beat Snitch A in this way; he'll beat Snitch B in that way. Then, he finds that the prosecution has lined up *five* snitches to take the witness stand. The prosecution has "turned" (made them into informants) the bottom echelon to get the top, or even in some cases the top echelon to get the bottom, whatever it takes to convict the particular defendant. Every criminal-defense lawyer has heard the call: "Come to us, be our witness, roll over on your friends. You're only the first of three tiers we've got here." At that point, what does the defense attorney have left? One tactic and one tactic only: nullification.

Serra searches, sometimes desperately, for something, some lawful instruction, some legal precept, on which to hang an acquittal. He doesn't, he can't, look at the criminal event for which a defendant is on trial. If he does, he's dead before he even starts. He knows he has to take the jurors outside of the small box that comprises the crime. He avoids or ignores entirely issues relevant to the trial, in favor of pulling some rabbit out of his hat and make it the main theme of the case. Anything that he puts a frame around becomes the picture.

Certain themes can be emphasized to encourage nullification. Perjury, as mentioned earlier, is a powerful motif. If a witness is willfully false in the material part of his or her testimony, it can be rejected in its entirety. Sometimes that's all Serra has in a case, but he considers it a "fabulous strength." As soon as he catches a snitch or adverse witness in a lie, he can go after the testimony with a vengeance: "false in one, false in all."

He can work the perjury angle from the beginning. "In this case, ladies and gentleman, you'll be hearing perjured testimony." Meanwhile, he's building the moral plateau. "Ladies and gentlemen, there are certain values in life that we hold closest to our hearts as the most meaningful, closest to our culture as the most worthwhile. Let's start with family as the most significant value in the personal and cultural hierarchy. And maybe under that is religion. Then education. Then, perhaps, justice. A society is only as great as the system of justice it bestows upon itself. I think we can all agree that the pursuit of justice is one of the top five values on which every culture is constructed.

"So, the way we dispense justice in this country has to be significant to you. And in our court system, truth is a hallowed principle. We believe that truth is beauty, and beauty is truth, and truth will set us free.

"But in this case, you've heard inconsistency. You've heard falsity. You've heard perjury! And in this hallowed hall, where we venerate values, the prosecution is asking for you ultimately to predicate justice not on truth, but on lies!"

Perjury is usually the strongest theme by which you can erect the structure of the morality play unofficially titled nullification.

"I once had a case in federal court," Serra explains. "A high-echelon member of a black prison gang in San Quentin turned over on other gang members regarding activities related to drugs on the outside. Previously, in a death-penalty case, he'd testified against one of the other members, admitting that he'd not only ordered the killing of various people, but he'd also participated in various killings at San Quentin. I encountered him a year and a half later in a different federal case in San Francisco. The prosecution failed to provide him with a transcript of his own testimony in the previous case, so it was easy.

"There he was, up on the witness stand, and I asked him, 'You were given immunity for murders?'

"The witness replied, 'I never murdered.'

"So then I asked, 'You were given immunity for ordering murders?'

"He retorts, 'I never ordered any murders.'

"'But on August 24 of last year, you not only ordered a murder, you participated in the murder! Didn't you?'

"I pulled out the transcript and impeached him, and that was the end of him! What comes next I had to learn the hard way. I used to like to think that, when I'd catch a guy lying, when I proved perjury, suddenly the whole room would shake, like in an earthquake. The chandeliers would start clanking; the artwork on the walls would fall. The whole courtroom would erupt, like some kind of a score from the fifty-yard line! Now I know that if I don't ring my own bell, if I don't shake and rattle it, the moment just passes. It's up to me to make the perjury meaningful, to make it the core of my case. This is nullification. I shout to the jury, 'You can't believe him! He's a paid witness and he's perjured himself! His word is not to be counted and you cannot convict on his word!'"

When Serra is working an inconsistency or a perjury angle, he has to know his witness inside out, upside down, and backwards. He has to not only get his hands on, not only read, but actually memorize every transcript of every testimony, every police report of every statement. Snitches and informants, he's found, are never consistent. They're not into words, the semantic order of reality. They don't have the best memories to begin with and it's very hard to remember lies. They won't remember what they said before, or they'll say things in the same transcript that can be interpreted differently. And then look out, because Tony Serra knows nothing if he doesn't know how to seize a moment. He's always ready to pounce, to turn any misstep from the prosecution's side right into performance art. He bellows, "You're lying! You're lying right now! Aren't you? Today, here, under oath, you say you didn't order any murders. You say you didn't commit any murders. But last year, you admitted to both ordering and committing murders! You're lying through your teeth!"

This is how Tony Serra has acquired his reputation for being a madman, a foaming-at-the mouth lunatic, in a courtroom. He doesn't wait until later to impeach a witness. No. He impeaches him, then screams him right off the stand.

And then he turns to the jury. He pushes out his chest. He huffs and puffs. *He* makes the court shake. *He's* the earthquake.

Later, he argues the morality. Most jurors won't convict based on perjurious testimony. In this case, they didn't. Jurors are human. They think, I wouldn't want someone to convict *my* kid based on lies from some bought-and-paid for witness. I wouldn't want *my* husband convicted by some lying son of a bitch.

. . .

Defense attorneys can't get admitted into evidence at trial many of the specific acts of misconduct committed by an informant who's testifying for the prosecution. Most prosecutors know all the tactics for guarding against it. But Serra knows that jurors and judges love to hear dirt.

They love to see dirty laundry aired out in the open. Everyone does. Often, it has nothing to do with the case, but it's the most important part for the jury. So he tells his investigators, "Get me the shit on this guy." And then he just jams it into evidence.

In one case in San Diego, Serra discovered that the snitch was in a sexual relationship with a 13-year-old girl. He had the snitch on the stand and worked it in. The snitch, a major drug smuggler snitching on everyone, was testifying about counting a lot of money. Serra asked, "Who was with you when you were counting the money? Wasn't it so-and-so?"

The witness said, "Yes. So-and-so was with me."

Then he mentioned the girl. "And wasn't she with you at that time you were counting the money?"

The witness saw it coming, and turned a little white, right in front of Serra's eyes. "And you're counting drug money in front of her. And you were having an affair with her, weren't you? You'd been having an affair with her when she was—" he blurted it out "—thirteen!"

"No!" he blanched. "No! No!"

But at that moment, Serra's investigator walked right into the court, with this little girl by the hand. Everyone in the jury knew that he'd been having sex with her and that she was only thirteen. It had nothing to do with the case. But that was the end of this witness. The jury hated him. And that killed the case for the prosecution.

Another example. Serra was cross-examining another snitch, a fiendish sadist. He used to rent limousines in which he and his friends had a big orgy with a bunch of strippers and hookers. Lots of cocaine, everyone naked, wild sex. At the end of the orgy, he actually threw the prostitutes out on the street, either scantily clad or stark naked, and then he'd take target practice on them with his taser. Serra worked it all in. Even though it was completely inadmissible, the judge loved it; it turned out the judge was himself a sadist, and anywhere pain and suffering could be created, these were the earmarks of truth for him. So that was the end of another snitch. No one was going to convict on this miscreant's word.

Sure, Serra's defendant was guilty. But after such a revelation about the sadistic witness, the jury no longer cared about that. Showing the bad character of the witness, however unrelated to the issues before the court, is a form of jury nullification, a theme Serra plays so loudly that it dominates.

.   .   .

Another popular form of nullification that has many variations is the insanity defense. "Diminished capacity" is a defense based on the fact that the client was mentally incompetent at the time of the offense.

Serra had a case in Santa Cruz, California. The defendant was on a big cocaine and alcohol binge when he took a prostitute into his bedroom. Something went wrong between them and Serra's client beat her into a pulp with a tire iron—a terrible ghastly crime.

The case turned into a psychiatric slugfest; 14 shrinks testified in it. Most cases require two or three shrinks; some escalate to five shrinks; this case had 14 of them.

Why so many? Because with a terrible, ugly, deformed crime such as this one, the chances of a conviction are high. Almost any jury you can name will bury this guy. With a diminished-capacity nullification defense, however, a good defense attorney calls for a higher awareness: that there are neurological misfirings, that people can commit horrendous crimes outside of or beyond any conscious awareness. And in this case, it was true. The defendant went into a bona fide amnesiac state; he didn't remember a thing about what happened. One of the testifying psychiatrists suggested that Serra's client couldn't get an erection and that perhaps the woman said something that he magnified completely out of context and went berserk. Whatever happened, it was a total drug and alcohol blackout.

In this case, Serra knew he couldn't try the event. Instead, he had to focus on the mental capacity of the defendant, then call the jury to a higher moral purpose.

"Are we enforcing the law of an eye for an eye and a tooth for a tooth? Are we seeking vengeance and revenge? Is that what we're doing here? Is that what a jury is about? Do you administer justice? Do you take into account scientific truth? Do you honor and dignify the profession of psychiatry? Or do you abandon that and revert to the animal that he was at the time of the crime?"

By challenging the jurors to call upon their sense of higher moral judgment, he managed to hang the jury. He knew he couldn't win the case, but at least he didn't lose it outright.

. . .

Coercion is another basis for nullification. Coercion is an affirmative defense at the state-court level; sometimes, as is the case with the issue of entrapment in the federal court, the prosecution must prove beyond a reasonable doubt that there was no coercion or the defense wins.

Serra used coercion in an LWOP (life without possibility of parole) case in which an ex-con with two drug priors was arrested after nine months on parole for selling 10 kilos of cocaine to an undercover officer, with a gun in his possession when he was arrested. The narcs had him dead. That's an LWOP even without the gun, so not much defense is available in such a case.

Still, a bit of investigation showed that some coercion was involved. The defendant, in fact, was being forced by the Colombians to return to the cocaine business to pay them back for the money he lost when he was arrested the previous time. They threatened him, his wife, and his mother with death if he didn't pay up.

Like diminished capacity, coercion is another state-of-mind defense. A good defense attorney will go into hearsay and a defendant's fears.

"Were you coerced? Were you in fear of your life? Were you in fear of someone else's life? Did you have any reasonable alternatives?"

Serra appealed to jurors who believe Colombians are vicious killers. The mother testified, crying, because she was actually threatened by the Colombians. Once again, it was a higher calling. This guy would never have touched 10 kilos of coke; he was out of prison only nine months. He had to do it or ruthless assassins would kill his mother.

It was nullification because Serra redirected the focus of the case away from the illegal transaction; instead, he convinced the jury that people who are coerced are acting involuntarily.

"Forget about the ten kilos," he demanded. "Forget about the gun in his belt. Instead, look into his mind, ladies and gentlemen of the jury. Was he coerced? Was he forced to do it beyond his will? Did he heed his mother, who called him crying? 'Do anything, son! They're going to kill me!' Was he worried sick about his wife, who was having a nervous breakdown over the whole thing?"

In the back of their minds, the jurors know this guy will go to prison for life. The extreme prospect of life without even the possibility of parole enhances the chances of reasonable doubt.

Again, Serra knew he was going for a hung jury at best. He figured he could only get one or two jurors to see things his way. Nullification is the process of transcending the facts of the case, in order to make at least one member of the jury empathize with the plight of the client.

. . .

Similar to coercion is entrapment, which always carries a large potential for nullification. Serra loves entrapment defenses, because he can really get into the mind of the accused. He puts the wife on the stand and asks, "Before this happened, what was he telling you? Did he come home one day and say, 'I'm doing this because they say it'll cure our son's sight'?"

Serra had one case where the informant promised money to the defendant in order to allow his son, who was blind, to have an operation. It was a tough case to build, but he constructed it brick by brick by sharing the defendant's expression of his thoughts with his children or his wife or his mother. All the things he thought and said were an exception to hearsay. He erected a moral edifice out of a defendant's hearsay to his family.

Another entrapment case took place in Marin County, which is one of the wealthiest counties in the United States and is mostly white. There is, however, a black ghetto, Marin City. "While everyone else is soaking in their hot tubs and driving in their BMWs and sailing in their yachts," Serra explains, "the blacks don't have enough money to buy groceries. But the fucking DEA formed a plan to go into Marin City and tell the following bullshit story. 'We can sell you a kilo,' they say, 'because we're a big organization from Colombia. We'll sell you kilos at half the market price because we're opening up new territory. If you guys can get enough bread together to buy a few kilos from us, we'll guarantee you this territory, we'll guarantee you this low price, we'll even guarantee you protection.'

"Well, these are poor people. You throw a piece of meat to hungry dogs, they'll bite, even if they know the meat is poisoned. It's instinct. It took the guys in the ghetto about two or three months to raise twenty thousand dollars for a few kilos, and then the DEA busted everybody. What a chickenshit thing to do and a half-ass prosecution! But it was a great entrapment case. In every entrapment case there's government overreach, falsity, corroboration; there are lying snitches in every single entrapment case. Entrapment is the keynote type of case for jury nullification. As always we can't call it that, but that's exactly what it is."

. . .

Still another angle is the necessity defense. These are hard cases to get. But as more and more ground in the traditional zones of defense is lost, defense attorneys have to be creative enough to find new zones. Necessity, in its legal context, means trying to avert a greater evil by committing a crime. Traditionally, the necessity defense has been applied to escape cases: A prisoner will escape because he's about to be killed or raped, or he's been raped and doesn't want to be repeatedly raped.

Serra once had what he calls "a beautiful necessity-defense case." In California it's illegal, a misdemeanor, to possess hypodermic needles. Now, the Clean Needle Exchange has worked throughout the world, especially Europe, to prevent AIDS by exchanging the dirty needles of drug users for clean needles. The Exchanges set up their stands in public places. Although it's against the law in California, the more civilized jurisdictions allow it de facto; they just look the other way. In San Francisco, in fact, the police are in favor of it, so the Exchange can distribute thousands and thousands of needles unimpeded. It has a definite impact, demonstrated statistically, in reducing the spread of HIV through dirty needles.

In San Mateo, though, dedicated Exchange workers set up a station and started dispensing the clean needles, and the police busted them. These were all social workers, humanitarian to the core, and Serra participated in what he calls a "showcase of a trial." They were allowed the necessity defense and brought in experts from all over the west: doctors and educators and social workers, all with impeccable pedigrees, who had all done self-sacrificial work for the community through various AIDS projects; people who advised the legislature; even HIV-positive needle users. In short, the defense was completely overwhelming.

Obviously, they weren't talking about the simple possession of hypodermic needles. They were talking about the state of science as it relates to saving lives. Serra held up a dirty needle and exclaimed, "Look at this! This is an instrument of death. Look at it! People are dying within ten blocks of this courtroom. Someone's shooting heroin into his arm with a needle used by someone else with HIV, and that needle is passed to someone else, and the police and city fathers of San Mateo want to prohibit the distribution of clean needles to these people."

Though the legal base for it is necessity, it's classic jury nullification. Again, the defense embraces the moral high ground with social, medical, life-and-death issues. In a way, it's the consummate nullification argument.

. . .

Character witnesses embody another classic defense. Character witnesses alone can raise reasonable doubt. If the defendant doesn't possess or has never exhibited the type of character required for the crime, innocence can be inferred. Serra blows it up, frames it, turns it into his whole case. He throws every character witness he can get his hands on at the case, knowing that what they say will have a cumulative effect. The prosecution, also knowing this is the heart of the defense, fights it, so Serra asks for 10 character witnesses and gets five. If he's lucky, they'll give him six.

The origin of character witnesses, like all of our law, is thought to come from England, from the common law. But if you look closely, according to Serra, it goes back a lot further, all the way back to the Codex Hammurabi, a code of law that survives to this day on a seven-foot-tall basalt stele that dates back to 1790 B.C.E., nearly 4,000 years ago, from the Babylonian civilization.

Serra carefully explains all this to the jurors. "In Babylon, nearly forty centuries ago, trials really were by one's peers. Everyone knew everyone, so that if someone was charged with a crime, there was a highly public trial. It was swift and direct—you know, the convicted criminal was stood in front of the stoning wall at noon and his head was on a stick by sunset. It was just, under Babylonian law, to stone that person to death. After all, he'd been condemned by their form of due process.

"But if someone from the community—some leader, some wise man, some religious figure, someone respected—walked forward and stood in front of the condemned and said, 'I vouch for this man! I've known him all his life. I know his family. And he is not, cannot be, guilty of this crime. He does not deserve to die,' well then, the villagers had two choices. They could let the condemned person go or they could stone both of them. That's how the custom of listening to character witnesses started.

"Then I say, 'Ladies and gentlemen, whom have we brought you in this case? We've brought to the stoning wall a priest. We've brought to the stoning wall a rabbi. We've brought to the stoning wall the minister, the mayor, the mother …' I go on. I beg. 'These character witnesses, they are honored respected citizens. They have achieved success. They're wise. They have integrity. Do you think they would have stepped forward for a drug dealer? After all, it's their reputations on the line." Now that raises reasonable doubt.

"In every case, if the client has a good family, I bring them all to court. I show the defendant's wife. I put her on the stand every time. I put the mother on the stand; I'll find some relevance. If my client wants to get up there and cry, he gets up there and cries! Are his children going to break forward, running to him, crying, "Daddy!" while he's in custody? Good! I plan it. I put my arm around the accused in front of the jury. If the defendant is out on bail, I have him walk proudly. I have him look at the jury, appearing righteous. I find out where the jury members eat their lunch and we go thoro. I show myself, I show my client. No downcast eyes. No lurking around in shame. I tell my client, 'Be proud. Stand with self-confidence. Don't look like you're guilty. Don't shrink. Don't divert your eyes. Look at them, man to man, man to woman. You have no moral taint. Don't try to fulfill the role of outcast.

"So again, it's a morality play. Jury nullification is always a morality play. I'm building morality on character witnesses: 'The defendant is a good wholesome person. He works. He's a good husband, a good father, a good son. Why would he get involved in an illegal transaction? He didn't do the transaction. The informant says he did, but there's no adequate corroboration. There are no photographs. There are no fingerprints. It's just activity consistent with guilt or consistent with innocence; if there are two reasonable interpretations of the circumstantial evidence, one for guilt, one for innocence, you must vote for innocence.' I give the jury that pitch. It works. It nullifies."

. . .

Four possibilities for jury nullification include black rage, battered-woman syndrome, racism, and genocide. These can all either stand as defenses on their own or can be woven into the defense.

"Nothing is more exciting, more uplifting," Serra says, "than one of those types of cases where the tail wags the dog."

He gets up for the opening argument and looks all the jurors in the eye. He's always hoping for some blacks, some Chicanos, a stray Native American on the jury, and he tells them that it isn't a drug case, or an assault case, or a burglary case, or whatever crime the defendant is accused of committing. Rather, this is racism they're going to hear about. When he says racism, or genocide, or black rage, or battered-woman syndrome, he's again calling jurors into the higher arena. It wasn't just any random woman who killed a man; it was a battered woman. She did it, he admits. She killed the guy. But only after years of being abused and battered and broken. Likewise, in desperation, the victim of racism, filled with black rage, robbed the bank. He did do it. But Serra shifts the focus from the mere "facts" of the case onto the mental component of the crime. Often he's trying to reduce what the defendant is guilty of to a lesser crime. Other times he's trying for an acquittal through nullification, or a hung jury.

In Oakland, California, for example, as soon as he says racism or black rage, that's the end of the case. In the U.S., citizens are inculcated, however simplistically, that racism and discrimination in every form are evil. Most Americans believe that. That's where, he believes, we have the most regrets in this country, where we feel the most guilt. And if Serra

129

can touch that soft part of a juror's mind, it's nullification. He doesn't, to be sure, touch it gently. He contacts it with a hot iron. He burns it into them.

"The calling of a trial lawyer is half-evangelical," Serra preaches. "Jurors don't want to hear this specious legalese. They're not equipped to understand it and defense lawyers are way off on a tangent when they engage in it. It's got to be straightforward. It's got to be honest. It's got to be from my spirit to their spirit. That's the heart and soul of jury nullification."

. . .

"Mere presence" and "mere association" also provide nullification defenses. A person who is merely present at a crime or merely associates with criminals is not guilty of the crime itself. Serra had such a case in Fresno, California.

The modus operandi was to steal airplanes, fill them with stolen machine guns, fly down to Mexico to a clandestine airstrip, exchange the weapons for marijuana, fly the marijuana back, and abandon the airplane, which was a B-25, a big aircraft. It held a lot of guns and a lot of pot. Serra was defending a guy who had literally published his way out of prison. He wrote a book while in San Quentin and he was a street denizen; he'd been in prison most of his life, 18 out of his 30 years. In the old days the prisoners couldn't have unlimited paper, so he used every last open space on a page, both sides, all the top, bottom, and side margins, and he actually got the manuscript published. He made a lot of money on the book and, as a result, he got paroled.

His brother was a heavy in the guns-for-pot smuggling venture. So one time he went along with his brother. They all got popped and wound up on trial in Fresno. Serra's defense was that he was merely there. He asked one of the other defendants, "He was there?"

"Yeah."

"You never saw him carry the marijuana, did you?"

"No, I don't think I ever saw him carry it."

"You didn't see him even touch it, did you?"

"No, I don't think I ever saw him touch it."

"His brother, Roger, carried it, didn't he?"

"Yeah, I think his brother did."

Then Serra brought up his client's status as a published author, having him testify that he went down there with the smugglers to write another book, not to participate in the transaction. He brought in a literary agent who said that the book, on marijuana smuggling, was getting published.

Serra actually read some of the manuscript to the jury, in which the defendant was describing the pilot going to Mexican bars and doing some unsavory things. The prosecution raised the issue of when he wrote the manuscript, before or after he was busted. But Serra redirected that to the "mere presence" defense. He said his client was a writer, a published author. Why would he go back to a life of crime when he was making good money writing and he had a contract to write another book? He was acquitted.

"We all want to believe that there's goodness in everyone and creativity in every domain of life, and that every dimension has its shining stars, and this was one of those times. I asked the jury, 'Do you want to put him back in prison after he's made such a success of himself?' We transcended the legal issue with a moral issue and won the case."

· · ·

Finally, police misconduct. It happens *all* the time, often in conjunction with police inconsistency and perjury and informants who are paid a lot of money, as much as $25,000. Under these circumstances, nullifying a jury involves making a classic switch: Rather than defending his client, the defense attorney puts the police and prosecution on trial.

Serra handled a Mafia case in Miami. The Mafia, he says, brings out the worst in the FBI. They unleash all restraints. In this case, the FBI put a recording device under the bed and kitchen table of his client, an old Italian who was married. They got deep into his private life, listening to its most intimate aspects. There were also surveillance video, paid informants, and a sting operation.

The case involved Serra's client taking a baseball bat in a pizza parlor and smashing another mob guy in the nose. When the guy went down, the defendant hit him a few more times with the bat. The victim was rushed to the hospital, where he became an informant. He called Serra's client, who didn't know he was being recorded; Serra's guy said on tape, "You motherfucker, you were supposed to be dead, but you're still alive. We'll get you."

The hair stood straight up on the back of Serra's head when he heard it in court. He thought his guy was a goner. But the generic defense theme was the corruption of the authorities, the fact that a totalitarian state always strips you of your rights. Serra turned it into a situation where a guilty vote was a vote for the Gestapo. A guilty vote was a vote for more wiretaps and invasion of privacy and sting operations. It was almost straightforward jury nullification and he didn't win, but he hung the jury, with two holdouts. The case was never tried again, mainly due to the expense of it and the embarrassment of FBI misconduct. So it was a win.

"To get two jurors holding out on a purely jury-nullification defense is a triumph, believe me!" Serra says. "In a nullification case, I really feel at the apex of my professional ability. Win, lose, or draw, it makes me feel proud that I'm a lawyer."

Chapter 8

The Psychological Elements of Crime

It's a busy intersection in a busy part of the downtown of a busy city. A man in a suit and hat is driving a newish convertible, with a woman in an evening gown beside him. Suddenly, the trunk of the car kicks open and you see a body, bound and gagged, struggling. The man in the suit stops the car mid-intersection. Everyone in their cars and on the sidewalk is looking at him. He walks to the back of the car and puts five bullets into the squirming figure. He returns to the car, grabs a bag and the woman, and they run from the car, disappearing down the street and leaving the convertible in mid-intersection with its trunk open and the gagged male dead inside.

This looks like cold calculated first-degree murder, doesn't it? But this case was the archetypal example of revenge, one of the psychological elements of crime that so fascinate Tony Serra.

It turns out that the killer was a major heroin dealer and the woman was his girlfriend. One New Year's Eve, a dozen armed men burst into this dealer's home, demanding to know where his stash of cash was hidden. The man in fact had hundreds of thousands of dollars in the house, but he wouldn't tell the robbers where it was. So they handcuffed him and beat him up; then they turned on a floor heater and stuck his head in it. Then they cut off his ear.

When he still wouldn't tell them where the money was, they turned their attentions to his girlfriend and, one after another, raped her in front of him. She was screaming, but he still refused to give up the cash.

They were about to kill them both, when one of the robbers found the cache of several hundred thousand dollars. They were so happy with the find that they scrambled out of the house with all of the money—far more than they ever dreamed was there—and left the man and the woman tied up, beaten, bleeding, broken, raped, crying, in extreme agony.

The dealer and his girlfriend managed to untie themselves. The man knew his fortune was gone and his woman was spoiled. His life was shattered. He was in a morbid, depressed, and vengeful state of mind. He figured it was an inside job, that someone who bought from him knew he had a stash and was vulnerable. He pretended that nothing had happened. He told no one of the robbery or rape. He went about his business.

It further turned out that the money had a scent. Stored under the house in a vault, the money had a little mildew, so periodically the dealer sprayed it with perfume. Day after day, week after week, month after month, the dealer sniffed the money he exchanged for heroin. Finally, some of the robbed money came back to him from one of his people. The aggrieved dealer hit the betrayer on the head with the butt of a rifle and got his confession.

That was the man in the trunk.

"My client and his girlfriend were caught a couple of months later. At the time of the trial, my client's girlfriend was pregnant from the rape. My client was sterile—we proved it at trial—and therefore he couldn't have impregnated her," Serra picks up the story.

"My client was charged with first-degree murder and I defended him on the basis that he was in the heat of the passion of revenge. Even though he'd premeditated this over a long period of time, during which he'd smelled the money coming in, the presence of the heat of revenge was strong here. During the closing argument, I tried to put the jury into the mind of the defendant by describing how *any* human being would feel after what had happened to him: his woman raped repeatedly, his head pushed into this fiery floor heater, his ear cut off. Ultimately, the jury had the feeling that he had the right—under the old law, *lex talios*, an eye for an eye—to kill his betrayer. And they returned a manslaughter verdict.

"This is one example of the successful use of a psychological element—the heat of passion; in this case, revenge—in the defense of a client. It helped eliminate many years in prison for a human being who, at one level, premeditatedly and determinedly and ruthlessly took the life of a fellow human being.

"Lawyers always argue logically and rationally. They appeal to the reasonable person, to the Aristotelian notion of 'common sense,' to the universal belief that rational processes will net rational results." Tony was illustrating his use, similar to jury nullification, of the psychological elements of crime. "But when we, as defense lawyers, proceed in this manner, we are ultimately sowing the seeds of our own failure as the sentinels of social justice. We're abdicating our responsibility if we pretend that *reason* is the most significant aspect of law. The forbidden fruit is always the most meaningful, the most desirable, the most compelling. And the forbidden fruit, in law, is *passion*. The forbidden fruit is *emotion*. Fear, jealousy, revenge, hatred, drug madness, all of these sub-cerebral states of mind, these agitations, these obsessions are the forbidden fruits of the court, of the law, of the judicial system."

It became clear to me that the power of Serra's tactical arsenal was the loaded weapon of *passion* in an arena where most lawyers pride themselves on logic and reason. "The instruction to the jury in every criminal trial goes something like this: 'You cannot consider passion or discuss pity or feel compassion in your deliberations. You cannot allow bias, prejudice, or any sense of identification.' But a good criminal-defense lawyer uses all of them! *That's* our realm, the sub-cerebral—passion, compassion, emotion. The criminal-defense attorney who emotes controls the courtroom, *because* it's forbidden. If the lawyer can somehow pull that cat out of the bag, he or she will always be an authoritative figure in the judicial system. Manifestations of outrage and protest and defiance—all overwhelming emotional states of mind—are what move the common people. I'll say it again: The lawyer who controls emotions controls the case.

"We defense lawyers are the purveyors of myth, and myth is the vehicle that supports and elicits emotion. In fact, myth is a greater metaphysical truth than the small microcosm of empirical data that under-lie every trial. Indeed, every trial attempts to reproduce this empirical data—the event—that happened out there in real life. A good defense lawyer takes up those elements that appeared in the real event and makes symbols of them.

"These myths are anti-intellectual, anti-rational, but they're the most meaningful elements that can be worked by the defense attorney. It is the high calling of the attorney to create emotionally laden myth out of the factual matrix of a case."

. . .

One of Tony Serra's cases was the archetypal example of revenge.

The letter of the law, as it relates to self-defense, is quite simple: It requires a good-faith and reasonable fear that you're about to suffer an *immediate* attack in which you'll be subjected to great bodily injury or death. But the law always burdens simple concepts with what Tony calls "profuse, protracted, and puzzling extensions."

The requirement is that the fear has to be "reasonable," meaning any reasonable person will have the same fear that the accused had under like circumstances, that he was in imminent peril of harm. Frequently, however, that fear isn't reasonable. It's paranoid. It's induced by drugs or sleeplessness or hallucinations. "That kind of a case," Serra says, "is called 'imperfect self-defense.'" Still, it reduces murder to manslaughter and attempted murder to attempted manslaughter. Even if your belief that you're in immediate mortal danger is unreasonable, the law says your state of mind isn't as culpable as that of a person who has no bona fide belief of being in peril. Serra defended a murderer who really be-lieved that the mailman was some kind of assassin; he killed the mail-man, convinced that he was coming to his home to kill him. That's an example of imperfect self-defense: The peril is neither real nor realistic.

Serra has had every variety of self-defense case. He admits to losing some, especially when the victim was unarmed or had a lesser weapon than the defendant—for example, a club versus a gun. "Juries don't like that," he says. "They like an even fight, that the defense of self must be commensurate with the attack. Traditionally, this means fist versus fist, club versus club, knife versus knife, gun versus gun. When that balance is altered, first we sometimes won't get a self-defense instruction from the court and, second, juries don't like it. They don't like shooting an unarmed man."

One case in particular stands out in his mind that he says was really self-defense, but wound up as second-degree murder.

The incident took place at a junkie hotel, a flophouse on Broadway in San Francisco. He represented a young, intelligent, educated white man from a good family who'd come to San Francisco in the '60s and become addicted to heroin. He was down on his luck when he checked into this flophouse. In a room down the hall was another heroin addict, a big tall physically fit black man with a ferocious reputation for acts of violence. As junkies often do, these two men established a relationship of sorts around the hypodermic needle and the cooking spoon. At one point, the black guy stole Serra's client's gun and they had an argument about it.

"You stole my gun!" the client accused.

"Naw, I didn't steal your gun."

"I'm gonna get it back."

"You come around me, I'll *kill* you," the man from down the hall said.

"My client truly believed that his gun had been stolen by his addict associate. He also believed that if he came around the guy, he'd be killed. So my guy got *another* gun, went up to the other guy's door, and kicked it open. The black guy was lying on the bed, zonked out on heroin. When my guy busted in, the other guy jumped up in alarm, his arms thrust out, looking to my client like he had the gun. My client shot and killed an unarmed man, under the influence of heroin, who was *not*, in actuality, a threat at the time.

"But the defendant *had* a reasonable belief, based on the other guy's reputation, the fact that he *had* stolen the gun, and that he'd threatened his life. When the guy jumped up so suddenly, it was reasonable to believe he did so to shoot more accurately. It was dark and he rose and his arms flailed out, so one could reasonably interpret that he had the gun and he was about to shoot it. This is a situation where it's all or nothing. The prosecution probably offered us manslaughter because of the overall situation. And I'm sure that we said, 'No! Let's go for self-defense here.'

"In the end, we asked for too much. The jury didn't like any of it.

They didn't like the heroin scene, the fact that my guy had a gun to begin with, that the victim was a poor addicted black man and my client was a rich white guy. But most of all, they disliked the shooting of an unarmed man. Unfortunately, this client is still in prison, convicted of second-degree murder. He's probably been in between ten and fifteen years. It was just a bad *hour* in his life when he wanted to get his gun back, but it took an inordinate part of his life away. He'll get out, probably, when he's fifty."

. . .

Another example of a strong psychological element of a crime, involving self-defense and fear, comes from one of Tony Serra's most celebrated, successful, and creative trials, the 1982 death-penalty case of Patrick "Hooty" Croy. Writer David Talbot, in the *Los Angeles Times Magazine*, called it "the ballad of Hooty Croy, as sung by his operatic attorney."

A paralegal who had worked with Serra on the Choo Sol Lee retrial alerted him to the case, which at the time, Serra considered the greatest cause of his career. "It was a case that every lawyer waits a lifetime to get. Because very seldom do you get a case, let alone a death-penalty case, with such socially significant issues and where your client, from any perspective, is innocent. So you feel honored, you feel graced, you feel like your karma is good—that you got chosen for such a case. It's a wonderful thing."

Croy, a young Native American Karuk from Shasta, California, was one of several Indians involved in a late-night altercation with the owner of a mini-mart in Siskiyou County in northwestern California. The owner believed the Indians stole a box of ammunition. The police were alerted and chased the Indians' car into the surrounding hills. By the time the car came to a stop near Hooty's grandmother's rickety cabin, in a ravine nestled between two rolling hills that led up to the mountains, several police cars were in hot pursuit.

Hooty, his sister, and a cousin ran up the hill that looked down on the cabin. Officers from approximately 20 police cars, with their semi-automatic weapons and all kinds of heavy armament, started shooting

138

the three Indians armed with an old-model .22 rifle. Investigators determined that seven shots came from the Indians and more than 220 rounds were fired by the police officers.

During a cease-fire, Hooty came down from his hiding place to see if his grandmother had been injured in the crossfire. As he was crawling through an open window in the back of the cabin, a police officer, Bo Hittson, came up behind him and fired a few shots, striking Hooty twice, once in the leg, once in the back. Hooty spun around with the .22, fired in defense of his life, and shot Hittson through the heart; he died. Hitton's blood alcohol count was .08 at the time of his death; he was off duty and had been drinking when he was called in for the action. Hooty was charged with the killing of a police officer, which carries the death penalty.

Hooty was convicted in the first trial. The public defender's office went with a diminished-capacity defense, claiming that Croy was just a drunken Indian. He was quickly convicted and given the death penalty. But the decision was reversed on appeal, which was when Tony Serra got involved.

First, he asked for and received a change of venue to San Francisco. Next, he went with the plea of not guilty, arguing self-defense and fear. With 28 cops firing 220 rounds and Hooty shot in the back, it was a straight case of Hooty experiencing imminent mortal peril.

But this trial also involved what's come to be called a "cultural defense," which is where the psychological element of fear entered the picture. Serra used fear to counter the deep-seated and well-established principle that flight from the scene of an alleged crime and pursuing police officers is indicative of guilt. Prosecutors make much of it and juries easily buy the fact that someone who runs has a sense of culpability and is fleeing in order to avoid detection or arrest.

In the case of Hooty Croy, there were two instances of flight: one from the mini-mart in Yreka; the other when they got to the cabin and ran away to hide on the hillside. So Serra and the defense had to repudiate the unspoken belief that the flight was evidence of guilt.

"Ultimately, this point became the tail that wagged the whole dog, the most significant element of the case," Serra explains. "The prosecution probably made a calamitous strategic error when they introduced the Indians' flight and failure to surrender as an indication of guilt, because it opened the door for us to put on what is now called the 'cultural defense.'"

The defense was allowed to explain how a young rural Native, living in a predominantly white culture, has a historically valid reason to be afraid of police officers. Even when a Native American hasn't committed any crime and has no guilty or culpable state of mind, that Native American will *run*. Native Americans will *not* surrender. Hooty Croy is emblematic of this psychology, due to what he'd heard from his elders in the great oral tradition, stories told and retold over many generations around the campfire, at the gatherings, at the powwows.

Serra and his team were able to present, in the retrial in Department 28 in San Francisco Superior Court, evidence of the perpetration by whites—frontiersmen, miners, settlers, military, vigilantes, and ultimately police—of a systematic genocide of Native Americans.

"That word, 'genocide,' resounded through the Hooty Croy trial like a giant Indian drum that was pounded incessantly into the jury's ears," Serra recalls. "We were able to enter into evidence the fact that when the whites first came to the Pacific Northwest, they poisoned the Indians by feeding them contaminated meat at the ceremonies they invited them to attend; they went through the Indian camp and mercilessly killed the young children, the old, and the infirm who couldn't run from their onslaught; they gave the Indians blankets in the winter, ostensibly as a gesture of friendship, that were laced with smallpox bacteria. I talked about how the government paid for scalps in those days and that so many scalps were taken, the government actually ran out of money to pay for them. The white people and their white government cleared the Indians from the Pacific Northwest as if they were getting rid of wolves or coyotes to establish a sheep farm.

"Then I moved on to the present: how the Indians have no property, no employment, how they've been dispossessed of everything and are constantly subjected to racism, harassment, and brutality by the police. Indians have no respect for the white-man's law because the white man has broken every single treaty ever made with them; the white man has ultimately taken all of their property and left them outside our cultural hierarchy. They have no position whatsoever. They are *still* outcasts.

"We set out this history of treachery and annihilation to explain the fear of Hooty Croy and the other Indians, which was historically based and justified. To prove it, we put on professors—mostly long-haired, solemn, dignified Indians, Ph.D.s from Harvard—who documented the genocide over the past hundred years. Hooty testified that even at four or five years old, when police showed up in the Indian community, he would run, for no 'rational' reason, just from pure unmitigated fear, fear of the oppressor, fear of the white man, fear of the white police officer, and throw himself into the river that was covered with ice, and he would hide under the ice, almost freezing to death, just because he was so frightened. And not only hadn't he done anything, no one else had either. But the white police came onto the reservation just to harass, to arrest, to assault. In those days the Natives had no redress whatsoever. And to a shamefully large extent, this is *still* true."

In the *Los Angeles Times Magazine* of June 24, 1990, the writer David Talbot described the scene. "Serra is humming with the full power of history. His energy threatens to burst the seams of his thrift-store suit that is, like all of his courtroom outfits, one full size too small for him. The snug-fitting suits make him look bigger than he is, and he's a big man. He flirts with clownishness with his floodwater pants ..." —a style that Talbot labeled "conspicuous underconsumption" and that journalist Alex Roth noted were "so frayed that his underwear sometimes showed through"—"... but all eyes in the courtroom are riveted on him."

Serra got the jury to go inside Hooty Croy's mind, from historical, sociological, and psychological points of view. "I gave the jurors deep issues to think about. I both sensitized and traumatized them. In my closing argument, I focused on the genocide that ultimately produced this naked and reflexive fear in Hooty Croy, so that he *would not* stop the car even though they had stolen nothing; he *would not* surrender even though the officers were firing at him; he would rather *die* up on the hill than be brought in and imprisoned or killed for what he knew were false charges.

"The element of fear in his state of mind cast a great shadow over the prosecution's entire case. And although this fear was not a necessary element to be adjudicated in that trial, it was allowed in order to explain why Hooty Croy had a reasonable belief that his life was in imminent peril, which gave him the right to defend himself; it also explained why he fled and did not surrender.

"This case was an instance in which, by singling out what I would call a discrete emotion and litigating that emotion exhaustively, I was able to enter the juror's hearts and minds and tap into their deep compassion and their deep guilt about Native Americans, in general, to a triumphant conclusion. At least four were crying during the closing argument.

"Not all cases, obviously, can focus on emotion with such success."

The actor Gene Hackman agreed. He was in the gallery to prepare for his movie *Class Action,* in which he portrayed a crusading defense attorney. Serra's law office was used as the set for Hackman's office in the movie, in which Tony also had a bit part. "He's really something, isn't he?" Hackman commented after the trial. "Actors always suffer in comparison to the real thing. They're never quite as dramatic."

· · ·

Drug impairment is another state-of-mind defense that has many applications to jury-trial work. Just as the heat of passion can reduce a verdict of murder to manslaughter, drug impairment can also change a verdict. When a person is so drug-impaired that he can appreciate neither the nature of his actions nor the distinction between right and wrong, then a verdict of not guilty by reason of insanity is possible. In some cases, drug impairment can be a complete defense: The person was so far gone that he didn't have the required state of mind for murder or, as is frequently the situation, even manslaughter.

For example, the person may have been in a state of what's now recognized as "stimulant psychosis" (in general, this condition occurs with the use of PCP and excessive use of methamphetamine or cocaine). Heroin addiction can reach this stage, but more often it counterindicates the states of minds required for murder: malice aforethought, premeditation, and deliberation; usually, when Tony Serra defends a heroin addict on a murder charge, he seeks to reduce the charges, rather than exonerate the defendant.

Some drug-impairment state-of-mind defenses actually involve the purchase and sale of drugs. A heroin addict, for example, is easy prey to an informant or an undercover officer, becoming that person's agent in purchasing or reselling drugs, in order to get hold of some for himself or to gain a little money to support his habit.

This defense isn't utilized enough, in Tony Serra's opinion, in cases where an addict becomes a buyer for or even a seller to law enforcement. The defense of entrapment is available and there's good law in that area, he says. The drug impairment in this type of defense doesn't have to be as severe as it does to obtain a verdict of not guilty by reason of insanity.

Drug impairment can also eliminate all states of mind that are required in a number of crimes where willfulness and knowledge are issues or where a person's comprehension of the ramifications of his or her conduct is litigated. Serra calls this "one side of the street": using the defendant's drug impairment as a defense. On the "other side of the street," he frequently uses the drug-impairment theme to do battle with snitches.

"The court system, as is well-known, has been infiltrated by informants [see Chapter 9 for a full discussion on informants]. These witnesses will say anything to save their own skin. All criminal defense attorneys find themselves constantly cross-examining informants in order to show that they're lying, that they don't remember, that they're making up their testimony in order to satisfy the prosecutor and to obtain favorable recommendations for leniency in their own cases. Sometimes I feel I betray my sympathy for drug addicts when I use the knowledge and information I've acquired through that sympathy in a harsh and adversarial manner against an informant. I'm sort of turning the blade, because most of the informants in the drug field have themselves abused drugs."

On both sides—exoneration of a drug-addled defendant and invalidation of the drug-using informant—of the street, defense attorneys have to know more than the defendant or witness about the drug that he or she uses. If it's heroin, the litigator has to know everything about heroin: how it affects psychology and physiology, what the symptoms are, what the *DSM-IV* says about it, what experiments have been done relating to all kinds of physical reactions and all kinds of psychological dispositions; he has to know when it creates psychosis and when the effect is merely a transitory state. And he has to make it very real for a jury.

"When I'm talking to a chronic crack user," Serra says, "I can converse with him about the imagined worms infesting his skin; I talk about the scabs or the scars on his flesh from scratching these imaginary worms; and I let the jury see the scars or the infested sores so that it becomes very graphic. I'll ask the witness to roll up his sleeve and show the track marks in his veins. Or I'll ask a witness to open her mouth and show us her teeth, which, because of the crack, are missing or black and discolored.

"When I talk about an addict shooting in parts of his body other than his arms, it becomes very graphic and I have to know everything about it. I've got to know where he buys the drug and the manner and the method of use, whether he uses it alone in the closet or in a group, whether it's street-level drug use or upper-class use.

"All of this has to be real for the defense attorney, not imaginary, and if we're going to be really effective, it cannot be secondhand. A witness will know immediately whether I know what I'm talking about or not when it comes to drugs. And that witness won't fall prey to my line of examination unless he or she feels that I—by virtue of my knowledge—command authority over him or her.

"For me," Tony says, "it's been easy. I've been involved in all sociological levels of the drug culture from the days of the Haight-Ashbury forward. I've combined a lot of case studies and a lot of literature with a lot of personal observations and that, I believe, is what makes this one of the most effective weapons in my arsenal: the fact that I know every type of marijuana grown, what the plants look like, how they're cultivated, how hashish is produced, how hashish is smoked. I'm familiar with all the cocaine paraphernalia, the manifold ways methamphetamine is produced. I know all the lingo that comes from the street and from the drug subculture and, on top of that, I've acquired a professional vocabulary and interest in the subject that have been unabated for the past thirty years. So this is an area that I use quite frequently."

The last maneuver of the defense attorney is to dress up a position with an expert witness, the best he can get. Serra frequently uses the nationally renowned Dr. David Smith of the Haight-Ashbury Clinic, but every good criminal-defense attorney who practices in the drug field knows at least a half-dozen board certified psychiatrists or psychologists with in-depth experience, both clinical and forensic, who've worked in hospital settings and conducted laboratory experiments. And just like the attorney, they have to have an insider's view. They have to know the subject matter from the ground up.

For the right kind of jury, these experts can offer the most fascinating types of evidence, because they combine the color of the street with the academic overview. Their testimony in a sense serves as the basis for the closing argument. They give the most credible description of the drug-addict's state of mind and whether that person is to be believed or not (yes if it's about the defendant, no if it's about a snitch), whether he's reliable or has gaps in memory, whether or not he's confabulating, whether or not he's been manipulated or coerced.

The in-depth presentation for a drug-impaired state of mind requires more preparation than most other defenses. Tony explains, "At one level, I have to dot every rational 'i' and at another level, I have to sensitize a jury emotionally. In this area of drug impairment, the defense attorney is both the director and the producer of a mini-drama, a mini-trial in itself."

It is, he insists, the most psychological of the psychological elements of crime.

Chapter 9

To Snitch or Not to Snitch: The Informant System

I don't go to bullfights. I don't go to cockfights. I don't even go to combative sporting events, such as prizefighting. I deem bloodletting and violence as entertainment repugnant.

But for some reason, I relish watching Tony Serra eviscerate snitches on the witness stand. There's something fundamentally satisfying about witnessing betrayers meet their fate at the hands of this man. With informants for the prosecution, Serra is merciless. In a slow and relentless process, he meticulously peels away layer after layer of the government's covert informant system, right down to its core. He stalks the snitch through the dark corridors of his deceit and toys with him as he dodges about in search of shadows of safety. Serra exposes the snitch as he cowers in the private caves of his lies, then draws him back into the glare of his intense scrutiny, before he rips out the belly of his alibi. Finally, Serra trots the snitch around by the scruff of his shame for the judge, the jury, and all of the spectators to despise.

Who among the patient plodding crowd that dutifully files into the courtroom on a given morning can know that a man will be fed to a lion before the lunch break? There will be no trace of blood, no dust-strewn struggle, no anguished screams that so disquiet the senses, yet one among us will never be the same again.

Tony Serra is famous for his cross-examination of snitches. He's masterful at asking just the right questions and eliciting the most distasteful, vile, despicable answers. The snitch, who has walked into court as nonchalantly as any spectator, is laid bare on the witness stand and forced to commit judicial suicide by the friendly fire of his own words.

Attorney Michael Stepanian recounted to Burr Snider of *San Francisco Magazine* that "Serra takes the most rough-and-tumble cases you can imagine and tries them better than anybody in America. He's been crawling up the rectum of snitches and rats for his entire career, working his way through the warmest part of the body until he gets to the heart, and then he destroys the beast."

Most ironically, perhaps, one of Serra's most prevalent preoccupations as a defense attorney is to be a prosecutor. He prosecutes informants.

. . .

The definition of an informant is a person who cooperates with law enforcement in order to have a suspect (real or imagined) arrested and convicted. For his cooperation, the informant receives "consideration" from the government and, on occasion, from the court system.

Informants are a dominant part of a prosecution's presentation in federal and state cases relating to drugs and political activities. They're used for background data, leading to search warrants and/or grand-jury investigations. Informants sometimes participate in the alleged criminal conduct, either as witnesses or hands-on, in a reverse-sting operation, for example. Especially in investigations of so-called dissident and subversive political factions, government infiltrators and informants themselves have promulgated a lot of criminal activity; they've had the ultimate inside perspective on what was occurring, because they'd instigated it. This was especially true, in Tony Serra's experience, of the Black Panthers and the Symbionese Liberation Army.

Informants sometimes claim to have seen possession of contraband or the sale of drugs; they sometimes claim to have heard incriminating statements from suspects. They're sometimes wired to record their conversations with suspects. Sometimes they testify; other times they're never revealed.

In return, informants aren't charged with crimes from which they've been arrested or receive up to dozens of years off their sentences for convictions. Informants sometimes receive payment in cash, immunity from past crimes, and when required, a change of identity and address. Informants have worked their way into the judicial system in ever-increasing numbers.

. . .

"Most of my cases have involved informants and I've gone after them for so long now that I do it unthinkingly. It's not intellect; it's just raw nerve instinct. It's Pavlovian."

J. Tony Serra leaned on the speaker's podium as he addressed a group of lawyers and law students.

"And it's filled with bitterness and pain. I have a very strong view that it's bad morally and practically; it's bad in *every* way. Presently, there's a blizzard of informants. Every major drug case involves them as key witnesses. It's a blight on our judicial system."

Serra's voice softened as he revisited some pain. "A few weeks ago, I went to see a person in prison who'd recently been busted. He was twenty-one, had one prior, and was facing a mandatory sentence of twenty years to life. I sat with him for about two hours. He was young and immature in worldly terms. His role in this bust had been trivial. He'd been a courier and had received a very small amount of money. But for him, it was going to be twenty to life. Twenty to *life!*" Serra pounded his fists on the podium for emphasis, then threw them up into the air as though throwing away a life.

"It was a contact visit, and we were at a real narrow table, face to face. He just *cried,* man." Serra paused, cupping the pathos of the situation in his hand and feeling the weight of it. "He cried for about an hour and a half. Here's this child really, not a man yet, and he's crying for an hour and a half, sobbing in front of me."

Serra's voice changed from somber to pleading as he switched roles.

"And he's saying, 'They want me to roll on my *best friend*, Tony. I don't wanna *roll* on him; I don't wanna inform on him.' His tears are coming down and he's saying, 'But I don't wanna go, either! I'm only twenty-one, and I won't get out till I'm forty, and I have an old lady and we want to have babies.' Ah, it was so heavy! 'What'll I *do?*' He poses it right there: 'What'll I do? I don't *wanna* roll! Can we beat the case, Tony? Can we beat it?'"

Serra's head dropped and he stared at the floor; the impact this had on him was apparent. When he lifted his head, his face was twisted with his own emotion upon recounting this story.

"And here I am, the champion of the anti-snitch position, a guy who *dreams* about snitches! What do I *do?* I can't emotionalize. I have to be Zen. This situation called for just being present. So I say, 'Let's look at it. Let's see the tapes that were body-wired on the cooperating defendant for the alleged time of pickup.' Ultimately, my client didn't snitch, and ultimately, they didn't indict him. He was *very* lucky."

The tension in the room gave way to relief.

"Let me give an example to show how strongly I feel on this issue. I've got five kids, including twin boys who are about the same age as this kid in jail. I love my kids as much as anyone's capable of loving his children. So let's just pretend I see my own kid in this position. And I say to myself, 'Well, what would you do, Tony? What would you do if it was your *own* kid?' And this is the conclusion I've come to: I would tell him how I really feel," he confided to the audience, growing more attentive word by word.

"But you can't talk to your clients like that. You don't preach ideology to your clients. You're their agent. You can't tell them whether to snitch or not to snitch on someone. I'm a trial lawyer; that's not my prerogative. So if a person wants to cooperate with the feds, I just walk away. That *is* my prerogative. I don't represent snitches. I never have and I never will. Not *knowingly,* anyway, because sometimes they're snitches and they're even snitching on *you* and you don't know it!"

Serra shifted position as if to take a solid stance.

"So this is what I would tell my kid. I would say, 'No! No! We *fight* it. We *always* fight it. We fight it *all the way!*'" His hand, clenched into a fist, vibrated the force of his statement.

"'But Dad!' I *hope* my son wouldn't be crying, but he could be, when he says, 'You *know* we're gonna lose. They got me wired! There's gonna be two witnesses against me. We're gonna *lose!* I'm gonna go for *twenty years!*'"

Tony Serra's voice deepened as he changed roles from son to the authoritative father figure. "And then I would say, 'We'll fight it all the way. Maybe we'll get lucky. I've gotten lucky before. Maybe we can do something. Maybe we'll hang it. Maybe the judge will commit reversible error. Maybe a miracle will happen. But we'll *fight it,* son!'"

Then, switching quickly back to the role of his son, he said, "'But I'm gonna be gone for twenty *years,* Dad!'" Then back again to father. "'If that happens, we'll visit you. We'll *love* you! We'll *respect* you! We'll *honor your name!* Your picture will hang on our walls. We'll pay tribute to you. You will be *beloved* amongst us, your family and your friends. You will *never* be forgotten! It will all be waiting for you when you're outside again. Everything within our grasp that we can give we will *give.*'

"And then if he says, 'I can't do it, Dad; I can't do it. I can't *do* twenty years,' I would say, 'Then *I* will bring you the hemlock! You don't have to do it. You *can't* do twenty years? Then die! If you can't do it, it's better that you *die!* Die *honorable.*'

"This I would say to my son. I don't say this to my client. But I want you to know the strength of the emotional involvement I have in this issue! 'You die and we will revere your image forever! We will hallow your image. We'll tell everyone how brave you are, how courageous you are! What a warrior you are. How loyal you are! How strong you are! We will *love* you! And you'll be born again. But you die a *lion!* You do not *live* the life of a dog!'" His hand pounded out these shocking words on the podium.

"That's what I would tell my *son!*" He again pointed emphatically. "That's the honest truth! I would sacrifice son, I would sacrifice self, I would never *never* countenance within my *blood,* within my family, what I call the Judas Syndrome. *That's* how strongly I feel!"

Continuing in a softer tone, he said, "Then I would tell him, 'Hey! Half of the world has always been nuns and monks. Don't you see? You've been *chosen!* A large burden has been lifted from you, though an equally large burden has been given to you. But now you can master

Hesse; you can master Shakespeare, Schopenhauer. You can read all of Socrates. You can create poetry! You can create literature! You can look into yourself. You can find *huge* free zones within meditation. It's not so *bad* to be in there twenty years!' I would tell that to my son."

In an aside to the audience, he said, "Obviously, the other polarity of incarceration is loss; it's defeat, self-destruction, death. This is the symbol that we lawyers can't countenance."

Serra paused for a moment, letting one wave of passion ebb as he began to ride the next one. "But to my son, I would say, 'You're given the sun that shines. The *same* sun that shines outside shines in prison. The winds that blow the spirits, that murmur and purr to you within your spirit, can't *ever* be confined. They will come *to* you. All the eternal truths are in as well as outside prison. In Buddhist societies, more than fifty percent of the society are monks. They live in cells. The privations and deprivations of jail are the same privations they *choose!* You've been given a holy life! See *that* part of it.'

"You see, we're all Western materialists, so we have this notion about confinement. There is no confinement. There is never confinement. That's an illusion. The mind is free! And the inner mind is *vast!*"

The mood of the room quivered in grim silence. An uncomfortable tension was now apparent; some of the lawyers in this audience represented snitches as a policy.

Serra turned to soul-searching. "Why do I feel this strongly? What are the underpinnings. What's the rationale? The theory? The logic? Why am I preaching this kind of view? I'll describe it in stages.

"You take the person who turns, who rats, who becomes a snitch, who participates in the Judas Syndrome. The person who *turns over* his friends, his family, his mother, maybe his father, maybe his brother. Take that person. Is society doing any good for that person by making him an informant? Is it something wholesome? Are we rehabilitating him? Are we regenerating his moral values? No! We've destroyed that person! We've totally *destroyed* him! Have you ever seen a tree that has snapped in the wind? It still has a stark kind of stature of boldness and strength. There's a courage in the broken trunk. But the tree that's bent by the wind, the tree that no longer stands upright, that's sad. That's depressing. No one wants to look at that!

"Loyalty is connected to survival of the species, to natural selection. Loyalty. Loyalty to family. Loyalty to tribe. Loyalty to your environment. Loyalty, ultimately, to nation. It's a deep-seated universal instinct. That's why treason has always been viewed as so heinous a crime. That's why the Judas image has always horrified everyone. That's why, in every society, disloyal people are banned. They're killed—we *still* kill them if they turn treasonous in battle!

"The highest crime has *always* been to go against your family, your friends, your ideology, those who have nurtured you, those who have supported you, the ones who will perpetuate your species. That's why— *always*—the courageous have died to allow family, or tribe, or friends to exist. You *must* sacrifice yourself! So that's another deep-seated instinct. It's a deep-seated conditioned response. Loyalty is a universal moral precept; it exists on all levels of civilization. Death to anyone who disowns, devalues, or undermines the right of his or her tribe, family, to exist!"

In a calmer voice, he said, "The universal moral precept of loyalty is so strong that when a person gives that up, he destroys *himself*. He's never the same. As a lawyer, do you think you've done him some good by encouraging him to snitch? Do you think you've turned him around? Do you think you've rehabilitated him? You've done nothing but *kill* him! He would have been prouder in prison. His friends would have saluted him. He would have been a symbol of strength and courage and resistance. But now, as the lawyer who has turned him over, *you* have participated in his Judas Syndrome. *You* have totally annihilated him as a moral human being, because he's now gone against everything that's instilled in the youth in every society: loyalty.

"So that's the first question I ask: Does snitching better a person in any way?"

Serra had churned up the room again. It was apparent that he was hitting below the belt of the comfort level of many people present, the snitch lawyers in particular.

"Let's look next at the judicial system. Imagine a judicial system in which one side goes out and buys witnesses. It buys one witness here for ten thousand dollars, another one there for twenty thousand, three over here a little cheaper: three for fifteen thousand. And then the *other* side goes out and buys as many witnesses as it can get, and the witnesses testify for the pay that they get. Would any intelligent sane person consider that to be a *wise* way to run a judiciary system? Is that the truth-seeking process at its finest hour?

"Justice has to be a meaningful attribute of every culture. And within that society's system of justice is the truth-seeking process. And if that process is based on the employment of paid witnesses on both sides, then what does 'truth' mean in that civilization? What does 'justice' mean? They mean *nothing*!" The room reverberated with the force of this statement. I looked around to see if anyone would walk out, but no one did. It was as if everyone was held captive on a speeding locomotive.

Serra was accusatory now. "What are we doing, especially in the federal courts? We're saying that *one* side can go out and buy witnesses. But if the other side, if *we* buy witnesses, that's a fucking *crime*! We would be prosecuted for it! *They* buy witnesses, not so crudely as with cash money, although that has occurred. I've had cases where they've given up to thirty thousand *cash* in a suitcase. Just like a dope deal. The narcs are giving it to their informant, who's heading for some unknown federal-witness-protection place. But no! Far more precious than money, they give *liberty*! 'We'll give you *ten* years of your liberty. We'll give you *twenty* years of your liberty,'" he said in a cunning seductive voice. "'You'll be anonymous and you'll be completely *free*! Nobody will know!'

"We're creating a judicial system that's predicated on paid informants, who are paid in the currency of liberty, the most precious commodity that exists. And dare we say that *that*'s justice? Dare we say that that's the underpinning, the foundation, for a just system? No! It's an utter disgrace. It's a mockery. It's ridiculed from *any* intellectual perspective, by other countries, by history itself.

"Someday historians will look back at these times as a very dark and gloomy period for the American judicial system. And if other judicial systems follow in our footsteps—with witnesses paid to testify with their liberty—then the notion of justice and the notion of freedom certainly will have to go!

"So what I say is, first, the individual who participates in this system is destroyed and second, the judicial system that participates in it is destroyed."

Serra built up such a force in his oratory that it seemed as if the room was banking like a plane, with its passengers bracing against the disequilibrium.

"The third level is far worse!" he shouted at the audience. "This is *really* why I'd let my kid become a heroic penal-colony member, why I'd let him *die*, before I'd let him snitch. *Informing destroys the adversary system.* You forfeit that which you think you embrace. And it's already coming to that: The dissident voice is being silenced by the snitch system.

"I'll get a case and I'll think, Oh, there's just one snitch against me. Oh, well, what's one motherfucking snitch? I can beat one snitch! And by the time I get to trial, there are *five* snitches. They *all* rolled! Rolled the top on my client, rolled the bottom on my client, rolled the side on my client. Total oppression!

"Total conquest is what's in the mind of the government. Total victory. They want to vanquish *all* opposition. And they don't give a shit if the snitch is lying or if the snitch is telling the truth! What they want is *total control*. They're not lawyers; they're oppressors in the U.S. Attorney's Office who go into this phony fiction that this is serving an adversarial function. But what happens, ultimately, is that there's only one side. You who think you're serving the defense, you serve the *prosecution!* There won't *be* an adversary system. *Everyone* will submit. Everyone will be vanquished. There will be no two sides. Everyone will turn over.

"And what does that mean? That means *totalitarianism!* That's where we're going. Don't you *see* that? The snitch, the informant, the conspiracy concepts, the reverse-sting concept—these are our gutters leading toward totalitarianism: eliminating the adversarial system, eliminating trial by jury, ultimately eliminating us lawyers!

"Don't you think that when they get through snitching on everyone else, they're gonna be snitching on us? Aren't they snitching on us now? Have you had a good open conversation with someone you didn't know lately? Do you walk around the block, like I do? You've got to walk around the goddamned block! Make sure traffic is noisy, turn up the radio, talk to them over the noise of the fucking radio. They've attempted to snitch on *me!* I've had them show up wired in my office carrying a fucking kilo of cocaine, saying, 'Hey, man, I owe you some *bread*.' And right downstairs is the DEA just ready to pounce.

"What do snitch lawyers say about informants? The snitch lawyers' general rationalization for aiding and abetting frequently perjurious informants is that their first commitment is to the welfare of their client, and the client's receiving a lenient sentence, or not being prosecuted at all, is the best possible result. Therefore, their representation of an informant is in the highest calling of criminal-defense lawyer.

"This, from my perspective, is a lot of bullshit. Most 'snitch lawyers' sub-specialize in the category. A body of law has built up around what manner informants and cooperating witnesses can be legally rewarded, and therefore there's a bargaining process that occurs in many instances before a snitch will take the stand. The lawyer is negotiating for the optimum that his client can receive, either in terms of a reduced sentence or financial compensation. Therefore, a snitch lawyer doesn't really practice criminal-defense law. He doesn't write motions, he doesn't vigorously cross-examine witnesses, he doesn't go to jury trial; he's part of secret negotiations in the bowels of the prosecutor's office, most of which never fully come to light. However, has he really served his client's interests well?

"These informants are subject to severe punishment by their peers, both in the prison system and out. Many of them can never go 'home' again. Many are estranged from their friends and relatives, even their children. Many develop psychiatric disorders after becoming informants. Many of them find themselves halfway between their old world and some new legal lifestyle that they cannot readily adapt to. Down deep, law enforcement doesn't respect them. The prosecutors don't respect them. They're vilified by everyone.

"And they should be. They're guilty of the Judas Syndrome, which is deep-seated in all of humankind. Betrayal has always been severely dealt with by all cultures. So instead of giving 'life' to clients who are encouraged to snitch by their lawyers, they're starting them on a downward cycle of depression and self-destruction. That's what I have seen and why I don't participate at any level in creating snitches.

"They hurt themselves; they hurt others. They're frequently so pressured that they'll lie, make things up out of whole cloth, bend and extend their narratives to suit law enforcement, so that law enforcement will give what they have promised. It undermines the integrity of the judicial process. It's an Orwellian spy society that has come into actuality. It is, ultimately, the KGBing of America.

"In fact, it's worse than buying witnesses with money. Buying witnesses with freedom is the least reliable form of witness testimony. It should be stricken from any judicial system that seeks for truth.

"In every criminal case in our alleged system of justice, some form of spy mentality is now present. There are degrees of informants. We probably have more nomenclature for informants than any other culture. We have citizen informants, confidential informants, confidential reliable informants, unnamed anonymous informants, informants who are percipient, informants who are participatory, informants who are merely eyewitnesses, informants who are co-defendants, informants who precipitate charges by reverse stings. We are confronting informants and cooperating witnesses at every level: preliminary hearings, grand juries, and state and federal jury trials. Our system of justice is permeated by the witness or the provocateur who is paid by government for a role in either revealing or instigating crime. It's probably the greatest tragedy of my career, in terms of whether or not justice is really pursued and whether truth is a foundation for actualizing justice."

. . .

I vividly recall Tony Serra's handling of one such informant. The snitch was called to the witness stand. There was nothing remarkable about him, nothing that singled him out. In fact, the most notable thing about him was that one would never suspect him to be different from anyone else. He bore no markings of the Judas goat.

Tony Serra squared off his stance at the podium for his cross-examination. The room went silent. I wondered who present in the spectator section of the courtroom was aware of the vivisection that was about to occur.

"Your plea agreement specifies that you were charged by indictment in a case where you could receive twenty years to life. Is that true?"

The snitch, unthreatened, calmly answered, "Yes."

Serra continued in his lawyerly manner, "And further, that the twenty years are mandatory. That is, you could not receive one day less than the mandatory twenty years to life. You understood that, didn't you?"

The snitch responded to these apparently non-threatening questions without hesitation. "Yes."

A rhythm established, Serra pushed on. "Further, is it a fact that presently you have not been sentenced?"

Again, an affirmative answer came right on cue.

Now Serra augured a little deeper. He lowered his head and fixed a hard stare on the snitch. "And that you will be sentenced at a date *subsequent* to your testimony in this trial *against my client*. That's your understanding, isn't it?"

This sudden stripping of the covert cover made the snitch squirm in discomfort. He hesitated, breaking the cadence of question and reply. The pause was apparent, the silence awkward. "Yes," he replied, reluctantly, as though he tripped and was groping to restore his equilibrium.

Serra fed on his malaise and further pinched the nerve. "And that you could receive, under your plea agreement, as low as five years on a downward departure for your cooperation in this case. You understand that your plea agreement allows that, don't you?"

The snitch feigned a cough and rubbed his nose, buying him nanoseconds of time, while searching for the right words that would save him from glowing with the falsity of his reply. He didn't find any. He was cornered, and his silence was damning unto itself. "Yes," he replied.

The spectators shifted in their seats as it became apparent what was occurring here.

Another tweak of the nerve by Serra. "And you understand the nature of the plea agreement: The U.S. Attorney will make the recommendation to the court, whether or not your sentence will be twenty to life, or your sentence will be five years. You understand, by your plea agreement, that you must *please* the prosecutor in order to get this most favorable recommendation, don't you?" Serra had him now and was hammering on him, and the only way out was through this damnable house of mirrors that reflected every motive and move of the entire sell-out.

The snitch, realizing his position at the center of this mortifying exposure, answered sheepishly, "Yes."

Now Serra amped up his volume as he moved in toward a deliberate denuding. "You further understand that the prosecutor wants testimony from you that incriminates *my client*, don't you! That's what he wants; don't you *know* that?"

This was like being caught with the murder weapon belching smoke. The snitch seemed to shrink before our eyes as he answered, "Yes." He'd suddenly become a prisoner of the government and a hostage of J. Tony Serra.

Never breaking his intense beam on the snitch, Serra gouged deeper with his semantic sword. "And that if you don't give the prosecutor the testimony that he seeks to incriminate my client, you won't get your reward of fifteen years, or more, off your prison sentence. Isn't that *true?*"

The snitch's face flushed tell-tale red. He squirmed with discomfort in his seat, in search of a position that looked natural. He was being stalked in a minefield of incriminating questions and he simply didn't know how to proceed. Again, there was an awkward break of the question-answer rhythm and the whole room perceived his distress. Staring downward, he said to the floor, "Well, not exactly. I was told that if I told the truth, that, uh, that's all I had to do." He looked up to see if anyone bought it.

Now Serra lightened the tension a bit. "The truth is known only to you and my client, for the most part, in connection with your testimony. Would you agree to that?"

Relieved for the reprieve of intensity, the snitch ably answered, "Yes."

But Serra's leniency was only a tease, the cat toying with the mouse, allowing the mouse to think the cat has lost interest; Serra now returned with unmitigating force. "You would do *anything* not to go to prison for twenty years to life, wouldn't you?"

The snitch, caught in his own trap, uttered a knowing sigh of doom and responded weakly, "Well, not really, not *anything.*"

Serra's voice darkened, turning ominous and overshadowing, as he said, "You don't want to go to prison for twenty to life, do you? You would die in prison; you're forty-five years old now."

The snitch, trying to fake his composure, was coming unraveled, while his eyes shifted nervously from side to side before they fixed on a point on the table where he stabilized himself; he pulled at his collar, as though feeling the tension of an invisible noose around his neck and shifted position in the chair. He shrank before our eyes. Clearing his throat, his voice a little too high, audibly strained, he said, "Yes, it's obvious I don't want to go to prison for the rest of my life," then hurriedly added, "but I'm not lying."

Serra imposed his next question. "Wouldn't you *lie* in order to save yourself ..." here Serra paused for dramatic effect, "... *fifteen* years?"

Gauging the consequences of his answer, the snitch quickly replied, "No."

Serra flexed his claws into the mouse once again to render just the desired response to imprint upon the memory of the jury. "Isn't it a fact that you have been *lying* in order to save yourself fifteen years?"

Again the defensive reactionary reply, "No!"

Serra's claws pierced deeper. "Isn't it a fact that you have been pressured to *lie* to escape a sentence of twenty years to *life?*"

With eyes dull as dust, the snitch rotely responded, "No."

Serra turned up the heat. "Isn't it a fact that the case agent and the U.S. Attorney have explained to you, over and over, your legal position?"

A robotic voice said, "Yes."

Serra underlined his theme one last time. "And that legal position is that if you don't get their recommendation based on your testimony today, you'll go twenty to life. That's what you have been told on numerous occasions, isn't it?"

Once again the shudder of cover-up, betrayal, sell-out, deceit surrounded the snitch like a vile aura. And the snitch, succumbed to a posture of defeat, obediently answered, "Yes."

Serra's fury cut loose in full Old Testament accusatory volume. "And you're quite willing to *lie* to this jury in order to save your own skin, aren't you?!"

A dull "No."

As Serra's final exclamation, he riveted his rage at the snitch, pointed his finger like a gun directly at him, and point-blank exploded, "You're lying right now, aren't you!?"

Only a stunned silence ensued. The bailiff escorted the snitch out of the courtroom.

. . .

"It's a direct equation: the more informants, the fewer constitutional rights. And so, in a certain sense, as they say in our ecology, 'The canaries are dying!' Our canaries of freedom are dying in the stench of the informant system. Each canary is a case—a drug case, a civil-rights case, a political case—and as each case falls prey to the informant witness system, our precious liberties die with it.

"So I close with a *warning:* Wherever there is a clash of ideology, wherever there is warfare, there are always going to be some people who succumb, some who compromise, some who betray, some who, through cowardice or self-motivation, will be disloyal. That's encountered everywhere. But we are in a war. The metaphor of the war on drugs, the war on terror, the war on patriotism brings up the metaphor of lawyers as warriors! It's better to die honorably with courage and self-respect than to live on as a token of victory for the oppressors."

Chapter 10

Maternal Justice: The Ellie Nesler Case

"Mama! Mama! Don't let him get me. Don't let him do it again!"

Tony Serra's voice was anguished, pleading, pitiful; his body was crunched in a fetal curve of self-protection with his hand a shield in self-defense, as he portrayed six-year-old Willie Nesler to the jury in his opening statements of the Ellie Nesler trial.

Then Serra's posture straightened to full manly size, his demeanor darkened, his powerful arm reached out, and one large hand froze in a grasping position like a five-fingered claw. In a deep menacing voice, he growled, "I'm gonna getcha, and if you squeal to anyone I'll kill you and your mama! Do you understand?"

The jury watched horror-stricken as Serra now stabbed his hands and piercing voice directly at them, in staccato, in their faces. "Do you know ... what it feels like ... to be sodomized ... by a two-hundred-thirty-pound, six-foot-tall, thirty-two-year-old man ... when you are ... a little ... six-year-old boy? ... It *hurts!*"

Gasps filled the courtroom and people shifted uncomfortably in their seats.

Tony Serra was getting down and dirty. He'd ripped open a wound and he wouldn't stitch it up again until it had spilled its contents all over the hearts and minds of the jury by turning the historic courtroom in Sonora, California, into a theater of rape, murder, insanity, and righteous revenge. In the process, he was deliberately creeping out the jurors and spectators with details of why Ellie Nesler fatally shot, right in court, Daniel Driver, the molester of her son.

My brush raced over the 11- by 14-inch artist pad on my knees to capture on paper this one-man morality play of good and evil, enacted before our eyes. Serra was switching between the roles, the molester and the child, in rapid succession. I used a style of multiple images to portray his many expressions. His hands were everywhere, now grasping in a sinister grip, now reaching out in desperation for protection. His expression was fiendish. He was innocence and evil personified. Other artists were seated on either side of me in the front row of the packed courtroom. We were all working as fast as we could to have our art camera-ready for the morning TV deadline. The close proximity of one another's inks and paints or pastels precariously balanced on our knees was an accident waiting to happen; the risk of destroying one another's work with an errant ink blotch or blob of paint was great. Cutthroat competition in this dying courtroom-artist career almost made it a temptation.

Tony Serra had invited me to be his artist on the high-profile case of a single-mother's shots heard round the world. They echoed the sentiments of mothers everywhere. The case was rife with controversy: Was it was about vigilante justice in a small gold-mining town in the foothills of the Sierras? Or was it the annihilation of a convicted pedophile who was likely be set free to perpetrate more harm upon the lives and to scar the psyches of more innocent children, as he had done to Ellie's young son, Willie? Was God's message to her to love and forgive, or had He given her a sign to rid the world of this rotten scumbag? Was she sane or insane? Would history remember her as a folk hero, as a mother acting from her core maternal instinct in protection of her young, or as a drugged-out maniac taking the law into her own hands?

One thing was certain: The onslaught of flowers and support as a result of Ellie's arrest after the shooting indicated that the public favored *her* over her victim. It was projected that there would be difficulty finding an unprejudiced jury among the population of 4,000 or so area

residents. A total stranger paid her $500,000 bail. Two banks set up El-
lie Nesler defense funds, together with local tourist shops on the main
street of town collecting cash donations in large glass jars. Forty-thou-
sand dollars was raised in funds for her defense. T-shirts and bumper
stickers appeared that read, "Nice Shootin', Ellie" and "L.E. Law." One
local mother got a "Support Ellie" tattoo on her ankle. Hollywood producers offered her big money for her story. Talk shows clamored for her. So
many calls of support poured in from all across the country, as well as
from Canada, Italy, Spain, and Denmark, that the phone and fax lines
jammed. Ellie had to set up a special room at the Sonora Inn and hire an
assistant to deal with the gifts and calls.

Ellie Nesler was now an official legend, the pistol-packin' Mother
Lode mama who pulled the trigger to save the children. Her outrageous
deed prompted three western songs to be written and recorded about
her. Had her dizzy rise to folk-hero acclaim gone unchecked, she would
have taken her place beside other immortals of her ilk: Annie Oakley,
Calamity Jane, Belle Starr, Bonnie Parker, and Ma Barker.

. . .

Sonora is located 130 miles northeast of San Francisco in the foothills of the Sierra Nevada. A Gold Rush town dating back to the 1850s,
its wooden sidewalk, historic inn, stately courthouse, and especially the
effigy of a hanging man outside a bar are reminders of the days when
vigilante justice was better than no justice at all. The marble steps,
wrought-iron railings, and fine mahogany woodwork of the courthouse,
situated atop a small hill, emit an incense of history and an old-world
splendor. Melvin Belli, the famous defense attorney who took on many
celebrity, torts, and consumer-protection cases, was born here in 1907;
Belli's law firm was a neighbor of Serra's in the 1980s.

Tony Serra joined forces with local attorney Donald Segerstrom in
the defense of Ellie Nesler. Diana Samuelson, the death-penalty attorney from Serra's San Francisco office, completed the legal trio defending
Nesler on the grounds of temporary insanity. Ellie and Tony clicked together, a factor that strengthened his ability to represent her.

We all met for breakfast on the opening day of jury selection. The rising summer heat was already cranking up to cripple the day. Tony entered the air-conditioned coffee shop in good cheer, appearing especially crisp in his gray-and-white thrift-store seersucker suit. His charisma overshadowed the stains, tatters, and mismatched buttons.

Ellie joined us at the table and sidled in beside Tony. She was 41, but her vivacious energy was ageless. She seemed in the best of spirits. It was clear that she adored Tony and that he shared a fondness for her. They were both mavericks.

The street scene on this morning was otherworldly. Ellie and Tony moved slowly forward arm in arm through hordes of people pressing in from all sides, yelling and cheering. Cars honked, placards waved, banners flew, babies cried, dogs barked, shopkeepers shouted, media people ran in reverse. Everything and everyone were giving voice to this historic moment. Satellite vans representing all the major TV stations had antennae twisting into the sky. Ellie was in her element, enjoying her 15 minutes of fame, albeit for murder. Sonora was in its element. The Ellie Nesler trial, a mother's cry for justice, was the biggest thing to hit this town since the cry for gold back in the 1800s.

Inside the courthouse felt and smelled like an overstuffed sardine can. I didn't dare venture away from Tony in that crush of people. At one point, everyone in the spectator section of the packed courtroom was ordered out. It was jury selection, and due to the polling of 80 potential jurors, there wasn't enough room to accommodate all the press and the four courtroom artists. I was the only freelance artist, so I was automatically eliminated. But as soon as the courtroom doors closed behind me, Tony burst out, pointed at me to the bailiff, and had me escorted to a front-row seat.

It became apparent throughout the trial that Ellie had a "can't-bust-'em" sense of humor that shielded the painful reality of her life. With her indomitable spirit, Ellie Nesler could turn anything into a good laugh as her means of getting a handle on the situation. Even at her own murder trial, she acted coquettish and joked with the court officers. During a weapon check on everyone entering the courtroom, Ellie quipped, "Even *me?*" When a "guess-the-verdict" pool was organized by reporters, she joined in the fun. Her seemingly jubilant demeanor gave rise to suspicion from reporters. It was, after all, a murder trial and she could spend the rest of her life in prison. By the trial's end, I learned that Ellie was just one of those people who wore a grin to mask her pain. She told the press, "I could be on my deathbed, and I'd still have that shit-eating smile on my face."

. . .

The Ellie Nesler trial was divided into two phases. The first phase was guilty or innocent. Tony Serra structured his case for this first phase on the basis that Ellie's action was a classic case of post-traumatic stress disorder.

He wasn't interested in a so-called frontier-justice defense, the idea of Ellie Nesler taking the law into her own hands or being above the law or in nullification where the jury rejects the legal standard and applies its own moral code. He was interested only in the psychiatric truths: the true psychological causes of her condition at that time that produced her behavior. He truly believed she was not guilty by reason of temporary insanity.

Nesler herself had suffered the traumas of molestation and rape as a child and an adolescent, thus all the psychiatrists cited post-traumatic stress. Serra's defense was no different than if he'd been defending a soldier traumatized in war who'd gone berserk at the sound of something that sounded like a gunshot. Her past experiences had produced a condition in her that erupted into an instinctive blind assault on this child molester. All the psychiatrists who observed her said that this kind of event could catapult her into a realm of madness, of uncontrollable fury, passion, instinctive behavior.

So, with one premise that Ellie Nesler was herself a survivor of sexual abuse and another that Daniel Driver had sexually abused her young son, Serra entered the case with a preconceived perspective, based on many many psychiatric defenses in the past, that this would be an intellectual marriage between psychiatry and law, and that psychiatry would free Ellie Nesler, a woman who'd acted beyond her capacity to control herself. Serra did not take into account that the Sonora jury wasn't made up of intellectuals.

Throughout this trial, Serra humanized Ellie's action to kill Driver.

He peeled back her life to the time when she was a cute little three-year-old girl being sexually abused by her alcoholic father's drunken buddies while her passive mother did nothing to protect her. He impressed upon the jury what it felt like to be small and helpless in the grips of a dominant father figure whose dreams of quick wealth as a gold miner never measured up to reality, who turned to alcohol and womanizing as justification for his failures. He dramatized Ellie at the age of six to the jury, with gun in hand, standing up to her father for beating her mother. Ellie had learned to become an excellent shot. It was her form of empowerment for the sake of survival. Dysfunction, along with violence, was the only family life she'd ever known. She assumed the role of leader and protector of her two younger sisters. Her protector role extended to children in school who were victims of bullies. It got her into a lot of fights with scrappy boys, resulting in her nose being broken many times.

"That's why I had my nose job," she told reporters.

Serra recounted that by the time Ellie was 10, her father had left home and her mother was bedridden with a crippling back injury, leaving Ellie to take over parenting her two younger sisters. He said that Ellie shouldered the mantle of being a caretaker, enforcer, avenger, and protector of the defenseless. He pointed out that she was proud of having "brass balls" for a girl.

"It was my job," she said. "I was the oldest. I would beat up mean people."

Later, she learned the power of her sexuality as a means of manipulation and control. She had a way with men and men had a way with her. It served her well. She was friendly with people in important places.

Ellie's attraction for men with a wild streak and a flare for adventure led her into her first marriage, then her second. Her second husband, Bill Nesler, was a crop-dusting pilot and a gold miner. He spirited her and her son Willie away to Liberia in West Africa where they ran a gold-mining operation and charter-plane service. It was a hard life in a foreign country. Ellie, now saddled with two young kids and the deja vu of a womanizing husband, turned heel. She packed her children under her arms and left Bill and Africa behind to return home to the Mother Lode.

Not long after her return, her sister Jan's ex-husband introduced

Ellie to Danny Driver, whom he'd met at the Assembly of God church. It was later revealed that Driver had an interest in dating young mothers with sons.

Driver passed himself off as a Bible-touting lay minister; he always carried a Bible on the front seat of his impeccably clean car. He recited Bible verses verbatim.

Ellie considered Daniel a righteous God-fearing man whose appeal was that he was good with her son and handy with repairs—an irresistible combination for a single mom. She was thrilled to find a man with whom she could share the love of her children and her devotion to God. Driver became a regular at Ellie's house, where he led the children in Bible studies.

During the trial, Tony Serra reconstructed the pieces of Ellie's life that ultimately led to her emotional breakdown. Ellie listened to her life being played out before her and the jury, awash in tears.

. . .

It doesn't take much of a leap of imagination to envision that pivotal day. The sun rose bright with the promise of a good day ahead on the morning that Ellie packed the small suitcase for her beloved son Willie, heading off on his first trip to Bible camp, where Daniel Driver worked as a dishwasher. Driver had offered to drive Willie to camp to spare Ellie the trip, since he was working there anyway. Ellie didn't have any second thoughts about accepting his offer to take Willie to camp, and she felt that he'd be in good hands with his buddy Danny there to look after him. Spirits were high. With pride and gratitude, Ellie hoisted her six-year-old son into the passenger seat, kissing him good-bye. Willie, whose own father had been absent from his life, was sitting a little taller, feeling like a big boy on an adventure. Ellie and little Becky stood waving as the big car drove off into the distance, becoming smaller and smaller until it disappeared altogether.

What Ellie Nesler didn't know, as she stood there in the road, was that Daniel Driver was a convicted child molester.

Willie returned from Bible camp a very different child. It was apparent to both his mother and his aunt, Jan Adams, that something was terribly wrong. When asked what was troubling him, he became sullen and withdrawn, refusing to say.

"We could see that there was anger in him," Jan Adams told the jury. "He would ask strange questions like, 'What happens to bad people when they go to jail?' And 'If I killed somebody, would you break me out of jail?' We always told him no, that if he killed someone, he would have to stay in jail. We didn't know what he was talking about."

When Ellie entrusted Willie to Daniel Driver he was an innocent pristine little boy. He came back broken, paranoid, afraid of unknown dangers and unseen attackers. He was afraid of the dark, afraid of windows, afraid to leave the house. The terrible secret was kept safe by Driver's threat that he'd kill Willie's mother if he tattled.

The psychological wound augured deep and festered, spreading like a stain throughout his whole being. This beautiful boy, the sunshine of Ellie's life, was now subject to violent mood swings. He was secretive and refused to talk about anything. He was tormented by visions of Danny's face in passing cars. Not only did Daniel Driver continue to be a part of their lives, but Willie had to pretend nothing was wrong if he wanted his mother not to die.

Willie held out for as long as he could. By then, the molestations were occurring regularly, sometimes right in the back of Ellie's own home. It was apparent that Ellie's son was having profound psychological problems of a magnitude that was beyond her ability to remedy, yet far too serious to ignore.

Serra told the jury that a whole year passed before Willie was able to talk about what was taking place. He finally confided to his aunt under the promise that she would not tell anyone. The family alerted the authorities. But then they got to live under a four-year reign of terror that Driver would return and make good on his promise to kill them all: Driver ran from the law when charged. He went on the lam for three years.

This was his second arrest. He'd been convicted of molesting another boy in 1983 and sentenced to three months in jail, then probation. But it was not until he was charged with molesting Ellie's son and three other boys at the church Bible camp that he became a fugitive of the law.

"He was indisputably incurable and recidivistic," Serra told the jury. "Even his own mother denounced him."

The police couldn't find Driver. But Driver knew where to find Ellie and Willie Nesler.

Ellie was consumed by her pent-up rage, which spread deep like a toxic venom inside her. Her loathing of Daniel Driver scorched her very core. She was anguished, torn apart by the opposing forces of her all-consuming hatred of this man and the Christian ethic to love and to forgive. She prayed to God to help her to deal with her torment.

Driver was eventually arrested. On April 2, 1993, the day of his preliminary hearing, Ellie had reconciled with her God-torn conscience that she would try to find it in her heart to forgive Daniel Driver if he would repent, if he'd show remorse for all the damage he'd done to her and her little boy. Willie, now 11 years old, had decided of his own accord that he'd testify against Driver. It took maturity and courage. He was well aware that everyone in and beyond Sonora would know what he'd gone through, but he didn't want any other children to have to experience what he had.

This hearing was to be the day of reckoning.

$$\bullet \quad \bullet \quad \bullet$$

Daniel Driver's preliminary hearing was to take place in Jamesville, a small mining town about 10 miles from Sonora. The makeshift courtroom was located on the main street of town in the community hall that also served for town meetings and weddings. Driver was facing seven counts of child molestation with four different boys ages six through eight. The most serious charge was of sodomy to Ellie Nesler's son, Willie, when he was only six years old.

Ellie poured some white powder into her coffee before leaving for Jamesville. She was anticipating the worst day of her life and she needed all the bolstering she could get. Her sister Jan and another friend accompanied Ellie and Willie to the hearing.

They parked the car and were walking on the sidewalk when the police cruiser, with Daniel Driver in the back, pulled up alongside them, then over to the curb so that Driver could be escorted out. Driver looked Willie up and down, making eye contact with the boy, and he smirked.

171

"My little boy started puking and I lunged at this man. They had to pull me off," Ellie Nesler recounted.

Willie broke into uncontrollable crying and vomiting. He clung desperately to his mother's leg, begging pitifully to be excused from testifying.

The intimacy of the town-hall courtroom was appalling. A single folding table, six feet long and three feet wide, served to accommodate the judge, the lawyers, Daniel Driver, and the young victims and their mothers. They would all be face to face, like at a dinner table. A small room at the back of the hall served as the waiting room for the boys and their families until they were notified of their turn to testify. Each mother and son had to sit directly across from Driver to testify.

Serra told the jury, "Ellie's son would have to sit across a small table and look directly into the face of the man who had physically and psychologically tortured him. The boy would have to testify about the harrowing events."

Willie would be close enough to smell Driver. He would have to bear the shame of public exposure. This pressure was too much for him. He couldn't go there again, couldn't revisit the horrifying nightmare. He couldn't go through with it.

Driver's three other victims had already testified, though ineffectively. Their desperate mothers were beseeching Ellie for resolution to the inevitable outcome of Driver going free. Willie's testimony was critical to Driver's imprisonment. His offense was the most serious and he was their only hope to put Driver behind bars. But the boy was incapable of functioning.

Ellie was suddenly experiencing everyone's molestations converging at once: her own, her son's, the other young children's. She was trapped in a molestation hologram, though still torn by the polarities of her hatred of this man and the mercy of God. She felt herself being sucked into an emotional vortex of primal pain far more powerful than reason.

"She snaps!" Serra exclaimed to the jury. "Her boat is set adrift and it's headed toward the falls. She's swept away by it."

Serra's facial expression portrayed the horrific moment of someone struggling with losing her last battle with self-control. His face showed the fear and desperation of going over the edge of sanity. I captured this

metaphor in art. Serra's fingers are wide open, unable to contain the waterfall of emotion rushing through his open fingers; over the arch of the
water is a small boat with the stick figure of Ellie in it. Her arms are raised
upward in a gesture of powerlessness. There is a smear of the American
flag in this piece, a symbol of the law she will have to reckon with.

"Her mind is in a swirl. She asks for a sign from God."

The next words spoken came from her friend, deputy Giles New.
"Are you ready?" he asked.

It was the sign she had prayed for. It was absolutely clear to her that
now the finger of God was pointing to her.

Giles New, of course, was asking if Ellie was ready to enter the room
for Willie's testimony. But she took it to mean that the voice of God was
channeling through Giles New, giving her permission to kill Driver. In
her mind it was the only way; it was meant to be. God had ordained her
to rid the world of this evil in the name of the children. Did he not ask,
"Are you ready?"

Giles New had become a friend during his investigation of the molestation. He testified to what happened next. Ellie took him aside and
asked, "If something happened to Driver, would you guys be in trouble?"

"No, babe," he answered, wondering why he'd be in trouble if something happened to Driver. He told the jury that he didn't realize she had
a gun, but at the time she thought that he did.

According to Ellie, "I thought he was giving me the green light to
kill the guy."

There was a short recess before Willie was to be called to testify.
Unobserved by the deputies, Ellie reached into her sister's purse, hanging on a nearby chair. Her hand felt the cool metal and the pleasing
smoothness of the mother-of-pearl handle of the palm-sized 25-caliber
semi-automatic pistol, which her sister, Jan, had carried for protection
since the vandalism of her automobile. Ellie removed the pistol and deft-
ly transferred it to the pocket of her dark jumpsuit. The pistol was small
enough to be easily hidden.

She walked into the main room, past the deputies chatting among
themselves, past the cooler, past the piano that was used to play music
at weddings; she was unaware of her body, so intense was her focus on
the man sitting in the chair. There he was!

There was the man she'd once trusted and taken to heart, the man she now hated more than anyone one on Earth. He was handcuffed at the waist and shackled to the floor. He was sitting with his back to her, his large body slouched, his dark stubby hair shiny in the light. Her eyes bored into the back of his head. He sensed her presence, turned his head to look directly at her—there was that shit-eating smirk again! No remorse. None.

Ellie Nesler made hard eye contact with Driver. That instant of recognition said it all. She saw not the man, but evil incarnate. Her steady hand rose into perfect point-blank aim. Her tensions released as five bullets slammed into the side of Daniel Driver's head and neck. The sixth bullet hit the wall as Driver, lifeless, slumped off the chair.

She stood still, never altering her position, her eyes never flinching from the sight of him. The gun dropped to the floor. A strange and unexpected peace came over her, the peace of knowing that she had done all she could do. She had exterminated the brutal pervert. The children were saved.

Ellie Nesler stood there in the savage silence of her action, waiting to be arrested.

For an eternal instant, time stood still. Then all hell broke loose. The sound of gunshots alerted security and suddenly the room was crazed with the frenzy of guards and guns and shouting and handcuffs. Ellie's sister Jan threw herself between Ellie and the guards.

"If it wasn't for me, Ellie would have taken a bullet," Jan later recounted to the media. "I saw the cops' eyes."

The guards threw Ellie Nesler to the floor, handcuffed her, and led her away. She looked over her shoulder at her sobbing son and called out, "Whatever happens, know that I'll always love you!"

• • •

More than 100 reporters and curious people from all over the country fought for seats in the courtroom to witness the final arguments of this phase. Many of them were law students hoping to catch a first-hand glance of Tony Serra in action. For the frustrated dozens who didn't get in, Judge William Polley allowed a video camera to relay the in-court proceedings to a television set in the crowded hallway outside.

Closing arguments turned into a sparring match between two totally different ideologies. The prosecutor hammered away that Nesler was
a ruthless cold-blooded murderer; the defense maintained that she was
a psychologically damaged parent acting on instinct in the name of God.

Tony had Ellie stand beside him for the beginning of his closing argument. Her strong character, which had held together up till now, gave
way to an endless flow of tears as he reenacted her life and the role of her
son in this tragedy to the jury of five men and seven women.

He filled the room with her anger and despair, projecting her fear
that she was losing her mind; he emoted before their eyes the experience
of being sucked into a vortex of insanity, then reenacted the ultimate
scene.

Ellie later commented, "He was pulling my heart out. That was my
life. I don't cry often."

Witnessing Tony in the frenzy of portraying Ellie, I thought, this
time he's taken it too far. He's gotten too personal and it shows. I wondered if her outrageous deed somehow resonated with his own maverick
style of living on the edge, taking liberties with his sense of entitlement
for a just cause.

In my art, I portrayed Tony Serra's impassioned closing argument
by drawing him with three arms. One arm cradles Ellie Nesler in a protective gesture, while another hand proclaims the anguish of her situation with fingers fanned like exclamation marks. With the third arm, he
passes on his plea for empathy to the jury. His eyes are intense with the
urgency of their understanding.

Tony Serra's comment about this piece is: "I'm frenzied here, with
one hand exclaiming toward the jury while the other hand is protecting Ellie Nesler. What's captured here is the protective nature of my
argument, how I sought to shield her from the act of murder that had
occurred. It was a terrible act—unredeemable, isolated, and an act unto
itself. To shoot a shackled man five times in the head at short range? It
was extermination, utter assassination. So the gloom of that horror is
on her face.

"And I'm shielding her, trying to raise the consciousness of the jury,
to show that what she did came from the highest maternal instinct,

175

which is defined through the survival of the species. What I see in this drawing is almost an overzealous attempt to hide the calamity—or to turn it into something that society can view as noble, something that anyone can empathize with. That really was the meaning of the case; so many people in this country and around the world could empathize with her act of killing the man who had molested her child."

The prosecution urged the jury not to be swayed by empathy. "Empathy should never, *never*, encompass cold-blooded murder," prosecutor Jo Graves insisted in her closing argument. Graves, a mother herself, disenfranchised Nesler's fear that her son was unable to testify against Driver and that Driver might once again go free to do as he wished. Graves said that "a good parent" would have supported the child in court, regardless of the outcome, and reminded him that "the tough part is what you've already been through. Then you take him home, let him stay up late, have pizza, and everything will be fine."

"That's a fairy tale," Serra said to reporters. "'Cold-blooded murder' bullshit! She was too *hot* for cold-blooded murder! If she'd *planned* to kill her son's tormentor, she would have chosen a better occasion than the day of the preliminary hearing. Myself, I'd have taken the son of a bitch out—blown him away and thrown him down a mine shaft."

Serra said he felt Graves's comments trivialized the pain that a molested child and his mother would feel. Graves insisted that it was Serra's portrayal of Ellie Nesler that was the fictional part. She capitalized on Serra's use of the word "snapped" in explaining how the tragic events of Nesler's life, especially her own molestations as a child and then that of her son, culminated in the shooting. Graves cynically said, "It ought to be characterized as the longest snap in history" and that "he never ever says when this snapping is supposed to end."

Serra pointed to the seated prosecutor and fumed at her insistence that Ellie planned Driver's death and acted out of sheer malice. "She's deceiving you!" Serra yelled incredulously. "That's why she's looking at her notes. She can't look at you."

Graves remained cool and non-reactive.

· · ·

After five days of deliberation, the jury sided with Serra. They lessened Ellie's sentence from first-degree murder to voluntary manslaughter. A muffled "Yes! Yes!" could be heard from her supporters in the courtroom as Nesler's family members gripped one another in tears.

As a member of Serra's entourage, it was impossible not to become involved with Ellie and her family: her two children, her two sisters, and their children. The stress of this lengthy trial was hard on all of them. Ellie's sister Jan was in her last trimester of pregnancy during the trial. She attended court every day to lend support. There were times when she thought she would miscarry or go into premature labor from the trauma.

Ellie's true heroic stature became apparent in the way that she managed the complex responsibilities she faced. She had become an international icon, and now she was having to sustain that image on a daily basis under totally different circumstances. She grew before everyone's eyes to fill all the roles. Every aspect of her life at this critical time demanded her full attention and she rose magnificently to meet the challenge.

Her killing of Daniel Driver spoke to all mothers everywhere who had been rendered helpless by similar situations, victims who couldn't strike back at their predators. Ellie was their role model, the woman who refused to be disempowered by the law, or reason, a man, or anyone or anything.

Faxes, letters, gifts flooded in from mothers the world over. Her own phone lines jammed, so she rented a room at the Sonora Inn to deal with the deluge. Then she had to hire a secretary. It was imperative that she remain collected in court every day for the sake of the jury, when in fact she was being torn apart by forces that pulled her in all directions. Her interviews with the media, the many-times-a-day meetings with her lawyers, the daily demands of a single mom, paying the bills, not to mention getting adequate sleep, went on in spite of her new status as a national and international heroine. Her children needed her desperately. The grave possibility that she might be sent away to prison for a long term and thus separated from her children cast a menacing shadow over everyone's psyche. Every moment with her children was precious to her, even though their needs became ferociously demanding as the trial dragged on.

She placated the children's demands for love by giving them a large German shepherd puppy that was unhousebroken and a very large adult iguana. The kids were inseparable from their pets, which meant that they all spent a lot of time in the Sonora Inn. Willie enjoyed wearing the iguana around his neck like a colorful boa. It escaped at every opportunity. It's location could be detected by the screams of terrified guests encountering it lumbering down the hotel hallways, who surely must have thought they were hallucinating and imagining that its cousin the alligator, with a human limb in its mouth, wasn't far behind. So now, the serene Sonora Inn, which had so graciously accommodated Ellie's overflow of needs at a time when they were experiencing an overflow of guests, was now coping with the excrement of an untrained German Shepherd puppy and the terror of a large pre-historic reptile prowling its halls. It was a surreal nightmare.

I was extremely moved by this compelling family tragedy. I occasionally babysat the children and on one occasion, I took one of the elder children with whom I'd bonded, Ellie's niece Cassie, home with me to Bolinas for the weekend. This sensitive 12-year-old girl, herself an artist, had spent her entire summer vacation in court watching her aunt's murder trial. The thought of her returning to school in the fall and hearing about all the other children's accounts of their summer camping trips was too grim, so I plucked her out of that environment for a brief two days and brought her to Bolinas where she saw the ocean for the first time in her life.

I wanted to show her so much of the beauty of the area, but once she got to the beach, I couldn't pry her off a comfortable large rock that protruded out into the tide line. She sat on that rock, staring transfixed at the immensity of the sea with its endless sparkle of dancing light and listening to the music of the gentle lapping waves for what seemed like an eternity. She became spellbound by the rhythm of the waves, the sounds and fragrance of the sea. She saw that there was always another wave in the sea, that nothing was finite. She saw that the tide recedes in order to surge farther forward. She watched as the wind made scalloped patterns in the sand; she watched as the waves erased them; she watched as a lace-like filament of seaweed was deposited by a receding wave; she watched as a gull swooped down and picked up the seaweed, leaving a feather in its place; she watched as a passerby picked up the feather leaving a footprint in its place. She watched the continuum and the ebb and flow of life's poetry in motion in a world beyond the rigid rulings of the courtroom.

When the two days were over, I phoned Ellie's sister to come pick up Cassie. To my surprise, the whole family showed up with all the kids! They all wanted to escape the confines of the trial and to cavort for one elongated moment in the healing waves of the sea. They brought a tent and camped on the beach, freezing at night and getting terribly sunburned by day, but none of that mattered. They took home with them the sanity of the sea.

. . .

Ellie Nesler's rise to hero status was short-lived. Blood tests showed that she had .14 milligrams of methamphetamine per liter of blood in her system on the day that she shot Driver. The white powder she'd put into her coffee on the morning of the shooting was crank. Like a high tide receding back into the sea, suddenly her popularity and all the great offers based on a hero's story shrank away.

The jury empathized with her enough to reduce her sentence from first-degree murder to manslaughter, but the second phase of the trial was now about her sanity and the conservative jury was not about to be seduced by sentiment twice.

Tony and the defense team's reaction to the verdict in the guilt-innocence phase of the trial was mixed. They were relieved that the jury reduced the conviction to manslaughter, which carries a finite sentence. But they were disturbed that the jury didn't buy the entire defense.

In the second phase of the trial, the sanity phase, the challenge was to prove beyond reasonable doubt that Ellie Nesler was out of her mind when she shot Daniel Driver. "In the law," Tony explained, "McNaughton's standard is the basis used for determining insanity. Derived from an old English case, it established a standard in America in the 1800s that we still use today, antiquated as it is."

"According to McNaughton's standard, one measure for insanity is that the person doesn't know the quality and nature of his or her own behavior. That is, he or she is just way out of it. Well, we couldn't show that. Ellie Nesler knew what she was doing. She walked into the courtroom at an opportune time, took aim at Driver's head, and shot to kill. She positioned herself so only Daniel Driver was in the line of fire. She made sure she didn't shoot any other person, the bailiff, or the clerk. So we couldn't say she didn't know what she was doing.

"But the second leg of McNaughton's standard says that you know what you're doing, but you cannot at that moment distinguish between right and wrong. That's called 'moral blindness.' So this was a classic case of moral blindness, because she thought she was exterminating evil. She believed that God sanctioned her act, that He was the one guiding her and she was merely His instrument.

"Ellie was very religious. Driver had been her trusted friend. She'd entrusted him with the care of her little boy, to take him to Bible camp! In Nesler's eyes, Driver was worse than some ravaging diseased animal. He was evil incarnate and should be forever removed from endangering young children again. He should be exterminated."

For the closing arguments of the final phase, my art depicted Tony Serra with Ellie Nesler standing beside him in a kind of cameo. Serra, with his hands behind his back, has an expression of humility, vulnerability, an openness of face and body language as he stands before the jury. Nesler, her hands also behind her, is looking at Tony Serra with soulful sadness as he elevates her plight into poetry.

The jury deliberated for an unbearably long time. Tony, who has an ingrained sense of these things and who tends toward pessimism at best, was losing his pallor. He was due to open another trial in Montana, but he couldn't leave this one until it was completed. This trial was going over schedule and it was having a domino effect on his calendar, which added to his overall tension.

The time that a jury is out deliberating is a true limbo. No one dares venture too far from the courthouse, because the call could come at any moment that the jury has arrived at a verdict, and then there is only a scant half-hour of leeway to get to court and nab a good seat. Some people never left the halls of the courthouse at all. Others staked out places in the grassy park out front. The waiting seemed interminable.

The guilty verdict wasn't the only crushing blow to the defense. It was also revealed that Ellie had developed breast cancer at this time, but her strong facade kept this a secret from everyone. She made it through the whole ordeal in spite of a malignant breast tumor the size of an egg. Her doctors gave her five years to live.

The judge gave her ten years in prison.

As she was led away from the courthouse by the guards for the last time, she commented to the press, "It would have been fair if I wasn't critically ill. He [the judge] sentenced me to more time in prison than I have to live. It's a life sentence!"

Ellie Nesler was given 15 minutes to say goodbye to her family. Once again, her son sobbed as the police led his mom away from him in hand-cuffs.

· · ·

Lead prosecutor Jo Graves said she was "very pleased" by the verdict. Her colleague, Scott Thorpe, said the jury's decision wasn't about sanity or insanity, but "that you don't take the law into your own hands. We're talking about taking the justice system into her own hands, we're talking about the sanctity of the courtroom, we're talking about how you deal with rage and anger."

Tony commented to the press that he was bitterly disappointed when the jury adjudicated Nesler sane in the second phase. Tony forever maintained her innocence.

"I believe, in retrospect, that if we'd submitted the facts to some computer or some abstract judgmental mechanism, we would have won. She was morally blind. The court and the jury withheld this fairness from us, because they didn't want to appear too unsophisticated, too liberal. So they did a balancing act. They thought manslaughter was as far as they should go. One juror said, 'After all, you know, she killed someone in the courthouse.' As if that taboo was more important than the mental issue."

Tony went on to say, "Working with those aspects of the case, from my standpoint, was intellectually satisfying and morally satisfying, but ultimately it was legally dissatisfying, because the jury found her sane.

They should never have done that. This case was such a clear example of the power of maternal instinct. I had never seen anything like it before and I may never see it again. Maternal instinct isn't rational or legal. The maternal instinct is blind and always protective of its young. It's so strong that the parent will sacrifice him or herself willingly for the child. How magnificent that instinct is! How strong it was in Ellie. How fervent she was with it, how forceful! That was the glory of this case, seeing the strength of the maternal instinct personified in Ellie Nesler."

After the final press interviews that day, Tony disappeared. I found him by chance sitting alone in an empty room. He was hunched over in despair, his expressive hands now limp and lifeless on his knees. He seemed totally spent, drained, eviscerated. I wanted to say goodbye, to thank him, but it was clear this was not the moment to say anything. It was clear that he was alone because he didn't want to see anyone. It was clear that this moment was private for him and that he wanted me to get the hell out of there.

This image of him burned itself into my mind and five hours later, when I was back home in Bolinas, I drew the vision I'd retained. When the floodwaters of defeat had subsided, I showed Tony the drawing and asked him to comment on it.

He said, "Defeat on a case is much greater than a mere personal loss. Since cases are clashes of ideology, defeat means utter rejection in every sense, from the metaphysical to the physical, from the psychological to the ideological. It's overwhelming and paralyzing.

"This drawing depicts the external attributes of that feeling of nothingness. What I've learned to do when I lose a case is to go deep into my own mind. I find some refuge there, some sanctuary in the pockets of my mind that I reserve for defeat. Because the nature of battle, when you're a lawyer and not a real soldier, is that you die, only to be reborn in the next legal battle. And the only way to find your ultimate salvation is through victory the next time. If you're on a losing streak in court at the time, you keep pursuing victory like a ghost, until once more you're reborn through victory.

"So what's depicted in this drawing is the depression of defeat: the pain and agony over the metaphysical rejection, the emptiness, the horror of the loss. But what isn't depicted is the journey inward. The journey inward can be random: You can be searching for the face of your own youth or searching for the faces of youth that surround you, because in youth there is new life, rebirth, new energy. It can be any quest into your flickering consciousness to escape the harshness of the blow that has been struck. It's both an escape and a nurturing at the same time."

·   ·   ·

The Ellie Nesler trial had run over schedule. Tony was due to appear in Montana for his own contempt-of-court case (see Chapter 11), but before that, he had to make a quick jaunt to Hong Kong regarding another case. A much-needed weekend in Bolinas to pause and regroup was in order. He needed to touch base with the wild untamed elements of the wind and sea.

Driving up sacred Mount Tamalpais from the Sausalito-Mill Valley side, then over the top and down on the other side through forests wooded with redwoods, he could feel his tensions begin to untangle from the case. There was no time to splash in the reflection pool of the details; other cases were galloping close at his heels. The battle always rages on.

Rounding the gracious arching curve of Highway 1 into the western slope of Stinson Beach was always a breathtaking joy. It was the moment when he could feel the cold salt wind of the sea enter his lungs. The expansive blue sea with its white lace trim of waves rolling in from other continents put things back into proportion. He would walk on the beach and shed the mantle of residue from the trial. The drive from Stinson Beach to Bolinas was a benediction, a return to the beautiful. Blue Heron Lagoon reminded him of a vast Japanese woodcut with striations of salmon pink sunset on indigo dark water. Herons swooped in for a landing, stitching tracks on the water's surface. He would walk the beach at twilight. The evening fog would roll in, diminishing the broken cliffs from view. Seagulls would bank and dive against the wind. He would walk the rocky shore, allowing the wind to have its way with his long hair, blowing it this way and that. He would walk into the rising fog until he too vanished from view. All that would remain in the fog would be the hiss and draw of the surf.

. . .

A fictionalized TV film, *Judgment Day: The Ellie Nesler Story,* was made of the case, which starred Christine Lahti.

Nesler served three years of the 10-year sentence and was released on an appeal of jury misconduct. She later served another three years after a conviction on methamphetamine charges. She was released in 2006 and died in 2008 of breast cancer at age 56.

Willie Nesler also later went to prison on drug charges. Just one hour after his release, he stomped to death a neighbor hired to clean his family's property in Sonora and is now serving 25 years to life.

Chapter 11

Contempt of Court: Solidarity Among Lawyers

Criminal contempt-of-court charges, with a punishment of six months in prison and thousands of dollars a day in fines, awaited Tony Serra as jury deliberations on the high-profile Nesler case eclipsed his trial schedule. He was due to open a major case involving a Rastafarian marijuana-smuggling conspiracy in Billings, Montana, on September 27, 1993, but the jury deliberating the Nesler case was still out.

Serra had been butting heads with Judge Jack Shanstrom over the timing of the trial since he took on the marijuana case. The sanity phase of Nesler's case was set for early September; Tony wanted a November trial date. The judge insisted on September 20, citing a prior commitment in November. Word got around that Judge Shanstrom refused to reschedule the trial date due to a hunting trip he didn't want to cancel. One of Serra's associates had observed that the walls of Shanstrom's chambers looked like a gallery of endangered species.

Serra's office kept in constant contact with Judge Shanstrom in Billings regarding the defense-attorney's inability to represent his client, Calvin Treiber, on the appointed date, but the judge rejected Serra's unfinished commitment to the Nesler trial. As far as he was concerned,

Serra's co-counsel could stand in for him to await the Nesler verdict.

As the September 20 date drew closer, Serra sent messages to the Montana judge that it was impossible for him to abandon the Nesler case in time to begin jury selection for the drug-smuggling trial. Shanstrom pushed back the trial date to September 27 and ordered Serra to appear. When he didn't, the judge charged Serra with criminal contempt and referred the matter to the chief judge of Montana.

Serra's defense lawyers openly accused Judge Jack Shanstrom, a conservative Bush appointee, of petty and vindictive behavior. Serra told a reporter, "I truly believe that my prosecution is a manifestation of [the judge's] continuing bias toward the Rastafarians and the 'long-haired San Francisco radical lawyer.'"

The contempt trial was scheduled for July 11, 1994, before Montana's chief judge, Paul Hatfield. The National Association of Criminal Defense Lawyers filed a friend-of-the-court brief with Hatfield, decrying the contempt proceedings as a threat to the Sixth Amendment.

When Tony asked me if I wanted to "see this circus," I jumped at the opportunity to tag along. It promised to be an interesting twist of fate to witness Tony as the defendant in his own case. Tony called on an illustrious group of defense lawyers to testify on his behalf, the star of which was Gerry Spence.

"Super-lawyer" Gerry Spence is renowned for his courtroom victories, which include the estate of nuclear whistle-blower Karen Silkwood against Kerr-McGee, the defenses of white-separatist Randy Weaver against federal firearms and murder charges, and the defense of Imelda Marcos.

I was hoping to be on the same flight with Tony from San Francisco to Great Falls, but he was coming in from Hong Kong and his flight was late, causing him to miss his connecting flight to Montana, so he arranged to have one of his colleagues, Bill Pinkus, fly him to Montana in Pinkus's private plane.

On my flight, I found myself sitting directly behind Jo Graves, prosecutor of the Ellie Nesler case, who was testifying in Montana as to why it ran over schedule. We chatted openly about the case. It never occurred to me that she was the "enemy." She told me what she planned to say. It seemed harmless enough, so I made no effort to recall every word. I mentioned that although she and Tony held different viewpoints, a person would have to be a real jerk not to respect him. She gave a sort of grunt and a nod and asked me to have Tony contact her upon arrival.

It was late when Tony and his team arrived. I was taken aback by his appearance. His skin color was ashen with fatigue from the flight from Hong Kong; it had an added green overtone from hours of airsickness in the small one-engine plane in which he'd flown from San Francisco to Montana. Apparently, the small plane heaved and dipped all through the long night, Serra's stomach heaving right along with it, every dip of the way. He said he could write a book about all the places he'd vomited in the world.

We ended up at some all-night café for dinner. With what little energy Tony had left, the conversation focused mostly on the opening day of the contempt trial. This was a late night of travel-weary souls, gathered together like a clan of elephants in hunting season, trying to strategize their moves to save their chief.

Taking on the daunting task of defending Tony Serra was Palmer Hoovestahl, a bright young local attorney with whom Serra had worked on the Rastafarian case. Hoovestahl was relatively fresh out of law school and his trial experience lacked the tread of mileage and hard knocks. His eyes were still innocent with the soft velvet of youthful idealism. One felt the urge to protect *him* from the brutal injustices of the court system.

Tony coached him every step of the way: at breakfast meetings, at lunch breaks, at dinner sessions, bite-sized briefings during breaks for the immediate sessions ahead. To Tony, that seemed sufficient to enable Palmer to quickstep and outguess the dueling blows of the prosecution.

But what was easy for the master was colossal for the student. Palmer gave it his all and the pure goodness of his intention was endearing, but it became apparent that Tony was losing the battle. This court was in redneck country. Tony was a long-haired-hippie lawyer from California who had already aggravated the judge and this court was going to show him how the law treated that kind of behavior in a *real* man's country. What's more, throughout the trial, Tony never said a word in his own defense. He remained silent, seen but not heard, the semantic warrior without his sword, without his voice and words, without his power.

The trial was in its third day and things were looking bad. I was beginning to think that he might actually end up doing jail time. But there was still one last witness to testify.

"The defense," Palmer said, "calls Gerry Spence."

. . .

At the announcement of his name, the wooden doors of the courtroom swung open and Gerry Spence, who'd flown into town in his private plane from Jackson Hole, Wyoming, strode into court. Wearing his signature buckskin jacket with the long feathered trim and his large Stetson hat, his mere presence emanated a feeling of personal power and dread.

The mood in the courtroom changed dramatically.

Spence flung his hat down on the witness stand and took his seat. His stature didn't diminish by sitting down.

He responded to the routine questions establishing his identity and expertise. Then Gerry Spence leveled his unflinching no-nonsense stare on the judge and jury. Everyone sat a little straighter and stiffer in their seats. Suddenly, something bigger than the smug satisfaction of courtroom fines and punishments was happening. It seemed as if a thunderstorm was about to strike everyone. The whole mood of the trial changed in an instant. Up until that moment, the proceedings, clearly based on prejudice and a hunting trip, now took on an aspect that struck at the heart of conscience itself.

Holding them in the crosshairs of his vision, in his deep authoritative voice, Gerry Spence infused the room with disdain for this travesty interrupting his day at the office.

"For a defense lawyer to walk out on a trial before it has ended, just because he has another trial on calendar, is like a doctor who leaves the patient while that patient is still in the operating room and hasn't come off the anesthetic, and the post-operative procedures haven't been done. It's *that* important. A doctor who left under those circumstances would probably be guilty of malpractice. So would a lawyer be guilty of malpractice if he left his patient—his client—in those same circumstances."

Next Spence cut another mighty blow, this time aimed at the judge, saying, "In my opinion, no judge has the right or the authority to demand that an attorney violate his ethical duty to his client."

Palmer asked, "Would the attorney be violating his ethical and legal obligations to his client during the period of deliberations if he took off and went to the other case?"

Without hesitation, Spence retorted, "No question about that! It's very clear, very plain, that he would be, and he ought *not* to, and if he did, he would be in trouble with his client, and I think he would be in trouble with the Bar, and he certainly would be in trouble with his *soul*. I have never, in forty-two years, left a case to another member of the defense team!"

He pointed out that Serra's presence was crucial to Nesler during jury deliberations. "Juries often come back with questions and how they're answered may affect the case."

He continued, "Jury deliberations are often the most painful time for the client and it would be malpractice to abandon a client while the jury was still deliberating."

Then Gerry Spence set his sights again on the judge. "A judge has an obligation to keep his calendar moving, but not at the expense of justice and not at the expense of anyone's constitutional rights. And that judge knew that or should have known it!"

Within a matter of hours, the jury acquitted Tony Serra.

· · ·

The follow-up on Serra's relationship with Gerry Spence came to a sad falling-out when Spence asked Serra to give a weeklong seminar at Spence's summer camp for young lawyers. Serra accepted; his seminar was one of the main draws of the camp. Spence advertised it in the brochure. Then, at the last minute, Serra begged off, failing to show up because he was in trial. It was a direct slap in the face of solidarity.

When I first asked Spence to write the foreword to this book, he flatly refused. "You tell Tony he owes me one." But when I asked a second time, he had a change of heart. He showed his greatness and came through.

Chapter 12

Sex, Drugs, and Silver: The Ted Binion Murder Retrial

"Has the jury reached a verdict?"

Judge Joseph Bonaventure asked the critical question on November 23, 2004, the final day of Las Vegas's "Trial of the Century."

The small courtroom was packed to its limit, the overflow crowd waiting in anticipation in the hallways. Bailiffs stood like sentinels, with hands on their billy clubs, should this ungainly mob suddenly flare out of control. TV satellite vans lined the streets, their coiled antennas corkscrewing skyward ready to beam the news to every major network and cable-news station.

Inside the courtroom, "Court TV" monitors blinked record red on this last day of its gavel-to-gavel coverage. Producers from "Dateline NBC" were gathering material for its two-hour special on the case, scheduled to air in the spring.

National reporters from the *Wall Street Journal* and the *Washington Post* were present, as were local reporters and photographer Jeff Scheid, crime authors Cathy Scott and John L. Smith, and myself as the courtroom artist.

The Binion family, the Tabish family, the Murphy family, and their friends, along with Vegas political heavyweights, tourists, and general spectators in the gallery, all added tension to this critical and long-awaited moment.

Defendant Sandra Murphy turned to the wall and vomited into a trash container. Her attorney Michael Cristalli tried to comfort her, but he, too, needed comforting at the ominous possibility of a repeat guilty verdict that meant life in prison for his beautiful young client in this highest of profile trials that would likely make or break his young career. Co-defendant Rick Tabish sat ashen-faced, hoping for the best and ready for the worst. J. Tony Serra, lead lawyer for Rick Tabish, sat statue still, head bowed, his large expressive hands folded like birds in repose. Even his signature ponytail was stilled of all motion in the powerful silence.

"We have, Your Honor," declared the jury foreman.

"Will the defendants please rise?"

. . .

When Benny Binion took over the Eldorado and Apache casinos in downtown Las Vegas in 1951 and replaced them with Binion's Horseshoe, he transformed two sawdust joints into one carpet club. In the days when Vegas was young, only four blocks of Fremont Street were paved and gamblers often traveled to the casinos on horseback. They came by the droves, drawn to the holy shrine of gambling by the lights glittering off the big horseshoe above the marquee.

In those roughshod days, the Horseshoe had class. It had style. Each gambler was greeted by name on entering the casino. A million dollars in one hundred $10,000 bills were framed and hung on the back wall of the plush velvet-and-mahogany gambling hall; visitors had their photos taken standing beside it to take home as a souvenir. In the 1970s, Binion's became known for its World Series of Poker. The high-stakes tournaments attracted poker players from the world over. Those were the good-old days, and this trial marked their end.

The fall didn't happen all at once. It was a slow circling of the drain that began with the death of patriarch Benny Binion and continued with Ted Binion's penchant for heroin and strippers. The latter led to his live-in liaison with a beautiful and younger woman by 30 years, Sandra Murphy, whom he met at Cheetah's topless club.

Murphy was new to Vegas, an outsider from California, attracted by the glitter and easy money. She and Ted hit it off. Each had what the other wanted. Ted cleaned up his drug habit for a while, but whenever things got dicey, he took the easy way out. The price he paid for his habit was the loss of his gambling license, his marriage, and ultimately, his life.

· · ·

Sandra Murphy had been Ted Binion's live-in girlfriend for three years. Rick Tabish had been one of Binion's contract employees, hired to bury $14 million of the magnate's silver coins in an underground vault in the desert 60 miles away. In trouble with state gambling regulators for a drug habit and associations with criminals, Ted Binion managed to stay clean for years, but finally he failed a drug test. His old heroin habit resurfaced and his gambling license was revoked; he was now banned from even stepping foot in the casino he'd managed, owned, and grown up in. Naturally, his relationship with Sandy Murphy deteriorated.

Murphy turned to Rick Tabish for solace and friendship. In time, they became lovers. Their liaison was no secret and probably would have been no big deal, except that one afternoon in mid-September 1998, Ted Binion was found dead.

The autopsy and subsequent toxicology investigation determined that Binion died of a lethal combination of Xanax and heroin. Police initially classified the death as "probable suicide"; Murphy claimed Binion had been suicidal since he lost his gambling license, though Binion's sister Becky Behnen denied it. Also, homicide detectives believed the scene of Binion's death had been staged and Binion's stomach contained heroin, which looked suspicious. Finally, it was discovered that in his will, Ted had left his multi-million-dollar mansion and all its contents, including valuable objets d'art, as well as a $90,000 Mercedes Benz and $300,000 in cash, to his girlfriend Sandy.

This was unacceptable to the Binion family's way of thinking. They didn't want Murphy to have a single dime of the Binion money. Something had to be done about it. And it was. In May 1999, seven months after the fact, the Clark County coroner's office reclassified the death of Ted Binion to be homicide.

Next, the family hired a homicide detective turned private investigator, Tom Dillard, paying him $200,000 upfront, with the final payment of another $100,000 due on the conviction of Sandy Murphy and her lover Rick Tabish for the homicide of Ted Binion. Murphy and Tabish were charged with theft, in conjunction with Rick Tabish's efforts to dig up Binion's vault full of silver a few days after the death, conspiracy to murder, and first-degree murder.

Investigator Dillard's best friend, Deputy District Attorney David Rogers, was assigned as lead prosecutor at the trial. Rogers had a large photo in his office of an electric chair, a picture worth a thousand words to describe his legal leanings.

Key witnesses were bought and paid for, according to their respective value. It made the evening news, but no one raised an eyebrow.

In the first trial, the prosecution contended that Tabish and Murphy bound Binion, administered the overdose, then "burked" (suffocated) him. Dr. Michael Baden, considered one of the country's premier forensic pathologists, was the prosecution's key witness; he testified that abrasions on Binion's lip were consistent with his struggle against someone covering his mouth and that two small lesions on Binion's chest were caused by shirt buttons pressed into him as someone applied pressure to force the air out of his lungs. Baden also testified that Binion's eyes had hemorrhaging, common in asphyxia.

The jury bought the argument, convicting the pair after 68 hours of deliberation. Tabish was sentenced to 25 years to life in prison. Murphy received 22 years to life. Justice was served, Vegas-style. The Binion family got what they paid for and the young lovers each served four and a half years in prison before the shady dealings were brought to light and a retrial was granted.

. . .

Las Vegas, famous for having its own set of rules when it comes to ethics, the law, and justice, might as well be on a different planet. Vegas law is not unlike playing cards. Lawyers are shuffled and reshuffled with the same frequency that a blackjack dealer refreshes a deck.

It took a league of big-name lawyers from out of state to focus the attention of the Nevada Supreme Court, which then reversed the travesty of justice of the first trial, thus opening the door for a second.

A power-attorney dream-team of celebrity defense lawyers was dealt and assembled: Alan Dershowitz, renowned appellate attorney, author, and Harvard law professor was hired by Bill Fuller, Sandy Murphy's benefactor, to address the Supreme Court and get the murder charges overturned; local attorney William Terry joined forces with Dershowitz on behalf of defendant Rick Tabish. Their combined expertise successfully paved the way for a retrial.

Then the deck was shuffled.

The Houston celebrity attorney Dick DeGuerin, known as "the gladiator for hire," who admittedly enjoys "getting down and scrappin' with the best of 'em" and whose big Stetson hat and cowboy boots are his courtroom signature, was retained to represent Sandra Murphy. William Terry was replaced by J. Tony Serra to defend Rick Tabish. These two heavyweights sat side by side at the preliminary hearing: Stetsoned DeGuerin beside pony-tailed Serra, both hunched and ready for anything the court could punch their way. It was "High Noon" out west all over again with the big guns striding into town.

But no sooner had DeGuerin signed on and settled himself in the saddle, earning his gun notches by getting Murphy released from prison on bail, than the scurrilous actions of non-lawyer tampering and interference prompted a shuffling of the deck yet again: DeGuerin quit. Local attorney Michael Cristalli, a handsome young rookie among legal allstars, stepped in to fill DeGuerin's boots.

But the reshuffling shenanigans didn't stop there.

In what looked like retaliation in a pissing contest, defense lawyers Serra and Cristalli filed a motion asking that Judge Bonaventure be removed from the case: The judge had attended a Binion-murder booksigning event, they said, proving he favored the prosecution. The motion was denied.

Then the lead prosecutor attempted another riffling of the deck, seeking the removal of Tony Serra, revoking his right to practice law in

Nevada on the grounds of failure to pay California income tax in 1974 and 1985. A desperate ploy, it too failed.

Just before the trial started, as a gesture of true gamesmanship, Serra publicly said he was excited about arguing the case before Judge Bonaventure, because the jurist already knew the case inside and out.

The shuffling was over, the players were in place, and the match was ready to begin: J. Tony Serra and Michael Cristalli for the defense; Christopher Lalli and Robert Daskas for the prosecution. The final hand had been dealt and the Las Vegas game of law played itself out in what was known as the "Trial of the Century."

This case became the swan song of the old Las Vegas; it was the last big trial in the old downtown courthouse. The baby-blue concrete bunker was scheduled to be replaced by a handsome new edifice in a matter of months. The new courthouse was part of a downtown renewal program in which a whole array of expensive high-rise lofts and shopping complexes were changing the landscape. The old and the new were on a collision course with each other.

All the while, just two blocks from the courthouse, the bigger-than-life bronze statue of famed casino magnate Lester "Benny" Binion, founder of Binion's Horseshoe and patriarch of the Binion clan, withstood the changes, like an ornery ghost from the past, forever astride his bronze horse, corralled on Ogden Street, a block from Glitter Gulch. Once a force to be reckoned with in this roughshod town, all that remained of Benny Binion's reign of power was this statue, but his stern no-nonsense glare remained a testament to the fact that Vegas was still a cowboy town with cowboy values, a macho place where male chauvinism, the size of the wallet, and the caliber of the gun were all that mattered.

• • •

The retrial of the two defendants in the murder of Lonnie Theodore "Ted" Binion was the biggest trial ever to be held in Las Vegas. History was in the making. All the murder charges from the first trial, four and a half years earlier, had been overturned by the Nevada Supreme Court. Even though a murder conviction can be reversed, it's rare for the defense to gain acquittals. And it certainly couldn't happen in Vegas, where justice, like everything else, has its price and in this case had been handsomely bought and paid for.

The Binions were one of the oldest families in town. Binion's Horseshoe Hotel-Casino was one of the last privately owned casinos. The Binion family had broken their bank of amassed wealth in the infamous first trial, paying off witness' to testify against the two defendants. It was an act of desperation to twist the evidence of Ted Binion's fatal heroin addiction into a murder charge. The first Binion trial, in 2000, was such a big event that five books had been published about it and tourists made the courthouse one of their vacation stops.

The retrial lasted seven weeks. Every shred of evidence was painstakingly examined, though Binion's lawyer was disallowed from testifying, as he had in the first trial, that Binion had instructed him to "take Sandy out of the will, if she doesn't kill me tonight. If I'm dead, you'll know what happened."

Tony Serra set the scene and pulled in a slew of experts; together with co-defense counsel Michael Cristalli, they sowed the seeds of reasonable doubt. Serra's impassioned closing argument lasted nearly three hours.

"Why are we here? Holy cow! Why are we here?" Tony Serra implored the jury. "We're here because of one witness: [Dr. Michael] Baden. Baden stands alone. He stands isolated. He stands rejected by his peers."

Serra went on to remind the jury that a host of equally respected experts had rejected Baden's theory that Ted Binion's death was the result of "burking," a far-fetched form of murder involving two people, one blocking the airway of the victim while the other sits or kneels on the chest, causing the lungs to collapse.

"My client wasn't there! Dear God, do you understand that?" Serra beseeched the jury.

He then went on to project the Binion family's motive to frame Sandra Murphy and her lover Rick Tabish for the death of Ted Binion. Serra made the analogy of Vegas casinos to palaces in Roman times; he likened their owners to modern-day royalty. Once this overlay was in place, Serra went on a rant. "Mr. Ted Binion was a demigod: 'Hail Caesar! We will find an assailant. The head must be brought forth and placed on a stick by dusk. We will not allow a mistress to live in the hallowed ground of our royalty. The offense is that royalty has been insulted!"

Serra stomped before the jury box, shouting his proclamations. He waved his glasses like a flag before the jurors as though they were the citizenry of Rome itself. The image hit the mark and stuck.

Serra then stripped bare the testimony of witnesses paid with reward money ranging from $5,000 to $20,000, due on the conviction of Sandra Murphy and Rick Tabish. Serra was pulling some expensive plugs and a lot of money was washing down the proverbial drain.

. . .

As the defendants followed Judge Bonaventure's instructions and rose from their seats, the judge asked the jury foreman, "What say you?"

"On count one, murder in the second degree, we find the defendants, Sandra Murphy and Richard B. Tabish, not guilty."

"On count two, robbery, not guilty."

"On count three, conspiracy to commit murder and robbery, not guilty."

Gasps of surprise, sighs of relief, and murmurs of outrage arose throughout the room.

"Silence!" Judge Bonaventure demanded, hammering his gavel.

All the murder charges from the first trial had just been overturned. Even though a murder case can be overturned by a state supreme court, it's rare for the defense to gain acquittals. In this case, the attorneys not only got the murder convictions overturned, they got not-guilty verdicts for Murphy and Tabish. This was *huge*. No one expected it to turn out that way. This wasn't supposed to happen in Vegas where the price tag of justice had a "sold" sign on it.

This time, however, the jury wasn't hoodwinked by foul play. They also cited, among other things, a contaminated crime scene and prosecution witnesses who simply could not be believed.

The defendants were, however, found guilty of conspiring to commit and committing burglary and/or grand larceny. This conviction stemmed from Tabish's alleged attempt to steal the millions in cash and silver that Ted Binion had buried in an underground vault. Serra went to great lengths in the trial to prove that Tabish didn't need the money, that his business was doing well, that he was only acting under Ted Binion's orders to remove the silver should anything happen to him. Another of Tabish's lesser charges, extortion, was also upheld.

In March 2005, Murphy and Tabish were sentenced to one to five years for their burglary and larceny convictions. Murphy remained free on bail pending her appeal of the latest conviction; in April 2005, she was given credit for time served, which discharged her sentence on the theft-related convictions.

Tabish, however, had to finish serving his sentence for extortion before he could start doing his time for stealing the silver, meaning that he was facing a total of 2 to 15 more years in prison.

. . .

After the verdicts were declared, Judge Bonaventure took a moment to acknowledge Tony Serra and his handling of the retrial. In an unprecedented exchange of man-to-man respect, Judge Bonaventure said, "Mr. Serra, it's been an honor to have you in my courtroom. I've read about you. I've seen the movie 'True Believer.' I am honored to work with you."

Tony Serra stood facing the judge and with his hands to his chest in a prayer position, he bowed his head. It was a quiet exchange of mutual respect. For a hushed instant time stood still, and then the room erupted into pandemonium. Flashbulbs popped, reporters clamored for interviews with the two defendants. Parents wept tears of joy and rushed in to embrace their loved ones. The Binion clan cursed the day. Cell phones rang incessantly.

On the courtroom steps, Serra made this comment to reporters: "I took the case after I talked with Rick, talked with his parents, talked with his former lawyers. I felt he was innocent."

When asked how he felt about winning, Serra replied, "I don't take credit for the victory here. I feel what all lawyers feel at the end of a long case. I'm tired and a little numb."

Later that evening, at a celebration party in Michael Cristalli's million-dollar home, Serra was nowhere to be seen amongst the throng of revelers. Later, he was spotted sitting alone on a large rock by the pool, staring into the undulating water in the moonlight, like a solitary monk in deep meditation. Without ever mingling with the merry-makers, Serra made a quick exit to his San Francisco office, back to the trenches, to begin his next trial.

. . .

Two years later, Serra reflected on the Binion case. "The trial, the pomp and ceremony, the media and journalists, the casinos and the lawyers, the defendants and the decedent all stood for nothing: nothing profound, nothing symbolic, nothing political, nothing meaningful.

"The trial was a grandiloquent venting of power and egos, a pitting of the casino monarchy against a triangle of lovers, ultimately corruption versus perfidy, a tired trite formula inspiring only to Hollywood and the Las Vegas mentality. In retrospect, the case for me was like one long line of bad cocaine.

"There never really was a case. The litigation unmasked a fraud. Binion apologists sought a scapegoat. They searched high and low, finally found a humbug pathologist who dishonored his profession for fame and fortune and created a 'burking' death theory that relied on a button impression on the chest of decedent Binion. When the mark was blown up, only a fool could call it a pressure mark. That was the end of the trial. The Wizard of Oz had been exposed as a fraud.

"Six nationally prominent pathologists said what was obvious: Ted Binion had died of an overdose of heroin. After all, he'd purchased twelve balloons of high-grade Mexican black-tar heroin the night before his death. He had enough heroin in his blood to kill an elephant. Why was there even a trial? It's because Las Vegas is a fantasy and believes in fantasy and will pay for fantasy. Celebrity addiction is the mass hallucination of the milieu, so that logic and reason and common sense become subordinated to the illusion of romantic thinking. Only in Hollywood and Vegas would there have been a Binion case.

"What I got out of the case was a mixed metaphor. I received what I call, in hindsight, bad publicity, because by taking the case, I compromised my image as a radical lawyer. On the other hand, I encountered some extraordinary human beings. My client, Rick, had been convicted of a murder that he did not commit. Feeling his strength, tenacity, the force of his discipline and intelligence was well worth the ride. Judge Bonaventure is a great man: perceptive, honest, straightforward; he could be brash, emotional, harsh, and firm and at the same time empathetic, compassionate, understanding, and fair. It's a rare breed and I was enriched by his presence. Co-counsel Michael Cristalli was a fountain of good surprises—behind expensive suits—a real advocate, humane, personable, prepared, persistent; he really cracked the tinsel veneer of the prosecution's case. By the end, I was in awe of him.

"Would I do the case again? Would I involve myself with circus drama in a teacup one more time? You bet I would! Snorting bad cocaine with good people is my favorite pastime."

Chapter 13

A True Calling

Tony Serra was invited by the Monterey College of Law to give the graduation speech. The graduates and their parents were all turned out in their finest formal attire, while Tony, as always, stood out in his bright tie-dyed T-shirt and worn pants, looking more like a misdirected tourist than the honored speaker. As the procession of proud law students and their families filed to their seats for the ceremony, Serra shuffled alongside, his hand-painted sneakers with their stars and stripes forever flashing color from under his black robe.

•   •   •

"I have never engaged in a formal graduation ceremony. Somehow I missed my high school graduation, my college graduation, and my law-school ceremonies, so I step forward with unfounded anxiety this afternoon. Judging by my metabolism, I have tremendous trepidation.

"I wondered why I have such trepidation here, and I came to this conclusion: It's this black-robe thing. You see, I've never worn a black robe myself. I've accepted the black robe as the image of judicial authority, of strength, of judgment, of force, hopefully of wisdom and vision. But what *I've* done mostly is fight. Mostly, I'm an angry linguistic fist in the court.

"What I do as a career, as a profession, as a calling is: I *defy* authority. I engage authority. I oppose authority. I rage against authority. I represent the antithesis of any theme. I'm in the minority position, the opposition. I'm the one who is vanquished. I'm the one who collects the pain and suffering that ultimately is administered by the *black robe*.

"So I'm sitting here *surrounded* by black robes. It's like a nightmare for me. I think part of the reason I'm trembling is because I feel as if I'm in some kind of an afterlife where I'm being judged by *all* judges.

"The moral of this story is: Examine the manner, the attitude, the ideology with which you regard authority. Don't accept the obvious or easy path, which is submission to authority. Challenge, always, the concepts that are established. 'Rage! Rage!' as Dylan Thomas says, 'at the dying of the light.'

"When I came out of law school, the society was so different from today's. The ideology was so *different*. The eloquent words of Black Panther leader Huey Newton echoed in my ears: 'Service! Service to society! Service to ideology! Service to freedom and liberty! Service to those who lack the social and economic nourishment to proceed! Nourishment for the deprived! Nourishment for the underprivileged!' The demonstrations on the streets were happening everywhere; it was all political and it was all social. So it was *easy* to get enthused. Becoming a lawyer wasn't like going to get a job. It was like having a *cause*. It was a vocation that pulled on all the strings of idealism, all the strings of what I'll call the 'adolescent sentiments': those pristine beliefs that you come into adult life with, hoping that they can be fulfilled.

"You new lawyers entering this kind of environment have a lot of questions: 'How many lawyers are out there? Are there too many lawyers out there? Why are there so many lawyers? Is there a place for us? Are we welcome within the profession?'

"Let me tell you what I think. You're desperately needed now. Desperately *desperately* needed. What is needed out there are the purity and clarity of idealism. This should be your mantra:

"More *prosperity* for more people through law.

"More *rights* for more people through law.

"More *liberty* for more people through law.

"More *justice* for more people through law.

"You shouldn't be saying, 'I'm going to use my degree to embellish my *own* prosperity. I want to make more *money!*' I recognize that you have families. I recognize that there are second careers. I recognize all the sacrifices you and others make to do this, all the giving and the support and the love. It's a fabulous strong endeavor. Support has a synergistic effect: That is, the sum of the whole is much greater than the parts. You have a strength that is multiple and geometric rather than arithmetic. *Of course* you don't divorce yourself from that.

"Do you understand why there is public sentiment, respect, reverence about the 'crossing of the bar' in a courtroom, the bar that separates the lawyers from the spectators? Think about crossing the bar. The bar is the railing. The bar is the hindrance. The bar is the barrier. Only the lawyers go in front of the bar. And you've been invited now to cross the bar, to be in that judicial realm, to be among the privileged where reality and the promulgation of ideas converge, where sociology and political causes merge. Fabulous! Being a member of the court gives you a fantastic perspective on the totality of life. And you have merited the invitation into that realm.

"But see, it's a *calling*, and that means service. That means giving. Ultimately, that means *more* for more people. It means a different kind of sacrifice, a nobility of thought, a nobility of purpose. Prosperity is easy. It's not difficult to succeed. The material benefits are yours. The *real* targets are *reform,* evolution, change in a positive fashion. In any semantic battle, you must always think about the *higher* principle, the greater thought. That's the *true* calling. And we desperately need you! We need the revitalization you will provide. We need the strength of a fresh view. We need fragrant breezes blowing in the court. We need new voices.

"What happens to old lawyers like me? I no longer have words for love. I have no words for romance. I have no words to describe normal social interchanges. Old lawyers become so articulate that no one understands them *at all!* We become *lost* in the shadows of language. What we need is the freshness of perspective that you bring, the boldness!

"I've always surrounded myself with young lawyers. It's important to listen. In some societies, before the leaders go to counsel, they bring in the young children and they ask them, 'What did you dream? Tell us about your dreams.' And then they send the children out and they try to construct a law, a philosophy, a religion, and a political system *around those dreams*. Right now, you're the dream-carriers. You have the visions. That's what we need *desperately*.

"The eighties are over. The selfishness of the eighties is *over*! The yuppies have come and gone. They've feasted on our material prosperity and they've *destroyed* it for us. You come in a time of decline, where you have to raise the standard higher, where you have to be purer, you have to be better. *That* becomes the lawyer's true calling.

"What is the secret to survival in this intense field of practice? It's about staying balanced. Most trial lawyers either become alcoholics or drug habituated, or they only last about ten years. I'm talking about how to last *at the* peak of idealism, at the peak of mental acuity, of sensitivity. I'm talking about a willingness to battle day after day, a willingness to change ideology in response to changing times. I'm talking about being on the cusp, always being on the look of change, always being ready for battle. For me, that's very stressful and because I feel deeply, it's more pernicious, it's more destroying.

"So I'm telling you why I'm here, why it is that I've lasted so long in the trenches, case after case after case where the dominant consciousness of my life, as the weeks go on, is my *case*, my trial. I'm in a trial. It's a fourteen- to sixteen-hour day. Some people can't sleep under these unendingly intense circumstances. I've *lasted* because I have some sanctuary of mind and aesthetic. For me, it's the aesthetic. For some people it's spiritual, for others it can be literary, it can be athletic, it can be any number of facets. But you have to have a place where you go. It doesn't have to be a geographical place. It can be a mental state where you gather, where you pull it in, where you become at one with yourself, with your awareness, your environment.

"You must hold to your vision and ideals. Where do they come from? You've got to find them, you've got to make them. You take them from your law professor, you take them from the words of a famous jurist, you take them from literature, from philosophy, you take them from artists, poets, great teachers. You've got to fertilize your domain; otherwise you'll become stagnant and sterile in your thought processes. The lawyer's language is entangled with legalese and his idealism dies on the field of pragmatism. The lawyer who succumbs to those pressures is a fatal flaw in society.

"Let me give you an image. Imagine a knoll—a little rise, a little hill. And there's a path leading up to this knoll. Let's just pretend that this is the lawyer's knoll. You look up the hill and see a figure at the top. You note that over this hill a tempest is brewing, a storm. There are winds. The blackness of the rain obscures the knoll. And there is that solitary figure. You're amazed to see: It's winged! Its wings are beautiful, almost like what an angel would have, and it's looking up toward the heavens. And you think, 'Oh! This lawyer image is a beautiful thing! Look at that. It's ready to soar. It's going to fly above the storm. It has wings to depart, wings that will carry it to higher realms. It will have the overview. It will transcend the battle. It will transcend the chaos and the spontaneity. It will afford a vision of unity. The lawyer! Aren't we lucky!'

"You walk up the path. As you get closer to the image, you look at its face: You see that the face is broken, the face is scarred. You see the eyes and the eyes are crying. And then, lo, you notice that this figure has only *one* wing! He doesn't have *two* wings! She doesn't have two wings. It— the lawyer, the genius, the gifted, the clever—doesn't *have* two wings! It could *never* fly!

"Then you know the truth. It has taken off in an attempt to fly and has fallen and been broken so many times that its bones are maimed and its face is scarred. This! This is the *true* lawyer image: a broken crippled angel.

"You look up again, and now you see that there *are* flying figures above that have transcended the storm. These are the figures of the poet and of the teacher, of the priest and of the musician. And then you feel *damned* by the occupation. You feel that you've been cheated out of the larger prospect that humanity has bestowed on you as a potential, that you're mired in the realm of pragmatism: What *works* is what's right. What *acquits* is what is right. What *convicts* is what is wrong. Therefore,

you have to compromise. And therefore, inch by inch, you have to surrender, abdicate your pristine idealisms, give up the childhood dreams,
vanquish from your hopes the spiritual knighthood.

"You've got to remember that image of the lawyer's knoll, and think
of that, and not *be* that. What goes first is the idealism, the life-long
pursuit of knowledge. Maybe you've told yourself: 'I'm going to read all
of Herman Hesse this year. And next year I'm going to read all of Cas-
taneda. And I think I'm going to revisit Schopenhauer. And I always did
like Spinoza. I think I'm going to revisit him too. And I'm finally going
to get around to reading—again, now that I'm in the fullness of life—
Shakespeare, even Charles Dickens. You've got to do that. You've got to
keep your mind fresh. You've got to keep language usage fresh. You've
got to keep inspiration and idealism fresh.

"But these are the first things that *go*. You'll never read again. You'll
read transcript after transcript, Xeroxes of transcripts, until your eyes
go blind. There's never enough time.

"Please, don't give up the sources of inspiration—the literature, religion, the great works of art—that have to be fused into a lawyer's vision.
Don't surrender the quest.

"Next. Where do you acquire your strength? You walk the beach at
dawn. You walk the mountains at dusk. You take long walks, solitary
walks, introspective walks, thoughtful walks, during which you gain that
inner peace from which you can strike out against the forces that you
stipulate are the opponents. Yes, those walks will go too fast. So nurture
those walks. Don't give up those walks. Don't give up those strengths!

"And this one goes, I'll tell you: love and family. It is said, 'Law is a
jealous mistress.' No! Law *ain't* no jealous mistress! Law is dope! Law
is a narcotic! You become *addicted* to law! You'll be there early in the
morning. You'll be there late at night. You'll be there on the weekend.
You'll be reading and dictating Sunday morning. So the first thing that
goes is *family*. The first thing that goes in your life is *love*. The children—
you don't see them very often. The mate—there's less and less to talk
about. You become a human being *obsessed*. That's what the law does to
you. That's the strength of it, that's the calling of it, that's the *beauty* of
it. But you have to say *no!* Be better than your forebears—me, especially.
Carry with you the love and the support of the family. *Don't* give up your

humanity. It's your humanity that gives you the vision that will carry you forward.

"I believe that the presumption of innocence is a fabulous thing. It's perhaps the most cherished thing that we have given body to as a culture. Americans don't really stand for very much. We've invented the cowboy movie. We've certainly invented a lot of implements of destruction: military airplanes, deadly toxins, and bombs. We jealously guard our atomic weaponry and disallow everyone else to have it. But on the good side, we've given concrete form and expression to the concept of presumption of innocence and we're giving it now to the world. It's really one of the pillars of a free society. *We presume innocence.* We make the prosecution prove its case beyond a reasonable doubt, to a moral certainty. What a fabulous notion!

"Yet now society barely pays lip service to the presumption of innocence. It has become an idle construct of words, something that has no breath, no vitality. So what I say is, 'Your spiritual cup must flow over.' When a cup flows over, there's plenty for everyone. Part of that flow has to be, in our lives as lawyers, presumption of innocence. On a metaphysical level, presume every person innocent. Presume innocence always. Presume your family innocent. Presume your fellow lawyers innocent. Extend that presumption of innocence to *everyone*.

"See, we are all truly innocent. The dichotomy of 'guilt' or 'innocence' is an artifact of *words*. We're *all* either innocent or we're *all* guilty! And we cherish innocence. We have built a noble edifice, a constitutional mandate, to that idea. *Cherish* that idea. Bring that idea forward with you each day. Presumption of innocence—serve that concept! Serve it in large ways. Serve it in small ways. Serve it every day. Bestow it upon your fellow man and woman, and you will be *proud* to have become a member of the legal profession.

"You have to carry with you your own allegory, your own symbolism, your own metaphor. That's your strength. That's your wellspring. That's where the ultimate *creativity* originates.

"I'm going to give you a metaphor of mine. In Southeast Asia they have temples, Buddhist temples. They have them in all sizes and proportions. There is one style of Buddhist temple that looks like an igloo. It's a small, curved, cone-shaped temple. The outside is austere; there's only a little entryway, a little door, where you go in. You have to get down on your hands and knees to actually get in and you leave your shoes outside.

"As I said, the outside is rather plain, but inside! Inside are various images of the Buddha. Over the years—it could be centuries—people have left the offering of little gold leaves. Devotees go in there and place their gold leaf on the Buddhas and they place gold leaf all over the walls and on the floor. So when you look in there, what you see is a molten golden hue. The radiance pours out! It's far more than visual; it's viscous. It engulfs you. It envelops you. There's a density. It's not just gold, there's a *glow* to it. There's a religiosity connected to the color in there.

"You stand outside and get ready to kneel down and crawl in. Right next to the little low door beside you stand the poor people and their children. These people reflect the beauty of their souls in their eyes. The little children have big bright black eyes and they're looking at you. Then you see an old man and an old woman and they have the same eyes as the children. The woman is wrinkled and small, poverty-stricken. Her child is small, petite, sad in face and in form. They're sad in their form, but beautiful in their eyes. The eyes are black. The eyes are bright. The eyes are shiny. The eyes are alive! The eyes *glow!*

"These impoverished people look up at you. One holds out a little cage and in the cage is a bird. They sell these little birds in the cages made of straw. You see this bird in the cage and it's cowering, it's shivering, it's fluttering. It looks like it's kind of black or brown or dying. It's looking so scorned, so overlooked by providence, at that moment. They offer this up to you and you give them a coin that has no value in your culture.

"And what you do is, you open up this straw cage and the bird flies! The bird flies right over the cone, right over the top of the temple! And as it flies, you see—ah! And it fills you with wonder, with awe—that it isn't brown. It isn't black. It isn't scared. You see the undercoloring of the feathers as it flies, brilliant colors! The way these colors merge, blues and greens and yellows, it's like a rainbow in flight. And the bird is flying and it's free! It's shimmering in the light. It's the 'Ode to a Nightingale' objectified for you.

"Watching that bird fly prepares you psychologically, spiritually, to enter into the zone of holiness, into this Buddhist zone, this *golden* holiness, the temple.

"The giving of freedom—the act of freeing something from confinement, from a jail—restores life to it, transforms it. You *see* how it's transformed from something trembling and tenuous to something bright and flaming. The transformation occurs during its transition to freedom.

"The act of the giving of this freedom is the preamble, the precursor, that *allows* you to enter into this—I will say for the sake of the metaphor—'spiritual grace' that will engulf you in the temple.

"I tell this story to lawyers. And I sometimes tell it to juries when I want to encourage them to give the client the benefit of the doubt. Giving is a bountiful thing. It has to flow. It's strength. Your cup has to be filled. You have to be brimming over to *give* the benefit of the doubt. *Give* that doubt! It's a metaphysical thing, to give it! First your mind sees it, but then to give it! To give *freedom*! It's the precondition to holiness itself.

"That's what I believe criminal trial lawyers do when they're at their best. You know, we're good, bad, indifferent. I think we're all three-fourths mundane, but that last quarter? That's what life is all about, that last one-fourth! What the criminal-defense lawyer does is give that image of freedom! Of liberty! We set minds free, we set bodies free, we wrestle with the iron of the cage and pull it apart and let a human being go. Let it fly out! Let it evolve to a higher form.

"That person just freed might fly down the road and fall, or be shot by a hunter down the road, or fall on bad times and starve. That's not the lawyer's concern. The lawyer's purpose is to free. To give liberty! And that's a beautiful *strong* thing to do. No one ever has to be ashamed of that. To be a criminal-defense lawyer and to give freedom is a noble, an almost religious, calling.

"At this time in history, lawyers are being vilified by other quarters of society. But the lawyers who give freedom give the most precious gift that can be had. I think we can all be proud of that gift."

Chapter 14

A Day in the Life

J. Tony Serra   ©Paulette

The orange-purplish hues of sunset cast long shadows that striped the garden path as a sedate evening crowd of judges, lawyers, and invitees filed into the old reconstructed barn at the top of a knoll at the College of Marin. It was a handsome crowd, well-dressed, well-coifed, with perfect teeth—a stable full of yuppie thoroughbreds in this barn, as one might expect in Marin, one of the wealthiest counties in the country. An opulent buffet offering wholesome California cuisine, radiant fresh fruits and vegetables, exotic finger food, ripe cheeses, and cascading spring flowers was set on tables that stretched the length of two walls. Napa wines complemented the culinary choices.

Tony Serra, always a draw, was the keynote speaker on this occasion. Heads turned periodically to glance toward the big barn door, anticipating his arrival. But he'd already slipped in through a rear entrance, unnoticed, and remained in the shadows of an unoccupied grandstand at the back of the barn until the last moment.

Eyeing the crowd from this safe distance, he commented, "I don't engage in ceremonies. I retreat from ceremonies. I don't participate in social gatherings. I retreat from them. I don't object to them or anything; it's just the way I am. I once had a Russian wolfhound. Russian wolfhounds are not quite tame. They sit inside, but they sit way in the back so that they can get out the door fast. They don't want to become too domestic. They're still a little wild. In my romantic self-delusion, I'm like that in any kind of social contact: just a little wild."

Upon introduction, Tony Serra walked with his lively gait through the applauding crowd to the podium, wearing corduroy pants, high-top tennis shoes, and a shirt cut from a real American flag—an intentionally inflammatory choice of attire at a time when flag-burning was making headlines. Amused snickers and mumbles of disapproval rippled through the audience as he took his stance at the podium. But it wasn't long before we were all swept away by the force of his oratory.

. . .

"Here's what I think: We are, as individuals, no better and no worse than what we last did. That's the sum total of you, of me. That's the existential culmination of every causative factor that has brought us to this time and place. It is an allegorical point: Everything reflects everything. The bird in the birdcage experiences the same universality as the bird out of the cage. All have some form of limitations, but the universal is in every experience.

"So what I did in my last case, your last personal involvement in a meaningful event, my last meaningful thought, that's the sum total of me, of you—symbolically. The last moment incorporates all of the precedents: psychological, sociological, intellectual.

"I'm going to give you *Friday*, and I'm going to give it to you on several levels. The first level is literal. The next level is allegorical; it represents all lawyers. And the third level is symbolic of my life in particular. So just come with me, come with my Friday.

"Friday, I woke up. Oh God, I felt so good! Even though I've been practicing law for many decades now, I never tire at the excitement I feel. I had butterflies, anxiety, about the day. I woke up Friday and that's how I felt. It was as if something special was going to happen. I felt as if I was going to do something I could be proud of. I felt vigorous. I was going to court!

"I thought about it in the shower. I started arguing the case in my mind, carving out the words and the mannerisms I thought I'd use—although it never works out the way I think—but I like to at least formulate my approach.

"I used to wake up this way every day. For twenty years of practicing law, I used to wake up energized like that and it makes all the difference in the world. To go into court feeling excited, not beaten or crushed, but robust and energized, feeling strong, feeling capable, and desiring the conflict, desiring the argument: 'I *want* to do it! *Let* me do it! Yes! I'll take that one! I want to make six appearances today. I want to see everyone who comes into the office *free* today! *I want to do it!*'

"That's the way my Friday started.

"Friday started like that, because here's what I had on the docket: one of the first 'three-strikes-and-you're-out' cases. But I had the *victim!* I had a seventy- or eighty-year-old woman, an elder of the tribe, a beautiful, strong, clear-eyed woman with a serious heart condition. In law, you derive your analysis of people from your perception of them. It's a gestalt. It's nonverbal; you feel it when there's charisma. There are all kinds of auras. Well, I could feel her: She was wise and strong, courageous.

"Someone had stolen forty or fifty dollars worth of something out of her car. She said she hadn't even locked the car. But she'd been subpoenaed to testify at the preliminary hearing of the person being charged with his *third* felony. And the person was going to go to prison, potentially, for life without possibility of parole. And she didn't want to do it. She didn't want to be responsible for that. *She* wanted to go to jail rather than put him away for life. And by some karma, by some good fortune, I was going to be allowed to stand by her when she presented that image of resistance to an unfair law.

"The judge on this case was one whom I respect and love, but he's very finicky. So I had it all planned. I was going to say something like, 'Based on this woman's position, which is grounded in ethics and morality and conscience, *knowing* that this last felony was a trivial and non-venomous event in her life, she is unable to participate in this preliminary hearing. She *refuses* to.' And I had my medical letters all ready. 'She could suffer a heart attack if she's pressed.'

215

"Now this particular judge could say, 'Bullshit, she takes the stand or it's contempt of court!' Although he would say this in legalese.

"My view of the role of the lawyer is this: Always throw yourself on the wheel. That is, it's *our* domain; you don't sacrifice innocent people to the sanctions of our domain. Laymen don't understand, although this woman understood, but laymen may not even want to play along with our game. So I was going to say to the judge: 'I've advised her—this is advice of counsel—that you can't put a sanction on her. I've advised her that the three-strikes-and-you're-out law is unconstitutional. It's going to be declared, in part or in whole, unconstitutional; therefore, she legally does not have to participate in something that is unconstitutional. Therefore, put *me* in jail! Don't put her in jail. She's just following my advice, the advice of counsel for the defense.' I was jacked up for it! It was going to be a large event.

"The case was scheduled for eleven a.m."

Serra was revving up his intensity. His arms were punching and pointing. Now his tone changed dramatically as he launched into this next somber phase.

"Now, I've also been on a large federal case, though every goddamned federal case is a large case. I'd been down to Fort Worth on this case three times and I hadn't even seen the judge yet. He never even came out of his goddamned chamber. The case got transferred to northern California. So now it's nine a.m. on this Friday morning and I'm in federal court for the appearance on this case.

"Besides that, I start on a murder trial Monday, a hard one. So this was my week off. I say 'off': I'm going to all the courts and doing as much as I can do, but I'm not in jury trial.

"So I had about three or four appearances for Friday. My partner, Randy, did one for me. I was going to take this one and everyone was covering for me, but I had to get from one court to the other. They can tell the judge, 'He's coming!' But this was the last straw. This was the straw that kind of broke my camel that morning.

"So at nine a.m. I had to go to court on this federal case, which was a perfunctory appearance. But you see, there's no such thing in criminal law as 'perfunctory,' because my client is facing twenty-five to life! And I'm his lawyer. I'm his hope. And I'm not going to let him down, because if he gets twenty-five years in prison, I don't want any karma *ever* that I wasn't there. So he's got me *numero uno* and I know that. But I say to myself, 'This is just a short appearance. I'll get there at nine. I'll be held up until nine-thirty. This is a perfunctory thing. I'll be out in time for the other court at eleven.'

"I go in to the federal court first and, shit! There are about six things on the calendar and it's like survival of the fittest. I go up to the podium and I try to get my case in first. In the old days, I'd just grab that goddamned podium! I'd get there a little bit early and I'd just *grab* it! No one could get in front of me, so I would be first. They still allow this kind of Neanderthal behavior in some courts, so I was going to be first! Remember, I was *up* and I was excited. I had the argument in my mouth! Maybe I'll go to jail today!

"Then the marshals came in late *without* my client. The marshals were late. My client was coming, but he wasn't there yet. Now I find that in law, it's easy once you get to court. Well, not easy, but I know everything will get done. The hard thing is the logistics, when I've got to be four places at the same time, my car doesn't work, the traffic's bumper to bumper; that's the hard part. These times should be the contemplative pauses, the valleys of repose, but part of my metabolism and part of my mind are *racing* while the other part is trying to chill it. I'm acting cool on the outside, but inside, I'm *dripping*. Perspiration is dripping right down and I can feel my blood racing. I can feel it from my mind down to my stomach, and my digestion is affected. But outside, all is cool. I'm smiling. I appear calm. Everything is *all right*. But by now it's about 10:30, an hour and a half late! I'm beginning to feel sick with anticipation. I'm a wreck. Time is playing havoc with me.

"My client, the federal one, is young and handsome, and we've got a bona fide entrapment case, but it's going to be hard to win. And if we don't, he faces twenty-five to life. He has a beautiful young wife and two babies. I always encourage family members to be present, even when there's no jury, because the client feels the vibes, and the client feels stronger. Law is played out on a psychological level more potently than it is on a linguistic level. You have to understand that. The practice of law is *not* linguistic. If you think it's linguistic, then you're just going to be reading stuff you've written, which has no life to it.

"So his wife and kids are there, waiting to see him. He's been in Texas a long time. He's been in custody; he's been in a bad condition. Texas *ain't* no fun. We're waiting, we're talking, we're waiting. The judge is off the bench.

"There's a holding cell right next to the court. Normally, guards bring prisoners down by elevator and into court from the side. Now the marshals march my client in. There are a total of three defendants in the case and they're marching them in from the outside, from the hall. I see that my client is in handcuffs. They're leading him in like he's some kind of sheep going to slaughter, like some kind of animal.

"In the federal system, prisoners aren't brought into court in handcuffs, only in rare cases. My client is a passive hippie who traded a little acid for a little grass down in Texas, no weapons of any kind. It was a sting. Some informant, some big smuggler, said, 'Hey, come on down; we're givin' this shit away!' And my client went down there and got busted. That may be a simplified version, but still it's not fair. He's sure as shit not some brutal, flame-eating, heinous, destructive person.

"I look down and he's got the big rings on his wrists, handcuffs so tight they make a red mark, and I say, 'What the hell's all *that* about?'

"'Oh, well, they were late, man, so they just brought us right in through the front door.'

"And I'm looking at the young wife and the kids. They're watching their husband, their father, come in like that, with no dignity, brought in like some kind of prisoner of war or slave on a chain. So I'm pissed! And at the same time, I'm thinking, *Shit, I should be over in that other court.* I'm getting angry, I'm getting turmoil, and that's when I'm *good,* because when I get my juices going, I emote! But I'm not thinking that; I'm thinking, *This is fucked, man.* And then they called the case.

"Now comes the perfunctory ritual, the dance, in which all lawyers delight."

Serra moves from foot to foot like a boxer.

"It's a stream of words that's more like music; the words don't really have content. It's part of the ceremony that's been going on from time immemorial. Some lawyers do it suavely and some lawyers stumble. It's a fantastic thing to watch. It's a fabulous feeling being up at the podium. There I am, getting my chance to say my thing; this is *me,* the best part of me. It's who I am. Each of us brings to that podium our basic socio-logical background, whatever level of consciousness we have, the level of awareness we've attained, our powers of articulation. So the lawyers on Friday are full of words and some of them are good. They're talking about the nomenclature that's ultimately going to apply to this proce-dure. And now it's my turn to talk.

"Remember, this is all true, but it's also allegorical. What do I do? Do I join the refrain? Do I sing a purer song? Cleaner? Do I, in a cer-tain sense, reject it all? Manifest indifference? What do I do? Churning inside—this is *always* true—shall I be blatant? Shall I speak from the heart? Shall I speak from the gestalt of my being, from my guts, my an-ger? Or shall I join the refrain? Shall I join in without disturbing the air?

"I get up and I don't know what I'm going to do! I *never* know what I'm going to do. I rely on something, a spontaneity, in terms of the flow of words, and it *comes!* I think about things ahead of time and I've obvi-ously got to know the law, but then, when I'm up there, it has to flow, and if it doesn't flow, then it's mechanical. Then it becomes, at best, a skill. But skill blossoms into an art when there's a flow that's beyond my power to describe or control. The words just flow out of me. I never know, when I approach the podium, what's going to happen! Am I going to be conventional? Am I going to do what's expected? Will I say the 'right' words? Will I express the clearest position? What? This is why these mo-ments are so fabulous. It's like giving birth! I don't *know!* Will my speech have wings? Will it fly? Or will it crumple? Will there be a prince on my tongue when I open my mouth? Or will there just be an ugly frog? I don't know! And don't think that the mind is not faster than the speed of light, and that it's not kaleidoscopic, and that *everything* isn't always focused on the tip of my tongue at that one moment: my childhood, my humdrum concerns, everything. It's all there. I can't eliminate it, so I incorporate it somehow.

"I'm walking up to the podium and probably because I'm pissed off that I'm not at the other court, I say, 'Your Honor, respectfully, can I have permission to *grumble?* I want to grumble. I have to *grumble*, Your Honor.'

"She's a good judge. She's quitting, probably because she is a good judge. In the federal system, a lot of them stay there too long and they lose contact with their humanity—if they ever had contact.

"So I say to my client, 'Put your hands up.' He does, and he's got these big red marks. 'I want you, Your Honor, to look at his wrists. Let me tell you what happened. We waited and we waited for my client to be brought in.'

"'These marshals are an hour and a half late. Are we pretending that we're not even going to say anything about it? We waited in here an hour and a half! The marshals did not deliver. I don't know where the error was, whether it was with the jail or the marshals. I'm not casting aspersions on anyone. But I've got a client here who wasn't negligent in timeliness. I have a client here who didn't participate in the reasons for the delay. But *he's* the one who has been victimized, Your Honor. Look. *Look!* They've brought him in like an animal.'

"I just go off! I'm yelling, 'Why does *he* have to suffer? Why does his wife have to suffer because they'—I'm pointing to the marshals— 'delayed bringing him to court?' I'm probably pissed off because *I'm* the one who's being delayed! But they did screw with him. And always the question is, do you bring it out? Will there be a sanction? Will anyone care? Am I a little bit off center? Of course I am! But there's always that struggle: Shall I really address the issue or am I just going to do the dance? Am I going to go with it or am I going to fly in the face of it? Do I have something morally strong enough? I never know the answer to that. I do know that my client and the other two defendants aren't at fault. I take my cues from them; I don't take my cues from anyone else. I represent them. They're going to do the time.

"This fabulous judge, this fantastic judge ... See, normally the judge just goes, 'Pffft! Well, all right, Mr. Serra. You've documented your concerns. There's no jury here; you don't have to engage in these forensic displays. It's of no meaning to the court.' I expect that shit; that's the ritual. I expect the judge to flip me off. But *this* judge looks over at the defendant. She has these big sensitive eyes. She's beautiful and strong, and the key word here is *compassionate*. And she's feeling it, feeling compassionate. All those other assholes aren't feeling it. The marshals are looking at me smugly, like, 'We're gonna get you in the elevator, man! We'll get you, you motherfucker.' But this judge is so beautiful! She says, 'It's all the court's fault. It wasn't your fault at all. It's not your fault. And I apologize. I apologize sincerely. It was wrong that you were brought here late. It was terrible that you were brought through the public domain in handcuffs and in that suit. I apologize to your wife and I apologize to your family.'

"This is what the judge said! Was that fabulous? Holy shit! It was so unexpected that I was just aghast! It was so beautiful! She took that moment and she made something out of it. It was a different kind of high for me.

"Now remember, I'm due at the other court at eleven, but by now, it's already after eleven. I was told later that it was a major event at the other court, there was a lot of press, everyone was interviewed. But my client wouldn't participate. Her lawyer wasn't there; he couldn't make it. He was stuck in the other court.

"As I'm coming out of federal court, I'm trying to talk to my secretary on the phone. 'Stephanie! Stephanie, tell them I'm *coming*. Put it off to one-thirty! Tell them I'll be there!' I do this half my life: pant, pant, 'Hold the court for it! Call in to the court!' Half the time the court doesn't even acknowledge the message. They just give you the standard answer: 'Court's in session.' So there's all this futility and *that's* what's so stressful. It isn't the stress of doing the job; it's the stress of not being there, not getting there! That's what kills me all the time, not being able to be where I'm supposed to be.

"And so, to go on with the allegory, I come running out. And then I see a friend, a lawyer; we've known each other a long time. In the practice of criminal law, our lawyer allies are the most meaningful. You see, it *is* a war, and we're on one side, and the prosecutors are on the other side. So our allies are our strength. The strength in the numbers *on our side* is the most important thing. Defense attorneys should never be arrogant and never be indifferent; it's critical to acknowledge each other in passing, to reach out and greet each other. It's a way of merging, uniting, holding hands in some invisible way, saying we are one, we are together, and we are *fighting for the same thing,* we are part of the same calling. We're not 'yes' people or money whores. We're word warriors. It's a bond that's strong and deep. It's a camaraderie, like a brother-sister cohesion.

"My heart is pounding. I've got to get to the other place. But I see this friend and just like in court, I say to myself, 'Cool out, man. Give him a hug, talk at length, talk at length.' I believe in serving the present moment, serving the face that's in front of me, serving the need of whoever is there. I give of myself entirely in the moment that is present. If I constantly think the need is somewhere else, then I know I'll never serve anything! I believe that what's important is *always* whatever is in front of me. It's never anywhere else. It's never in the next court. It's never in the next argument. It's never in 'Next time I see you, hey, man, let's go to lunch; why don't you call me sometime?' That's all bullshit! That *dis*-integrates; that doesn't unify. The goal is to unify, to bring together, to hold onto something precious all together. For me, it's a *must* to acknowledge my brother and sister, to acknowledge them sincerely.

"So I run into my friend and I talk. Outwardly, I'm calm, social, happy, convivial, congenial, all of that. But I know time is ticking. I'm not going to make it to the other court. Then I run into a second friend as I'm nearing the elevator. I have to spend maybe twenty minutes with him. I shouldn't say *have to*; it was my joy to spend time with him. I hadn't seen him for a long time. He's a good lawyer. But by that time, it was too late to get to the other court.

"I didn't make it. I never made it to the other court. The proceeding went on without me. It will *always* go on with or without me. I'm *not* indispensable; sometimes I don't even count! I'm just a symbol, but I *think* I'm indispensable. Anyone bred on the maxims of existentialism thinks he is the *most* important element! After all, the lawyer is really the only one who wants to be there at all! The clients certainly don't want to be there. No one else wants to be there. But the lawyer—if you're a *real* lawyer—*wants* to be there! You get there early. You want to do it!

"At any rate, I was thrown into—I don't know what you'd call it— dark moody despair. Morbid self-reflection. I lost the rest of the day in a swirl of grayness. And I reflected on how just that morning I'd been singing! I had been *so* excited! And by that afternoon, I was in a state of quiet pain, desperation, convulsed thoughts. And that was yesterday. That was just *Friday!*

"So in trying to tell you what my day is like, I'm trying to tell you what I'm like, what my practice is like, what it has always been like for me, what the attributes of my mind and my perception and my value system are. Everything is always symbolic. Friday was symbolic. My larger aspirations, my vain hopes, my strengths, my weaknesses were manifest in my routine activities. It was the summary of all my days. Did I do anything significant—for myself, for others, for the cause? What have I done in life that has any fucking meaning at all? Once I had great expectations! I was always bright. I always got top grades. And I was an athlete. At a certain age, I was full of the vanity of life itself, poised and full! Full of promise! California was prosperous; the dollar was something. It was a fabulous time. But now the pendulum has swung. Defeat is my main diet. And through my failures, in my pain, in my agony, I shrivel psychologically into some insecure, self-doubting, fallen soldier.

"And that all happened in one day for me. This is certainly a fecund lifestyle."

Chapter 15

Closing Arguments

Ｈis motto is, "Pretend that you're on horseback—that is, don't use too many words, but direct your words like arrows or spears; always speak like you're on the back of a horse."

Tony Serra's closing arguments are theater at its best. The drama rises and swells like a storm, but in order for the storm to build in force, there first must be a moment of emptiness. Serra begins in a soft tone, barely audible, his hands clasped pensively behind his back in a posture of folded respect. He leans into the jury for intimacy as he thanks them for their time and attention. His words are well-chosen, measured, non-threatening. Drawing upon the imagery of great poets and prophets, he appeals to the higher consciousness of the jurors. Their senses dilate. His stream of imagery flows into their mind pool.

Then, as Serra weaves his tale, as the drama unfolds, he ignites. He erupts. As if by divine intervention, the lava of his words flow. The pyrotechnics of his passion are well-targeted. He's a blitzkrieg in the courtroom, a sudden squall, a torrent of emotion, hurling accusations, lunging his rage, stomping, jumping, rending the room with his fury. The jurors are spellbound or in shock, vitalized or repelled. Serra's intensity shatters the well-ordered glass menagerie of their minds and forces them into a deeper place: their humanity.

His voice crests and dives with the unnerving intensity of a siren.

And then there's silence. The silence is seismic. It's the resounding silence of aftermath. It's over. Few jurors, or anyone else for that matter, have ever experienced the impact of real live heat of passion at point-blank range as only an enraged Russian-Spanish-Moorish-Jew can evoke. It's a hard act to follow. The prosecution rebuttal always begins with respectful acknowledgment of Serra's eloquence and dramatics, along with a sheepish apology to the jurors that he or she cannot begin to match his style.

. . .

Tony Serra's closing arguments draw people from all over the country. Lawyers, law students, and laymen travel great distances to experience them, to learn from them. There's always an excitement in the air, an "opening-night" feeling when Serra delivers a closing argument. It's the hottest show in town.

Of course, behind every great performance is a tremendous amount of talent and skill. Here, speaking to an audience of lawyers and laymen for the Drug Policy Foundation, Serra shared the craft of a good closing argument.

"The theme that I want to address is how to regenerate the romance that existed between jurors and lawyers prior to my generation. I consider myself from the era of the late fifties, the sixties, seventies, eighties, nineties. But prior to that, lawyers were giants in the court and people desired to listen to great oration, eloquence, passion, and confrontational semantics."

His gaze narrowed as he looked off into the distance, beyond the confines of this starkly austere lecture hall to a vision in his mind's eye, a vision he held dear in his memory, of an appropriate setting for magnificent oratory.

"What I want to do is describe for you a court that's aesthetically beautiful. It's a federal court in Boise, Idaho, not a real old building, but it has a beautiful high ceiling, wood throughout the interior blended with marble, the smell of English lemon oil emanating off stately, glass-covered, mahogany tables. Looking into the counsel table I can see the reflection of the ceiling, of the chandeliers. Words seem to reverberate off the walls, requiring that one be throaty, that one cast his or her voice, because of the largeness."

Now, feeling the swell of his own descriptive prowess, Serra imagined a trial befit for such a setting.

"The trial is a long one. We're in the eleventh week. Let's just postulate that there are social issues, there are political issues, there was corruption in the investigation, the narcotics officer is corrupt, the informant has perjured himself, and we've been on the attack. The drama has attracted the media and aroused public attention.

"Now it's time for the closing argument. The court is packed. There are people outside, there are cameras inside. The moment comes when I, as the lawyer, am asked to rise to give the closing argument.

"I stride forth, and not with paper in hand. I have no outline close by. I use no eyeglasses to hide my eyes. I do not stand behind the podium. I do not stand behind the client. I believe that as the defense attorney, as *the* incarnate symbol of the pursuit of justice for the accused, I must step into the center. It's like an arena and there I am, right there in front of the jury, maybe ten feet away. There's that hushed moment and with my peripheral vision, I can see the D.A. or the U.S. Attorney. I can see my client sitting to the right side in the back. In that hushed moment, I experience all these fragments of feelings.

"I can feel myself *throbbing*. My metabolism is pumping and I know at that moment that I stand before all those assembled mentally *naked*. My mind is naked in front of them! And for me, as a lawyer, if that isn't the most thrilling ecstatic moment, if that isn't the moment of existential self-realization, if that isn't an experience of my highest calling, if that isn't my image of perfection, if I don't feel that this tableau of the defender before the jury is the ultimate symbol in every system that seeks to ascertain justice, if I don't think that this is the quintessence of the *calling* of a *noble* profession, then I'm *never* going to be able to communicate to the jury."

Serra paused to let the impact of his passion for the law permeate the psyche of his audience.

Charged by the magnitude of his own energy, Serra continued to crest his wave. "You see, it's *you*. You have to preserve—through case after case, through being battered, and defeated, and defamed—*you* have to preserve that awe, that *wonder!* The *thrill* of it!

"Obviously, you've manifested passion throughout the course of the trial in other ways, but now you step forward and you're out there alone. You're like the sentinel, you're like Don Quixote, you're the vigilante, and you're just about ready to speak, and if that isn't the most fabulous moment in life, if that isn't the culmination of everything that you desire to do, then you ain't gonna do it! Then there's not gonna be a regeneration, a nexus, a connection, between you and the jury.

"The point I'm trying to make is that the vitality comes from the *lawyer*. It doesn't come from the evidence or from the rulings of the court. That's the clay. You make the vase out of the clay. It's the charisma, the integrity, the sincerity, the true belief, the force, the *passion* of the attorney that are all summed up and symbolized in that moment.

"When I was much younger, I used to wonder, what would I like to be doing when I go out, that is, when I die. At a certain age I wanted to die making love; I wanted to go out on a *high* note. Then I changed my orientation; I wanted to be like Aldous Huxley and go out while peaking on LSD. And I may still culminate my life on that pillar of desire. But now my thoughts are, it would just be fine, it would just be noble, it would just be appropriate, if at that moment while standing before a jury, the white light would come down and flash me to whatever dimension exists beyond this one!

"As the closing argument begins, I step forward empty-handed into the center, in front of the jury. First I turn to the judge and I say, 'Thank you, Your Honor,' or just, 'Your Honor,' and his or her name. I look at him or her in the eye *if* he or she has manifested anything like compassion during the course of the trial. I don't lie, I don't cheat, you don't say something that ain't true. But if the judge has shown, dare I say, fairness, or partiality for the defense, then I thank him or her in a generic fashion. 'The defense, the accused, thanks *this court* for its indulgences, for its fairness.' I'm communicating with the jury, but also acknowledging the judge.

"Next I say, 'Counsel ...' And depending on what I'm going to do next, I handle this brief moment in a variety of ways. The game is to beat the U.S. Attorney or the D.A., to implant *reasonable doubt*, to instill in his or her mind from the inception that, by the end of the case, I'll be winning. Now he or she is a believer. He or she thinks there's reasonable doubt. He or she gave a very non-spectacular closing argument. Defeat is written on his or her face. Therefore, I can extend compassion and I will say in the salutation, 'Co-counsel,' and perhaps I'll call him or her by name. If I *don't* intend to extend this sense of connection, I'll call him or her, 'Mr. Prosecutor, Ms. Prosecutor'—you know, cold and cast off."

Serra's hands fling off the words as if they were something vile.

"Then I turn and bring my client into the invisible circle I've just created. Remember always that the important thing is to touch, to smile, to associate with the accused. He's not tainted. He isn't a piece of cold dead carnage. He's not someone to be avoided. He's someone to be embraced, respected, dignified. I have to communicate my regard for him in all of the variables of my interactions with him, verbal and nonverbal. That's got to be the message to the jury. Sometimes I'll stand him up and I'll bring him or her over to the jury box. I'll put my arm around the defendant, and I'll say, 'Mr. or Mrs. or Ms. So-and-So,' and I'll sit him down again. I want the jury to look at him *de novo*. Then I'll go back to the jury and say, 'Ladies and gentlemen of the jury.' I'm starting off by centering everything around an image of the accused that's filled with respect and dignity.

"I believe in what is called *tour de force*. In boxing, this means that you don't save your roundhouse, your heaviest sock, for the last round. You get out there and you *kick*. You get out there and you hit your opponent below the belt. You get out there and slug him in the face as fast as you can. You want to deliver the mortal blow sooner rather than later. Again, I'm trying to establish the connection, the nexus, the affinity with the jury, the empathy, the identification, the soul breaking out of division and into unity at that moment.

"'Ladies and gentlemen of the jury, I've prepared for you a closing argument, and the closing argument is probably going to take three hours.' I'm out there—no notes; it's all divided in my mind, an hour of this, an hour of that, an hour of the other. If I can't talk to the jury directly without notes, then I'm not going to be able to excite this nexus with the jury.

I've got to be out there naked, so that they can judge every bit of sincerity that I have to give. There's no hiding. I look them in the eye. I level with them. And the first thing I do is point to the U.S. Attorney or the D.A. and say, 'He *solicited it*. He *paid* for it. And he argued for it. What is *it*? What am I talking about? PERJURY!'

"In drug cases, informants are given so many many benefits and even a mild form of investigation will produce large or small statements that are perjurious. It happens. It can't be false for me to say it, so I lay it on them. 'This is a U.S. Attorney! And he's standing here as your symbol of representative government. *He's* the person who's supposed to have pursued the truth, the objective truth. *He's* the person who takes no sides. Yet *what* has he done? He's offered thousands of dollars to an informant, to *multiple* informants, and then he stands behind what everyone in this court *knows* is perjury. *Is* it perjury? Ladies and gentlemen, I'm going to evacuate my spleen at this point! I had prepared rationally. I had prepared based on the evidence. I have to tell you what a *disgrace* the prosecution's case was.'

"Closing arguments have to cover everything, and they have to rise and fall. All parts can't be passionate; all parts can't be emotional. But I'm talking about engendering a live *force* in the beginning so that *I'm* the electricity between the defendant and the jury. I like to give a death-blow at the weakest part of the prosecution's case right at the beginning and vent my passion. If you can't get pissed off, if you don't feel frustrated, if you don't feel anger and bitterness over a judicial system that *pays* informants with liberty, with money, a system that offers them credibility, that relocates them—and sometimes they're homicidal maniacs—into communities and calls them 'John Smith,' if that doesn't cause your blood to rise, then this isn't for you! It's not your calling! In order to bring that jury toward you, so that they're with *you*, the right energy has to be manifested. From my perspective, and maybe it's just *my* bag, the approach isn't intellectual. It doesn't come from speaking in any form of legalese or allegorical, metaphorical, symbolic language. It must consist of direct thrusts, like sword fighting.

"There is nothing more beautiful than a lawyer at that moment, because he represents—in any kind of a case—the barrier between truth and falsehood, between a judicial system that works and one that doesn't. Jurors will all respect you. They'll *listen*. Their ears will tune in to your words at that moment. If you can get the U.S. Attorney or the D.A. *ever* defending his own integrity, then you're halfway home! So I slam them at that point, then proceed to what I'll call a detailed analysis, and that for me is multifaceted—I have my own method, my own way of describing my cases. But that's not the topic here. The topic here is how to generate a feeling or to encourage some kind of sympathy between jury and lawyer.

"It's the integrity of the *lawyer* that's the main conduit. It's the lawyer. There's a beautiful word: impeccability. If you want to communicate, you have to be impeccable. The lawyer has to be impeccable. The members of the jury have to identify and project with the lawyer. They have to transfer all their idealism, all their adolescent beliefs in democracy and honor and truth and justice, to the lawyer. The lawyer is the bearer, the carrier of all that, so *we* have to be impeccable. Juries will judge the entire case by my word if I *have them*, if I've drawn them in during the course of the case and they trust me, and if I never lie to them.

"I tell them: 'This is the word of an informant. The word of an informant in any judicial process *cannot* be the basis of a conviction. You've got to look to the evidence extraneous to the word of an informant. You *always* have to excise what the informant says. Why?' And then I spend forty minutes on why snitches can't be accepted in any kind of a judicial system. They *can't!* Who can predicate a truth-seeking process on paid witnesses? If *we* paid witnesses, it'd be an obstruction of justice. If the system allowed both sides to pay witnesses, it would be mocked. It would be scorned.

"Yet we have a system whereby we *can't* pay witnesses under penalty of being arrested and prosecuted, while they *do!* All of their witnesses, in the major drug cases, are cooperating witnesses or informants. And they're paid off—more with liberty nowadays than with money, previously with money *and* liberty. But liberty is more precious than money. No judicial system can predicate a truth-seeking process on paid witnesses. I have my discourse on that topic. And the jury will *accept* it, no matter how brainwashed they are into disdaining drugs and people connected with drugs.

"Bullfights are a large allegory for me. The lawyer is the bullfighter.

He stands alone. He stands impeccable. He stands proud. He or she, whichever. The bull is the symbol of the dark forces, of primordial fear, of instincts that are self-destructive—everything that society fears. That's what a crime is. It's a manifestation, ultimately, of fear in terms of survival of the species. Now obviously, in the bullfight, one side cheats. The bull is drugged, so it's not a fair fight. What we do as defense lawyer is take the bull—and sometimes the bull is called racism, sometimes it's called poverty, sometimes it's called psychiatric deficiency—and conjure that bull into something that a jury can understand and appreciate and empathize and sympathize with. We're always bullfighters in that respect, and this means that we have to have the courage to be gored, to die. Maybe our cape is our way with words and our cross-examination. But ultimately in a trial, we're calling for direct confrontation. 'Toro! Toro!' We're not avoiding it.

"'This, ladies and gentlemen, is a case that involves *racism!* Racism in the District Attorney's office. Racism in the narcotics detail. Racism that they're trying to incite.'

"It works! Because the heart of the community is still good. If you can reach the people through the haze of brainwashing, through all of the indoctrination by the media, and law enforcement, and other authoritative images of enforcement, then you reach good pristine Americans. They believe in freedom. There really is a good rock-solid *core* there that a good lawyer can reach.

"The lawyer is the symbol, the litmus test, the filament, the light. He is what the jury is going to focus on. We have to be impeccable, we have to be forthright, we have to be confrontational, we have to be passionate. I'm talking about what I think is more significant than the verbiage. Jurors don't take in verbiage. We measure our words, we plan our metaphors, we think we've coined some innovative phrase, we're so thrilled with our insight or our literary allusion. The jurors don't give a shit about that! They're good fundamental people, strong people with a moral base.

"You want always to make your case a passion play involving morality. Make the case elemental. Take the high ground. Make a frame around your moral imperative, your moral priority. It's so easy in drug cases. Why? I do murder and drugs. In every major drug case, there *is* a bad snitch; the narcs *are* brutal and they *do* harass. There are Fourth Amendment issues that juries recognize. You can't legally put some of these constitutional issues before the jury, but you goddamned *do* put them before a jury. I've had jurors tell me, 'Well, we know that he was entrapped even when you couldn't say it.' There are all kinds of ways to slip in jury nullification. Be self-righteous. Be indignant about *something*. Tell the jury: 'You can never convict, because if you *do* convict, you're convicting on the word of a perjurer, on the word of a paid informant, on the word of a psychiatric-drug-despoiled mind.'

"A lawyer nowadays, especially a drug lawyer, is held in the lowest esteem. He has the status of a child molester in prison. If you do death-penalty work, you're not regarded as homicidal; you're lauded for it. If you represent a rapist, you're not accused to be a rapist yourself. The jury knows that. They're not going to impute the crime of the clientele to the lawyer. In the drug arena, however, it's quite different. They make all of these terrible inferences. 'You live off the fruits and the spoils of ill-gotten gains. You take money from these drug dealers. We know you use drugs. You probably sell drugs.' If you fulfill, in any respect, their preconception of you, you're *dead*. You are not doing your client any good.

"There's a caricature of the drug lawyer with the snakeskin-leather boots, and the flashy cars, and the gold chains, and the hot bags of cocaine falling out of his briefcase. That's the image in the jurors' minds.

"Naturally, I always gear myself toward the other end. I court the jury. When they're eating in the cafeteria, *I* eat in the cafeteria. When they're talking off to the side, *I* go off to the side. Where they park their cars, *I* park *my* car. If they go to church somewhere, *I* go to church somewhere. I walk amongst them. I have my client walk amongst them. I want to make contact. Just make sure you heed what the judge says at the beginning. He or she gives a formal order. Some say, 'No contact with jury members. All you can talk about is the weather' or something like that. 'Well, how's the weather, Mrs. Jones?' You can *talk!*

"I remember one large case in which one of the jurors was a woman who had twinkling eyes. This woman would go to the candy mart, where they sell little things in the courthouse. Every morning she'd be there.

Every morning *I'd* be there. We didn't say anything. She twinkled her eyes. I twinkled my eyes! It was a hard case. It was a Mafia case. It was in Miami and it *hung!*

"So I'm saying, 'Go.' There's a line; everyone knows where the line is. If you stay on the—dare I say—'right' side of the line, then you're not doing anything. If you're on the line, you're not doing anything. It's territorial. Be *over the line!* The game is to take a little bit of *territory.* So in terms of your interpersonal contact, the nonverbal is far more important than what's said.

"I drive old junks. I've driven old junks all my life. It's not something that I manipulate just for a jury. I can recall one case in particular. I had an old Ford Sentinel that would never start. It was a big case. And I had the jurors helping me; they were out there pushing this goddamned car that would never start! You know that you've got it then. At that time I had a partner who had some fancy red car. He came into the parking lot. I saw the juror looking at me as I talked to my partner and later she said, 'You know, you were talking to the person in the parking lot with that red car and that hurt you considerably. We thought you were connected'—I was talking to a *lawyer*—'to the drug world.' I got an acquittal, but I also took *note.*

"So what I'm saying is, wear the same suit. Wear a cheap suit. Don't have fancy suits. I'll wear the same suit at least twice a week or at least every third day. I'll take a shirt—all my shirts are old anyway—and make sure that the shirt has an ink spot on it, and then I'll wear it the second day so the jurors know it's the same shirt. *They* wear the same fucking shirts twice. You've got to get down on their level. They've got to identify. They don't want to think this cat is part of the syndicate. You can't have that. That works against you, just as moral impeccability works for you."

Chapter 16

"These Are My People"

" All rise!"

The command of the bailiff's voice hushed the anxious murmurs in the courtroom at the same time a room full of people rose to their feet all at once. They'd gathered to witness, lend support, or report on the sentencing hearing of J. Tony Serra for willful failure to file income taxes—for 40 years.

This was no ordinary group assembled in the spectator section of the July 2006 hearing. Big-name attorneys were there to ask federal Judge Joseph Spero to allow J. Tony Serra to serve out his time under home confinement rather than in prison. Jeff Adachi, head San Francisco public defender, suggested Serra be sentenced to working in his office, providing training for his attorneys. Family members, office staff, and friends were present; ex-clients and ex-cons were attending Tony's hearing.

A fearsome silence preceded Judge Spero's decision in this case.

Serra knew well the power of the law. He'd devoted his life to wrestling with its forces of light and darkness. The law was a force like none other. The courtroom was where a jury of twelve and a judge cloaked in black determined the fall of an axe or the flight of a caged bird. At age seventy-one, the remainder of Tony Serra's illustrious career now lay at the mercy of the law.

Lady Justice, atop her stone pedestal in front of the courthouse, seemed to cock an ear toward these proceedings. She was well-acquainted with Tony Serra, with his unpredictable and over-the-top theatrics, so effective with juries and such a reprieve from the tiresome wherefores and therefores of legalese, of hot air from dry mouths blowing smoke for personal gain. In the same way that he represented only one side of her scales, Serra was one-of-a-kind, with a lust for justice that trumped the lust for profit and prestige. Lady Justice, half-naked and blindfolded, smiled a knowing smile, and tilted her scales of stone.

Before announcing the sentence, Judge Spero lauded Tony Serra for his dedication to the cause of justice and admitted that his resistance to taxes was based on principle and not greed. Still, this was not the first time the IRS had prosecuted Serra. He'd spent four months in the minimum-security Federal Correctional Facility at Lompoc in 1974 and was convicted in 1988 of two further misdemeanors, willful failure to file taxes and willful late filing, which earned him several months of probation and the loss of his license to practice law for 30 days. At that time, he was found to owe $350,000 in back taxes and was paying $1,000 every couple of months. Thus, Spero sentenced Serra to another stretch, ten months, in Lompoc Prison Camp, his latest debt to society for failure to pay his "fair share."

There were gasps and tears among the crowd of spectators, but Serra himself shook off the dark specter of a withering fate, uttered a sigh of relief, and welcomed this relatively short sentence as a temporary vacation from his grueling calendar in the trenches of jury trials.

"I can do ten months standing on my head," he cheerfully proclaimed.

The media crowded around Serra for a comment about his notion of living with criminals for 10 months. "These are my people," he said. "I have more friends in prison than out. I've given my life to defending their causes. I love them and they love me."

. . .

Why did Tony Serra opt out of the taxation system? How did he get away with it for so long? Who dropped the hammer on him, forcing him to do time?

It's the way he's hardwired. Right from childhood, Serra was never interested in acquiring material assets or possessions. In the mid-1960s, amidst the free-form lifestyles of the hippie movement, psychedelics and Timothy Leary's drop-out syndrome, the Vietnam war, and all the political cases he was doing at that time, Serra determined to take an informal vow of poverty. He eschewed bank accounts. He foreswore insurance. He shunned investments and real estate.

He didn't believe in probate. He wouldn't acquire assets to pass on to another generation. He didn't (and doesn't to this day) believe in the private ownership of property. He considers himself like a Native American, believing that the Earth is our mother. You can't own parts of your mother. You can't pass parts of your mother to your children. You don't put parts of your mother into the bank.

Serra certainly didn't want to be a servant to possessions, in bondage to materialism. So he made enough money to satisfy his creditors. He paid his rent, he bought his food, he brought up his five kids, but he never bought anything new. Junk cars, clothes from the free boxes and thrift stores, a rent-controlled apartment, pro-bono cases—Tony Serra simply lived outside of the American dream.

When his kids wanted to give him birthday and holiday presents, they asked what he needed, and he always needed socks and underwear. They also went to the thrift and Goodwill stores and found him old suits and ties; they still do.

Thus, since he didn't make any real money and never took a profit from his legal work, and since he wasn't acquiring assets—no stocks, bonds, apartment houses, yachts, and so forth, nor any money in the bank—and since he didn't *have* anything, paying taxes made no sense to him. It was easy to slip into a mindset that, since he didn't make anything, since he didn't have anything, he had no reason to pay taxes.

Also, of course, he saw that taxation was ultimately a relationship between conqueror and conquered.

"When the Romans conquered territory," he explains, "the conquered locale had to pay an annual tax. If you didn't pay up, the Legions arrived and took your silver and gold and your women and your children. Taxation was the fruit of conquest, the relationship between you and the army that had conquered you. Translated into modern times, that relationship persists. Ultimately, who bears the tax load? We know that the corporations don't. The loopholes are *all* for them. Through their lobbyists, they're accorded liberal tax allowances. The working class, the underbelly, the economically enslaved, they're still the victims.

"I pledge myself to the working class, the underdog, the impoverished, and therefore I'm not a victim. I'm not Caesar's victim. Also, I've *always* paid my dues to society. So I made this kind of rationalization: I exempted myself—in some kind of grandiosity—from the tax."

Problem was, the system didn't exempt him. The taxman came after him. Government lawyers prosecuted him, once, then twice. That's when he started filing his taxes. He still wasn't paying, but he was submitting his records, however marginal they might be. Because after 45 years of poverty and conscientious objection, Tony Serra isn't about to start keeping a strict financial accounting of himself. He's not going to collect and file receipts for business expenses. He won't break down outlays for individual cases and disbursements of fees. He's not going to become a servant to the IRS.

He does report his gross income. He does deduct office and other expenses that can be calculated by his secretary and given to the accountant. He figured, what the hell were they going to do? And he was right: No one did anything. Twenty years passed between his two misdemeanor convictions and being sentenced to federal jail time.

How? He was simply considered financially dysfunctional. He didn't make anything, he didn't have anything, and they gave him a pass. Not that they didn't investigate him.

"They investigated the hell out of me!" he exclaims. "And what did they find? They found I'm honest. They found there really *isn't* anything there. There's no bank account in the Caymans. There's no Swiss annuity. And they concluded that I'm aberrant. I'm crazy."

But then, George W. Bush was elected. He appointed John Ashcroft as Attorney General. And Ashcroft wanted to take a stand against tax resistors.

"I wasn't outspoken. I was quietly going about my life. I was even filing. I just wasn't paying. What did I have to pay with? But Ashcroft came in and he wanted to make an example of high-profile people, in order to get everyone else to comply. There's a big compliance problem in this country, you know. You don't hear much about it, but millions of people don't file or under file or subsist in the underground economy. These are my people.

"But Caesar wanted his pound of flesh. He went after lawyers and doctors and Indian chiefs. It came from Washington, not locally. The local prosecutors would come up to me and say, 'Hey, man, it's not us. We're really sorry. We understand. We never would have done it.' It was compelling people who were considered dissident to the grand scheme of Bush.

"So I was prosecuted a third time and we entered into a plea agreement for me to do ten months."

As part of the agreement, Serra promised to pay $100,000 in back taxes at a rate of $20,000 per year for five years, as well as to pay future taxes.

"I will comply," he says, "because I've got ten more years of active trial work, at least fifty or sixty more cases in me. I *want* to do those. So I'll pay the devil his dues. But I won't be converted into an accountant. I'll have my secretary make sure she bugs me every time we get a new case, so that we can document it. If, in order to do fifty cases, I have to compromise a little bit on a lifestyle that started when I was young and has now become an alleged financial dysfunction, I will have my aides aid me in that dysfunction."

. . .

I didn't visit Tony in prison camp. He discouraged visits from everyone, even his family and close friends. Writer Burr Snider, however, went to see him and penned a story for the November 2006 issue of *San Francisco* magazine. And I corresponded with Tony.

Serra "settled into a comfortable, if dull, routine, lost twenty pounds, goes to bed early, and sleeps well, despite the non-stop cacophony in his 150-bed open dormitory. His prison job, which takes about four hours a day and pays $19.20 a month, is watering the grounds."

Snider wrote that Serra liked his job. "'After I was here a couple of weeks, one of the staff guys offered me a job as a clerk, but I turned him down. It was kind of delicate, because he thought he was doing me a favor. But I didn't want to be someone's flunky, and I wanted to be outside. Doing the watering, I'm on my own as long as I get the job done. Which means, you know, I get to space out a little. I dig just watching the way the sunlight refracts through the sprinkler spray.'"

Then Serra answered Snider's inevitable question about "the enforced cessation of Serra's prodigious marijuana consumption. 'Cold turkey, boom, no big thing. I've been offered a hit off a joint a couple times, but I just tell them, "No thanks, man. I'm a short-timer. I don't want to fuck up."'

Snider wrote that two months into the ten, Serra was one of the oldest prisoners in Lompoc, had lost weight. "'Down twenty pounds already,' [Serra] grins proudly. 'Not bad, huh? Or do I look too gaunt? When I get out, everyone will think these people have been starving me down here.'"

• • •

The following sections are culled from some of Tony's prison writings.

"What are you doing in here?" goes the refrain.

I tell them I'm only a misdemeanant. I got ten months for willful failure to pay taxes, not tax evasion, which is a felony.

Deep down, I'm a bit ashamed of being a mere misdemeanant. I have defended every category of felony, from marijuana to murder. I've represented the Hells Angels, the Nortenos, the Symbionese Liberation Army, the Black Panther Party, the Animal Liberation Front. I've defended the Devil himself. I know the secrets of the felons. My mind is a shelter for all serious crimes. I am the consummate deposit for all felony mentalities. I am the greatest felon of them all. But in this camp, I'm recognized only as a misdemeanant.

My work assignment is "groundskeeper." My specific responsibility is to water lawns and flowers. I set up temporary sprinklers, turn on and off permanent sprinkler systems, and water with long hoses by hand. By the end of the day, my shoes, socks, and feet are soaked.

I must appear as a solitary figure, way out on a lawn. I daydream through the spray. I smile at my reveries. I romanticize my prison work. It makes things easier to accept: to give life when life is taken.

If I am incarcerated, if one human being is incarcerated, everything is incarcerated—the loved ones, the friends, the birds, the flowers, and the grasses. The lonely waterer is the centerpiece of this captured and suppressed microcosm.

. . .

Anomaly is the general rule in prison camp. In my case, I eat food I wouldn't consider outside—hot dogs, sweet cereal, cold cuts, white rice, and endless canned fruit and vegetables. I go to bed at the same time every night and get up at the same time every morning. I receive mail at mail-call time. Outside, my life is irregular; inside, it conforms to the prison schedule.

But my strangest abnormality is my choice of friends. Outside, my associates and intimates all share my anti-materialistic egalitarian social values. But inside, I gravitate to inmates who are semantically oriented, knowledgeable of world events, and have traveled—who have been acculturated by education or experiences similar to my own. Oddly enough, these are all committed capitalists. Money drives them all. Opulence characterizes their lifestyles. They are all victors in the capitalistic world.

Our discussions are animated. We share anecdotes and humor. We have bonded. They know my social philosophy, but that hasn't deterred our friendship. Still, I strongly believe that on the outside, we will revert to having nothing in common and never see each other again.

I feel badly that I'm not close to the inmates who constitute the outlaw class I've always represented, who are abundantly present in camp. They're average-minded with average world experience, but not as interesting at a personal level as my friends the capitalists!

. . .

The camp chapel is multi-denominational: Islamic services on Friday, Jewish on Saturday, Catholic, Protestant, and Buddhist on Sunday. On weekdays, it's used for the small number of classes given at the camp and as a TV room. During free time, inmates play the small piano there.

An inmate friend, a 74-year-old doctor, told me in disgust that the Catholic priest had forbidden him from the using the piano, because it was part of the Catholic mass and therefore could only be used by them on Sundays. Thus, even the Catholic priest punishes the inmate.

. . .

It's well-known that I'm a marijuana activist and smoker. But in prison, I don't smoke. I will wait. I'm a short-timer. I don't want to be busted for a joint and do more time.

Marijuana is not an addictive drug; it doesn't enslave. It simply enhances awareness. It increases one's appreciation of beauty, and beauty is a component of truth and love. Abstinence doesn't enfeeble or destroy any portion of mind and body; it merely eliminates one blissful dream within the reality of one's life.

. . .

Camp-issued mattresses for our bunk beds are hard, probably stuffed with synthetic cotton. They don't soften to accommodate body pressure. It's like sleeping on the floor. At one time, the prison issued normal mattresses, but only a handful of inmates had these remnants by the time I arrived.

Recently, these old and comfortable mattresses were confiscated. There was no advance notice. The seizure was arbitrary and punitive. No prison objective was accomplished. Inmates get used to random cruelty perpetrated without logic.

. . .

Smoking cigarettes has been banned at Lompoc. Cartons, packs, even individual cigarettes used to be the inmate currency of exchange. Now U.S. postage stamps have taken the place of the cigarette as the coin of the realm.

If an inmate is caught with cigarettes, there are a number of possible sanctions: extra work assignments, suspended phone and/or commissary privileges, and the like. A popular young inmate was searched at his job and a few cigarettes were found. He was handcuffed at gunpoint by two guards and taken to the Hole.

. . .

About 20 inmates are assigned to assist the clean-up and maintenance of Vandenburg Air Force Base, which is a one-hour bus ride from camp. The inmates take bag lunches. Recently, four or five inmates filled out a form complaining that their lunches were deficient. When the complaints were considered by the administration, each complainant was placed in isolation and remained in the Hole for nine weeks. Their infraction was designated "inciting possible food riot or food strike."

. . .

In prison mentality, Judas exists in many roles. There's the informant who gets you arrested. There's the co-defendant who turns government witness and gets you convicted. There's the convicted inmate who names criminal suspects in exchange for a reduced sentence. And there's the jailhouse "rat" who snitches on fellow inmates. All these types are ostracized: sliced, stabbed, assaulted; clothes and bedding thrown out of the barracks; beds urinated on; shouts of "Rat-Rat" wherever one appears. Any kind of snitching in prison is reviled.

An inmate in a wheelchair, who'd been paralyzed by a drive-by gunshot, was taken into custody after a contraband cell phone was found on him. He knew that a rat had tipped the authorities on the phone. He was wheeled to the Hole.

The phone incident turned into a dormitory raid. The guards ordered all the inmates out of the barracks and searched each of us and our lockers. Dogs were brought in to smell for drugs. It was a show of force, overkill for a simple mobile-phone arrest.

Later that afternoon while I was watering, the camp administrator asked if I'd seen any cats around. They wanted to trap and remove all the strays. I knew where they were, but there was no way I'd inform on anything, not even on a cat!

. . .

At camp, fresh fruit is a rare luxury. Everyone knows that I help as much as I can with inmate legal problems, so on many occasions, I'm the recipient of the gift of an orange, banana, or peach.

The peaches come to me unripe and hard. I hide them in my locker under a white baseball cap. It takes about four days for them ripen. Then, they're juicy and sensuous. The juices spill down from my lips. The flavor impacts my taste buds with explosive force. I feel the vitamins buoying my health. For me, the peach is a sacrament. It connects me to the gracious lifestyle of the free outside.

. . .

A few of Tony's letters to me also reveal his state of mind and how he passed some time.

6/27/06
Paulette—

Greetings from Lompoc Prison Camp, a touch of Bolinas with a small wooden fence around it: eucalyptus trees, deer, raccoon, hawks, cranes, et al. Army-type barracks, a mess hall, a library, a chapel, and flowered gardens. Camp prisoners are non-violent, non-escape risk. We each have work assignments. I water lawns and flowers. I call myself the "River." Lots of time to read and write. I'm in the sun five hours a day; the routine is monotonous; my brain gets baked.

The inmates are fascinating—the camp is tolerable—the time will pass. My license will be restored in six months. When I get out, I have a murder trial already set to go!

My children and Vicki are adjusting to my absence, but the office is in shambles. We'll probably downsize considerably.

I'm losing weight, getting sunburned. My mind retrospects over my past lifetime. Law subordinates to sentiment. Thanks for your grand effort. I hope you are well.

My Best,
Tony

9/16/06
Paulette

Got your "Desert Landscape." Your art work adorns my gray barracks' cabinet wall (inside wall). Gives me a lift sometimes when the mind drips dreary.

I'm now four-tenths finished—it will be over soon. I'm leaner and stronger. I'm ready for my murder trial re-entry in March. I've had a sufficient "retreat"; I'm ripe to join the struggle once again.

I'm not having visitors, except for my children and professional visits. I don't like visits; they're disruptive for me. I don't like to see people in my prison green. Visits can pull my memory in nostalgic directions, which has an adverse affect. I'll be out soon— happy and strong—that's when I want to talk to friends!

Fondly,
Tony

1/13/07
Paulette

I have finally finished my writing objectives here at Camp. I've written two drafts of two books, both fictional, both amateurish, both good jail medication, but I did it! (I'll look at them again in six months, when I can be more objective.) Also, I've done about 50 poems and 50 "essays" on prison-camp insights, also in the amateurish category, but also good balm for monastic life.

I'm reading "Hegemony" that you sent; you were/are exceedingly generous in sending books. I didn't read them all, but other inmates did. I'll always fondly remember your gifts to me.

I'm in the San Francisco halfway house in less than a month! The uncaged tiger will attack!

Best,
Tony

2/10/07
Paulette

Thanks again and again for the books—just got another. The library here is enriched. What your generosity has done goes far beyond me personally!

My last epistle from exile! I'm wistful at departure: no more epicurean garden time; never again the freedom to pursue random literature and adolescent prose and poetry. Back to the delineation of the semantic warrior; blind focus; mindless fury; hot panting pursuit of elusive windmills!

See you or talk to you next time as a "free man!"
Tony

. . .

Tony sent me a few of the poems he wrote in prison. The following are a sampling.

Crushing Hope

I feed on man's poisons
His suffering and despair!
I sup on fear and trembling.
My expertise is terrorizing.
Punishing, giving pain and torture.

My art is deception and falsity.
I crush hope; I suck lives dry.
I specialize in revenge and retribution.
I am brutal and sadistic.
I am the Prison System.

Lawyer In Prison

For everyone who asked I did my best
It was my joy
I heard their case
Read their appeals
Helped write their writs.

I learned their secrets
I hated their judges and their prosecutors.
I gave my opinions, my advice.
I corrected spelling and grammar in their letters.
I increased their understanding of the law.
I consoled, I also grieved.

What can we pay you? they exclaimed.
Do you want cigarettes, or steaks, or postage stamps?
Can we wash your clothes, press your shirts?
What can we buy you from the commissary?

I responded I need nothing.
It is my joy to help.
But they gave me oranges
Because they knew
It was my favorite treat inside
And rarely provided to the inmate.

My locker now swells with oranges!

Faces

I see American Indian faces
I see black African faces
I see the faces of Europe, of Asia, even the faces of the South Pacific Islands.

I see young ignorant faces, I see wise faces
I see old faces, I see proud faces
I see the tough and the weak faces,
The faces of the defeated and the faces of the survivors.

All inmates with different bodies and minds
From different locations, different social and
Economic conditions; some educated, some not.

Many religions, many atheists, blue collar and white collar
Workers and executives, rich and poor;
All criminals, all smelted together in prison confinement.

Men who would never encounter one another
On the outside, living in a forced fusion.
Each one shaped by the strangeness of the other
Each accommodating the differences of the others;
Prison tempo pulsating through all.

The Not Guilty

We tread at a cadence
That hundreds have marched
For hundreds of years
From river to sea. We swarm, as
A tidal wave bursting upon
The false forums of injustice.
We walk with the dead, the dying

And the dead to come. We walk the prison circles.
We've been walking them for centuries;
Slain by lawyer and judge, buried alive by law and order
"Guilty" cried the jury.
"Not guilty" responds the marching voices
of the multitude of Not Guilty ghosts;
Toward the High Bench where
The black robed interrogators, buzzards perched for prey,
Administer their fatal oaths.
"Innocent" "Innocent" surge screams
of the wrongly convicted.
Their cries deluge the courthouse and
Swell destruction on its perfidy.

Prison Dimness

And the crows have no voice
And the sparrows no eyes.
The heart-beat of inmates hibernates
In endless gray dawns
Without sunrise,
Ash descending blinding and choking us.

The Birds Cage

Wild birds in a cage
Beating their wings against the bars.
Song birds in a cage
Sounding sweetly.
Wingless birds in a cage
Without memory of flight.
Dead birds in a cage
Shriveled and dry.

The Path Around The Prison

The prisoners walk the Ring of their confinement
Eyes forward, eyes down and eyes backward
Seeing nothing
No contrition, no remorse, no excuse.
Brazen Burly Bravado movement is their sustenance
Blinded eyes for freedoms of volition,
Past and future.
Posturing solely for the present in their trek.
Psychic shields and weapons discarded
Marching in a circle manly
Finding that the beginning and the end have joined.

The Long Termer

Twenty-seven years down
Gurgled the wide-eyed Boy
Now gray and wrinkled and withered.
His white-hot tears have flamed
Inwardly all this time
Bringing demise of hope and meaning.
Unnourished, his spirit has receded.
An automaton corpus is the residue.
Metal, brittle, mindless, enduring.
I scream wordlessly:
"Die, Vanish! You make Lepers of us all."
"You are a contagion."
But the Living Dead make no reply.

. . .

Tony Serra was released from his sentence on March 21, 2007. He held a press conference in his office on March 23, which I attended. True to promise, once his tiger was out of the cage, he *did* attack, this time with a new cause: suing over the low wages federal inmates earn. At the press conference, he cited the 19 cents an hour he received for watering the prison gardens and the five cents to $1.65 an hour other prisoners, whose work was much more arduous, were paid.

"I'm angry at a system that perpetuates, from my perspective, slave labor," he announced.

He also invoked federal labor law, insisting that it should entitle inmates to the federal minimum wage of $5.15 an hour (in 2007).

This news was covered extensively in the Bay Area, and even made the *International Herald Tribune.*

Chapter 17

The Double-Edged Sword

I had been amassing material about Tony for years. Piecing it all together became like quilting together parts of a dream, where the past
and the present merge in strange ways to create new kaleidoscopic patterns. This chapter is one of those.

. . .

"Let's go, Paulette! They're calling our flight!"

I was startled to hear Tony's commanding voice behind me at the
airport snack bar. We hadn't arrived at the airport together, but we
were scheduled to fly together to Salt Lake City, where he was keynote
speaker for a convocation of criminal-defense lawyers on the subject of
minorities. This speaking engagement cut into one of Tony's jury trials
and I wasn't sure if he'd make it.

I was dreading another teeth-gnashing no show/no call in my growing list of aborted rendezvous with Tony. Ducking out on me, and on
other appointments on his calendar, was part of his quirkiness; he has
a long track record of no shows of all sizes and levels of importance, as

evidenced with his contempt-of-court hearing for missing the opening of the drug-smuggling trial in Montana and subsequently failing to attend Gerry Spence's seminar in Wyoming. His office staff call it M.I.A.: missing in action.

Serra missed being guest speaker at a dinner because a jury probe ran way late into the night. He missed being the featured speaker on a radio show for court reasons and the program staff had to ad lib for an hour. He missed a pivotal hearing on the Sara Jane Olson case when he was held up at the airport. He attributed it to "bad karma." When I reserved my ticket, I asked his secretary, Stephanie Brown, if Tony would be on the plane to Utah for *sure*, to which she replied, "Never plan anything non-refundable with Tony Serra."

Not only was that not a comfort, I found it to be infuriating and frustrating as hell.

But there he was, straight out of the courtroom, looking rather frazzled, carrying only a small plastic backpack, all ready to go. His backpack was much smaller than my own carry-on shoulder bag into which I'd stuffed an overcoat for the chill of Salt Lake City in October, recording gear, camera equipment, my journal, a nightgown, and toiletries. I assumed he'd checked a larger bag at the ticket counter. But no, he assured me this was the way he always traveled, just this small blue-plastic backpack, whether he'll be gone for one night or six months.

"This bag's been everywhere," he proudly proclaimed.

The small size was deceptive; it was like a circus car that could produce an impossible number of clowns. He'd somehow compressed a fresh shirt for his speech and an entire casual outfit for the next day. Tony's mastery of the impossible, apparently, wasn't limited to the courtroom.

Traveling with Tony made me feel 10 feet tall. It was unprecedented to be invited to accompany him for a speech out of state. It was the first and only time he ever paid my way anywhere. I trotted along beside his large stride, barely able to contain my excitement. We found our seats and the plane rumbled down the tarmac for take off. Airborne with Tony Serra! Finally, uninterrupted time with him to discuss matters of this book.

But just as I turned to him to speak, I discovered Tony had once again "vanished," disappearing into his own world of thought. He took out a folded piece of cardboard, recycled from the packaging of his laundered shirts, and began scribbling notes for his speech that evening. These recycled shirt cardboards also served him in court in place of a yellow legal pad. They're larger than pads, but not too large. It was all part of Tony's ethic not to be wasteful or to use anything new. He filled the cardboard with his hieroglyphs, then fell sound asleep without a word. I was miffed. I felt as though I'd been left watching another long-awaited opportunity vanish before my eyes.

When we arrived at the airport in Utah, the person scheduled to meet us wasn't there. That's when I discovered that in Tony's world of practicalities, traveling with him included being his "gofer," the person who attends to all the little stuff.

He reached into his pocket and produced a fistful of loose change, urging me to make the contact call. I remembered that a reluctance to place telephone calls was one of his quirks. Even at home, he delegated other members of his family to place his calls for him, the residue of someone who has a staff of people doing his bidding.

I thought that because he'd invited me to the speech in Salt Lake City, there'd be some sort of exchange and interaction, that I could get answers to questions long ignored, but again, I found out differently. He had his own agenda and it was up to me to find my footing in it. At the same time, because of his anti-establishment attitude regarding credit cards and photo ID, I was the one who had to run interference in order for him to remain "pure" to this dysfunctional stance.

A lavish dinner preceded the program. The buffet was a carnivore's dream feast, filled with meats of all descriptions: roasted, fried, grilled, and layered in rich gravies, adorned with tufts of parsley and candied fruit. A plump pig had been roasted for the occasion and lay on its gourmet gurney in a prayer position, its flesh still crackling. Tony, a vegetarian, stood with an empty plate.

Prior to his speech, I carefully positioned my tape recorder on the speaker's podium for later transcription. I had gone to the out-of-pocket expense of purchasing a top-of-the-line new cassette recorder for the occasion. Tony repositioned it underneath the podium beside his feet. All that was audible was the stomping and shuffling of his lively feet. Not a word was decipherable. But what did imprint upon me was how infuriating and difficult and impossible he could be to work with. This trip gave me plenty of time and opportunity to reflect on his impossible side. I reflected on his ducking-out factor; it would be understandable if he ever bothered to call, but no. Then there was the not-returning-phone-calls factor, which, given that he has a staff of people with telephones, seemed to me an unnecessary sign of disrespect. Then there was the missing-important-appointments factor, of which there was a shocking array. They accumulated like parking tickets. Then there was his disappearing into his private world at the expense of social convention. I wondered what other dark spaces filled his most personal closet, so I threw out a net to see what information I could dredge up.

I found that regardless of what opinions or personal affronts people had about Tony, no one wanted to go public with stabbing him in his underbelly. Everyone, regardless of how they felt about him personally, respected him above all.

So, seizing this opportunity to tweak his guilt, I asked him to reveal the flaws in his own vessel. I asked him to talk about the issues that had most frustrated and eluded me: the arrogance of not respecting anyone's time but his own; his refusal to forgive; his tendency to excommunicate people with one swift slice of his iron judgment; the reasons he chooses the cases he does; and his drug use.

In other words, I asked him to go belly-up on himself.

In this soul-searching exposé, the warrior's sword, which cuts to the quick in the courtroom, appears to have a double edge. Here the sword attacks the warrior himself, stripping away the mystique and exposing what lies beneath. It's rare enough for a person in power to have such introspective vision, but it's rarer still for that person to openly admit to his deficits, and rarest of all for such a person to go public with this information.

I find his bald-faced honesty a strength and a revelation.

· · ·

"My overwhelming ego probably is my central religious failing. Although I respect, intellectually, the concept of selflessness, I can interpret everything I do as an ego trip. For the most part, I seek high-publicity cases, and this is obviously to feed my need for publicity and self-aggrandizement. Even most of the free cases I do offer some kind of publicity factor, media attention, or psychological hedonism; they bestow upon me what I'm going to call self-centered, egocentric, egotistic, and selfish motivation.

"I have a nouveau-riche office. I, the street lawyer who espouses non-materialism, am dripping in what I would call redundant images of prosperity: the grandiose hotel-lobby atmosphere, token images of adversarial causes for poor people while I abide in splendor, and the normal images of material prosperity." (As I reflected on the Pier 5 Law Offices on the Embarcadero, it was my understanding that for once the spacious comfort factor was chosen so that the *staff* and other lawyers wouldn't be so ridiculously cramped. For once, I thought, Tony was thinking of the needs of others, not just himself and his own image.)

"I need to be the center, I'm the show-off, the cock of the walk. I have all the deficits of the peacock, of the conceit.

"Even my old clothes and old cars and modest living habits are a way of gaining attention. They're a way of saying, 'I'll be more humble than you. I'll manifest a greater degree of humility. Therefore, *look at me.*'

"Basically, one who publicly professes non-materialism, as I do, then goes public and says, 'I'm the first lawyer to have a marijuana prescription,' even issuing a press release—you *know* that this is all basic nourishment for a self-centered egomaniac!"

. . .

"My arrogance, the sin and the vice, basically comes in two forms. First, I'm excessively judgmental. Though I profess relativity and empathy and compassion for all value systems and lifestyles, I, in the interior of my mind, have a very adolescent, rigid, moral structure. And it's very traditional, very conservative.

"One of these values is that the pursuit of knowledge, either through direct experience or study and education, is a superior path. The work ethic and self-discipline and the sacrifice that comes with them are a superior path. Fine arts, poetry, sculpture, and drama are a higher path. I publicly support the common man, the breadth of humanity as it comes from the lower classes and vitalizes the upper structures, but I have these beliefs that, for the most part, pertain to the establishment. Those outside the establishment, whom I serve, don't have these kinds of values. And so, down deep, I'm in *judgment* of the very persons and ideas that I publicly claim to serve.

"I'm cynical. I've been around the block and I think I know it *all*. I have little patience for inferior minds. I have little respect for materialists and those who don't respect that the true meaning of life is the pursuit of, say, a poetic lifestyle. I, like Karl Marx, love humanity, but *hate* mankind. It's a form of arrogance that isolates me, estranges me. I will talk the social talk and walk the social walk, but I feel deeply that somehow I'm *different* and *stronger* and more *perspicacious* than the norm, and this is an arrogance that colors my life.

"Once again, it's the image of the peacock on the walk, thinking down real deep how defiled the rest of humanity is for not having the flamboyant colors of his feathers."

· · ·

"Being busy, too busy, is my condition, my status, my karma. I'm too busy for all the street people and the outcasts and the rejected that I have an image of serving. I get twenty to fifty calls a day: I don't return them. People call and I don't even know what they're calling about or who they are. I don't have time to read my letters; I have to delegate them out.

"And so I've become too involved, too wrapped up in my ego, in my trial work, in my media, in my projection through speeches, to tend to the flock, to the people who have given me their lives and their ideas and off of whom I have become—let's just say—an icon. And I thereby *betray* them. I'm too busy for their cases, those poor people, too busy for the madness of their ideas, too busy to shake hands with them on the street and sit in alcoves and talk the crazy talk of the street people. I have cut myself off from my roots. I am spinning wildly in the skies; I'm falling and floating at the same time. Too busy! Too busy!"

. . .

"I *always* make a strength out of weaknesses. That's the way I approach my cases: The infirmity in the case has to be projected as the *strength*, as the core defense of the case. I do that in terms of my own drug addiction as well.

"I'm a marijuana addict. Like a cigarette addict, I want my marijuana *every day*. It pacifies me. In my subjective foolery, I believe that it stimulates my imagination and inspires my intellect. Well, that's what *all* drug addicts say.

"I know I've lost touch with the central core of humanity, because I'm filled with the flowers and bursting colors and harmonies of the psychedelic realm. Most of my mind lives in that realm and slips only sparsely and painfully into the realm of the law and the pain and suffering of the law. So I'm two-thirds abstracted in the psychedelic paradise, which is *the* self-serving definition of addiction. All addicts sing the same song. I brag about my past use of cocaine and methamphetamine, and I'll brandish my marijuana smoking before the world. But down deep, I practice with the divided mentality of a drug addict."

. . .

"I'm *not* filled with poetry. I'm *not* filled with drama and sculpture and fine literature. I *am* filled with pathology and sociopathology. I'm filled with sociopaths, madness, and the crazy aberrational behavior of my clients. I court the defense of 'not guilty by reason of insanity.' I court, for my alleged inspiration, the mad perspective of drug addicts. I court, in short, *aberrance*. I'm filled with aberrance. I devour aberrance. I, therefore, *am* aberrance. Aberrance *breeds* aberrance!

"If you only absorb what is absurd, rejected, insane, misfit; if you live on the mishap, on the unfortunate, on the crisis; if you feed with the carrion-devouring beak on the maladies and misfortunes of others, then you *are* that! You're no more or no less than what you empirically absorb. Down deep, I'm all the negative attributes of behavior and humanity.

That's the core of me. It won't ever be higher than that, and that core encases me in the false perspective. In reality, I'm blind.

"Some of the saddest words ever spoken to me came from my ex who said, 'You give more time to those weirdoes and crazies and drug addicts than you do to your family and me.'

"Yes, I court that dimension because I'm metaphysically sullied. In my opinion, that's the greatest indictment that I can bring upon myself."

"You're lyin' aren't cha!"

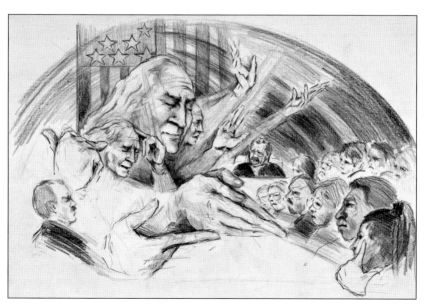

"Feel the condition so you know how this thing erupted."

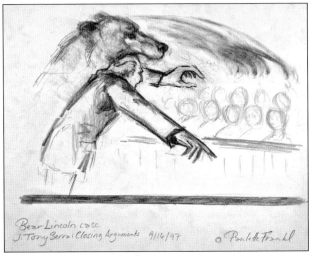

Bear Lincoln case
J. Tony Serra: Closing Arguments 9/16/97   © *Paulette Frankl*

Bear Lincoln case
J. Tony Serra defense
Closing Arguments   *9/16/97*   © *Paulette Frankl*

Bear Lincoln   *9/03/97*   *Paulette Frankl©*

Bear Lincoln

Lucille Lincoln   © *Paulette Frankl '97*

Lucille Lincoln

J. Tony Serra   Richard Serra

Brownie Mary

Espenal case
J. Tony Serra, defense
© Paulette Frankl

The Face of Madness

Cordova case   1/03/95   © Paulette Frankl

Barbir Singh Dolly case -
J. Tony Serra: defense: closing arguments   11/03/94   © Paulette Frankl

"This is all a mental shipwreck. This was a proud man who wanted respect . . . This is the setting: into this setting comes the bankruptcy that propels the situation into madness . . . it's anger and then it's PAIN. He was a swirling whirlwind of fragmentory thoughts. The heat of passion has turned into a WILDFIRE! And it has tossed him over the side." J.T.S.

"Sometimes people push you to the edge of the cliff, and then they look to see if you are going to fall over by yourself or if you'll take them with you!"

J. Tony Serra
Dr. Jeffrey Gutstadt -
Dohang case   5/10/95   © Paulette Frankl

Ellie Nesler case
J. Tony Serra : defense : Closing Arguments 5 August 1993 Paulette Frankl©

Ellie Nesler case
Ellie Nesler & J. Tony Serra 5 August 1993 Paulette Frankl©

"Her mind is in a swirl; she asks for a sign from God."

"She's going crazy. She's out of her mind. The boat is set adrift and it's going toward the falls!"

"Whatever happens, know that I'll always love you." —Ellie Nesler

Defeat

United States of America v. J. Tony Serra   11 July 1994   © Paulette Frankl
Palmer Hoovestol: Defense: Opening Statements

United States of America v. J. Tony Serra   12 July 1994   © Paulette Frankl
Gerry Spence: witness for defense
Palmer Hoovestol: defense

"A lawyer is like a captian of a ship. If the captain is ordered off his ship by the Port Authority to go on another ship, that ship is lost. If the lawyer leaves during deliberations he would be in trouble with his client, he would be in trouble with the Bar, and he would be in trouble with his *soul*!

"A judge has an obligation to keep his calendar moving, but not at the expense of justice, and not at the expense of the constitutional rights of anybody. And that judge knew that, or should have known it." —Gerry Spence

Dr. Michael Baden, witness

Tim Boileau, witness

"We have offended Caesar, the royalty of the casino!"

L to R: Lucille Lincoln, Paulette Frankl, Bia

L to R: Bernadette Zambrano, Diana Samuelson

Below Left: Left, Tony Serra; Right, Samantha Burkey, Investigator

L: Diana Samuelson, co-counsel in death-penalty cases

Center and below: Serra's office on Pier 5 of the Embarcadero

Penelope Rose (left), Stephanie Brown

Serra's apartment in North Beach

Office Halloween party

Paulette Frankl

Chapter 18

Beneath the Armor

Years had passed since my first encounter with Tony Serra in court. We had reached a familiarity and a comfort level with each other, so I invited him to come to my cabin in Bolinas, the small hippie town in west Marin County, north of San Francisco, where he spent weekends and I lived full-time.

Bolinas is a peninsula of land jutting out into the ocean, known as the place that time forgot, famous for its absence of road signs leading to it and the handmade lifestyle of its creative residents. Like the uncharted dirt roads of this off-beat town, I wanted to plumb the remaining depths of the Serra soul. Admitting his weaknesses had been a start, but I wanted to enter his uncharted areas, his forbidden territory.

My handmade cabin was very small, while Tony Serra was very large, both in stature and personality. I imagined the effect to be something like Gulliver visiting a Lilliputian.

The appointed hour came and went, and I wondered if I was going to be stood up, again. Then, suddenly, my garden gate swung open and I could hear Tony's familiar loud voice. "Paulette!"

He bent down to clear the low-hanging honeysuckle vines that created a fragrant passageway of flowers to my door. He entered my sunroom with an outburst of flattery and good cheer, obviously relaxed from his day away from the office and the stresses of his trial schedule. I expected my cats to go straight up the walls in his bombastic presence, but they didn't wake from their morning naps; they never twitched an ear or a whisker, attesting to Serra's inner comfort level. It was immediately apparent that Tony was a man truly at home in the country.

I smiled inwardly to note that he'd bothered to dress in his Sunday "best"—an old but clean pair of tattered white jeans mended at the knee with silver duct tape and a psychedelic Grateful Dead T-shirt. He looked boyish and fresh. He settled into the one comfortable chair in the room. I felt awkward turning this pleasant occasion into an interview, but Tony gave no indication of being annoyed. I gave him a cup of good, strong, homemade espresso and a joint and we were ready to roll.

"By nature," he began, seeming to start up where we'd left off, "I'm egotistic, self-centered, domineering, obsessive, and vain. Yet these are the qualities, shallow as they may be, that allow me to dominate in court."

"You've fused your image with that of a warrior," I said. "How does the warrior in you deal with the issues that this book addresses in your own life?"

Seeing him sitting so relaxed, so comfortably stoned in my cabin, nothing could be further removed from the warrior image at that moment. I was surprised that he could straddle the two paradigms at all, but he's a master at "spacing out" while keeping both feet on the ground, never losing touch with the reality at hand.

"This is how I justify it. If a warrior wants to propagate an ideology, he can disseminate the ideas that sustain his vision and his view. He may hope or even believe that this will change perspectives, add an increment to evolution, so he will speak to all those reasons that he fights in order, ultimately to effect reform, to change society.

"A lawyer in court, as a warrior, is doing the same thing. A warrior is seeking to make his ideology prevail over his antagonist's ideology.

"A warrior should have no interest in a book whatsoever. A warrior is involved in his battles. A book is for the edification or recreation of its readers. That said, through books, television, radio—it's not merely an ego trip that I involve myself in these things. They're all direct avenues to the collective mentality of society, and I want this ideology at least to be *available* in the marketplace of ideas. So I think that's the way that I, as a semantic warrior in court, justify making presentations in other media."

Tony seemed to be into the flow of his self-expression, so I pushed on, going a little deeper. "Many of your clients face murder charges. Some are looking at the death penalty. You've said that you're 'in denial' about death. You don't attend funerals, not even of those people who are close to you, such as your parents. How do you deal with your own physical mortality, your own physical frailty? How do you look upon death?"

Outside, the sun was pouring a glorious bright warmth through the foliage of trees, birds were chirping, and it was a rare and perfect day for the beach. This line of questioning seemed so out of context to the now, so contradictory to this setting and to this moment. But Tony graciously indulged me with his intense focus on my issues.

"I'm not in denial about death. I'm in denial about *aging*," Tony replied. "Aging, I guess, is the first shroud, the first fog, of death. It's an announcement of death, but it's *aging*, not death.

"As a warrior in a courtroom, every time I lose, I *die*. I die! I've been completely rejected, and everything that I've tried to do is in ashes, and I'm a depressed failure. These are symbolic deaths, but they're also very real. The fascinating thing is—and it's almost Hindu, almost Buddhist— the only way I can experience rebirth, the only time I can find my life's viability again, is through another case. I'm reborn in the next case. And there I may come to fruition or I may die *again!* And then, once again, out of the flame I arise. So it's kind of like the wheel of Samsara: We go through many *many* lifetimes, sometimes triumphant, a warrior-prince, and other times, death! Death and dishonor, disdain and misfortune. It's fabulous! I've died many times. I've been reborn many times. A warrior as a lawyer is reborn with each new case and he dies if that case results in conviction. That's one part of it.

"The next part is, how do I look upon death? Death is the narcotic! As a child, my greatest fantasy, what I really wanted to be—and once I was lithe and slender—was a bullfighter! And that's *exactly* what I'm doing in court, because my cases are very difficult. What I'm mostly noted for is taking the impossible cases. Every case I do nowadays is impossible. I win sometimes, I hang more times, but I lose most of the time. So like the bullfighter, I'm courting *death*. The bulls are large. And they don't have just two horns, they've got 24 horns! They're coming at me without being shot up with morphine. This is what gives me the *rush!*

"Who wants to be a prosecutor? They win most of the time. It's courting *death* that's exciting. It's courting the impossible dream of life, knowing that you're in the death throes. That's the narcotic that burns my psyche. A criminal-defense lawyer is always in the internal raw meat of the human condition. There's some kind of a masochistic thrill to it.

"To be a semantic warrior, a trial warrior, you've got to be hooked on the courting of death. I think it's like being a surgeon in the emergency room of a New York or some big-city hospital. The bodies roll in hour after hour in death throes. That's the narcotic that burns my psyche. A surgeon operates five times a night. Some are going to live and some are going to die, but the surgeon/lawyer is always up to his elbows in the blood, in the internal raw meat of the human condition. Some are dying as you sew them, but some are *living!* It's like that. We deal with death. For a warrior, death is a part of his everyday existence. Death *is* life!

"Think of the warriors of olden times. They went into battle. They knew most of them would die. Maybe one-tenth of them didn't die, but they saw their brothers dying. That's what I see every day in terms of jury trials and criminal cases."

All this up-to-the-elbows in blood and raw meat was vivid and real, happening in my living room, my one safe haven on Earth. Tony was clearly oblivious to his surroundings at this point, so I tried to sustain the spell.

"You've made the issue of freedom a driving force in your life," I said. "Freedom from imprisonment, freedom from confinement is your number-one priority, and you place its importance above that of family needs and love relationships, above everything except the health crises of your children. What drives you so hard to prioritize your life and compromise your family in this manner?"

Tony paused in his reply, as though he were turning a page in his thoughts, then replied in a slow and gravelly voice, serious and searching, a voice from the deep that he seemed to pull out of some unlit cave of profundity.

"I would like to say that my loyalty to my ideas, to my idealism, is so consuming, that I am so dedicated, that it is a platonic love of the first order: I will secure liberty and the metaphors of liberty for humanity. I'd like to say that it's some kind of a religion for me, like I'm a latter-day Sir Lancelot. This dedication comes first and everything else has to feed into that. I want to say that, I *want* to believe that. I'd love for other people to believe it."

Now, gaining momentum and levity, he added, "But this is what I truly think: I'm born that way! I've often thought that if I were a potato farmer, I'd have the same zest and commitment for what I do. I would say, 'Look! These potatoes symbolize easy, accessible, and economic nutriment for a whole culture.' I would get up early in the morning and hoe my rows and clean my potatoes. I would work Saturdays and Sundays. These potatoes are the most significant thing in my life, and everything has to funnel into them. My potato farm is good for everyone, there's nothing wrong with it, I don't capitalize on it, and good potatoes could save the Earth!

"I know I would be like that! I'm born with a zest or—I don't know what it is, a blindness on the other side—a belief that *what I do is important*. If I'm doing my homework as a child, *that's* the most important thing. Don't come bothering me. If I'm practicing baseball, *that's* the most important thing. If I'm walking the beach, I don't want to talk to anyone. *I'm* walking the beach. I'm thinking.

"I think it's in the nature of the person. Some people are obsessive and they forge that obsession with their life's work, their careers, their profession. Not everyone has that obsession. Some people have family obsessions. Some have artistic obsessions. But my obsession is my work, and my work, thankfully, in my feeling, helps people. It doesn't hurt people. And therefore it's a good obsession.

"Certainly, in many moments of my life, I'm sorry that I've sacrificed other things. Here's the hardest thing in my life: I've chosen not to make money. I've chosen not to be a materialistic, capitalistic, exploitative person. I've chosen to do a lot of pro bono cases. Early in my career, I did almost all pro bono. I still do a significant number. But when the fucking first of the month comes around, I can't pay any of my bills. I can't pay my rent. I don't have money to send to my kids. I'm behind in everything.

Then I get this little twinge that this *obsession* may well do me in! I always have my doubts about my priorities, but I can't evade them."

"Do you consider that a weakness, a flaw, in your character?"

"A warrior's life, his very existence, is predicated on winning, in battle and in court. You lose, you're dead. Weaknesses would betray me and ultimately create my downfall and demise. So, as a warrior, I cannot tolerate, if that's the word, weaknesses. That doesn't mean I don't have a lot of them. But I fear my weaknesses. I avoid my weaknesses. Hopefully, I overcome my weaknesses.

"Let me give you the scope of my weaknesses. I have a hunch they're the same or similar to weaknesses in everyone.

"First weakness: I don't work hard enough. I should work harder. If I were truly obsessed, I'd be ten times more disciplined in absorbing the material that I must master for trial. I'm real good, I'm real fast, I've got a good mind, I have a good memory, so what I do ultimately is like studying for a final exam: I get in there, I book in, and I've got it. But my weakness is one that will be voiced by any obsessed individual, that I'm not working hard enough and I'm wasting too much time."

He continued, "Another weakness is that I have real sentiment. That is, I get sad and angry. Those things manifest in court and they're not an act, they're not trumped up, and they're not phony or a sham. Well, that's a weakness, because the warrior must have many masks. The law, in the court context, is performance art at one level. And if the prosecution sees the true me beneath the performance, beneath the argument, beneath the courtroom decorum, then I'm vulnerable. I cry. I get angry. I get passionate. I blow it and go over the edge. In other words, I'm *vulnerable*. I've got to shield myself from their gaze. I've got to be sure they can never get to the inner core of me. I hold that aloof. That's not for them. My strength is in the mystery of the inner core. That's what makes the prosecution fear my presence. I have real sentiment.

"Sometimes that's real good for the juries, but it's also a weakness. Emotions are a weakness. Emotions should be anchored by reason. Emotions cannot be allowed to fly on their own. I'm not talking about on love's couch; I'm talking about in battle, in court, where there's life and death in an engagement between two sides that are enemies.

"I'll give you another weakness that has slowly emerged in the last fifteen years. Call it compassion for the other side. Everything has a psychiatric explanation. As I began to understand behavior, to see the causal connections among life, upbringing, environment, and ultimate behavior, I began to forgive the prosecutor, forgive the snitch, to understand the plight of the narc—all that kind of stuff. We're assassins. We try to slit the throats of our enemies at every opportunity. Once compassion and understanding and forgiveness seep into my mentality, it's over! I may not want to hurt the snitch as much as he should be hurt; in my cross-examination I may not want to pin him down and grind him and beat him into submission. When I extend compassion to the enemy, it's high spiritually, but it's a weakness in the heat of battle that can cause failure or demise.

"I probably have a zillion other weaknesses, and it's probably better that someone other than I talk about them. It's easy to shield ourselves from our weaknesses. They become black holes, and we don't even see them anymore."

•　•　•

Once Tony gets on a roll, I can hardly believe my ears as to what he divulges about himself. People want dirt about Tony Serra, but it seems to me that his own vivisection is much deeper than any second-hand gossip anyone else could produce. It elicits a feeling in me to protect him from himself, his own worst enemy. But instead, I ruthlessly pushed onward.

"Crime stems from people not being able to, or not knowing how to, cope with the dark forces of their emotions, commonly called their demons. These psychological elements of crime stem from anger, jealousy, hatred, envy, and revenge, as you expounded on in Chapter 8. How do you deal with these dark forces in your personal life?"

Tony candidly answered, "These kinds of confessions lack insight, because we all guard ourselves from self-knowledge, especially in these areas. But I just wrote an article in which I said, 'I really *hate* racism, police transgressions, laws that oppress poor people ...'—things like that. I got a letter from some D.A. who had read it and was trying to be compassionate and make me feel better, who said, 'Mr. Serra, you should let go of these hates. You'll be happier or bigger for it. Good luck!'

"I then had to think about it some more, and this is my self-image: I have no hate, no anger, no jealousy, no revenge, none of these demons that you talk about."

Whoa! Didn't he just say he was riddled with them and that he guarded against revealing them? Didn't he just say he vented his anger in court? I put aside my mental edit and listened to what he had further to say.

"I was a jock all my life and then a lawyer, which is the same kind of thing; it's kind of a competition with win-or-lose imagery. And as a jock, I only lost it twice, giving vent to uncontrollable anger, where you just lose it and you start going after the other person. I never lost it in boxing or baseball and I've never lost it in law. So perhaps there are demons that I don't see in the darkness of Plato's cave. I do know that I've only seen them pop out twice in anger and those were adolescent football emotions. I'm pretty cool.

"The only other time in my life when I was a little bit off-balance in the realm of human emotions was when Mary Edna (the mother of Serra's five children) split from me. I guess I felt unhappy, sad, kind of broken. But that didn't manifest in any heavy *action*. I mean, I didn't do anything. I probably snorted a bit too much cocaine at that stage, but that didn't get me into any really negative conduct. But I felt *emotion*."

"How interesting! Here you're known for your wild expressions of emotion in court, yet you're almost denying feeling it flat out."

"As a semantic warrior, you have to carry the emotions of your clients. You have to convey those emotions. You have to manifest their rage and their fears and their protests and their defiances. It's almost like being an actor. Let's say an actor knows Shakespeare really well. Well, part of him *is* Shakespeare. I used to think that I was Walt Whitman. I read everything there was of Whitman and I got into the spirit of the man and I *felt* him. I'm sure a part of me believed that I *was* Walt Whitman. So, I take on the emotions of my clients: I *become* their anger."

"How can you become something that you've never *felt*? I don't buy that."

"We're talking about my self-image. It's all subjective: instinctually, intuitively, I have been a Platonist. When I sit down and think about it in my rational pragmatic mind, I can't be a Platonist: It's almost like a religion in postulating realms of perfection beyond the grasp of mortal humans and I don't accept that kind of a theme. Instead, my theme is empirically based. When our experience ends, then our existence ends. But that's rational.

"Like I said, I'm an intuitive Platonist. An intuitive Platonist, through the observation of multiple projections or manifestations of a notion or idea, can learn, understand, fulfill that generic idea.

"Let's take sadness. Better yet, let's take rage. I know rage better than a person who rages knows it, even though I never have rage, which, in fact, I don't. But you think you know rage? Oh, you've had a little bit. You think this guy over here, who rages like an animal, knows rage? Well, he knows it a little bit. What I've done, empirically, is enter the realm where I've picked up rage! I've interviewed thousands! I've felt their rage! I've shot up their rage. A Platonist makes inferences and deductions from the available data: I have a greater Platonic grasp of the ideal, the idea, the notion of rage than those who rage! And that's because I *am* a Platonist, and I'm an *intuitive* Platonist."

My artist's eye envisioned a man cut off just below the neck with his head mouthing one thing and his truncated body flailing and raging another.

"So don't tell me that just because I don't rage, I don't know rage. I know rage more in depth—I know the corners of it, the mysteries of it— more than those people who sit in the corner and rage.

"To answer your question: How do the demons affect me? For me, they're not demons. For me, they're fascinating facets of human experience, of human behavior, that I utilize by projecting the applicable ones to a jury. That's part of the lawyer-performer. The lawyer is the conveyor of the client's feelings and emotions, because the client doesn't have the knowledge or experience to do it on his or her own. I'm not crippled by these dark forces and demons."

His clients are often murderers and drugged-out maniacs, so he certainly does have quite a big proxy party going on inside him.

I softened my line of questioning. "I think that a lot of these dark emotions can be boiled down to an insecurity of some sort, and in the time that I've known you, some years now, I haven't seen you feel insecure about much of anything. Self-deprecating, yes, but insecure, no."

Tony jumped right in. "Where I feel insecure doesn't necessarily relate to my behavior. This is where I chose the wrong path. I'm a cop-out, I've compromised, and I guess I'm envious, and I'm feeling guilt, which is the next topic. All my life I've had a pretty good mind. I was always a top student. I had an academic calling. I understood things that people didn't understand; like I said previously, I really 'knew' Walt Whitman. I had a grace or a gift in that respect.

"Going into law and dropping so many notches down to the warrior image meant giving up the particular grace I had, let's say, for interpreting poetry and philosophy. I surrendered all of that. I'm now nothing but a semantic sword! For me it's not demons but guilt, unfulfilled destiny, the path not chosen, that I mentally revisit. I chastise myself for not being purer or more perfect. I chastise myself for being intrigued by the world of sensation and sensorium, for living in the fast lane in the neon-light jungle, for courting the more vicious experiences of life, dropping into drugs and living at the edges of my sensations, encapsulating them as my universe.

"That's all a fall from grace. That means I'm going to have to be reborn and reborn. That means I *devolved*. I didn't *evolve*. I *rejected* the path that had been given to me as a form of enlightenment. I rejected it! You know, it's *easy* to go backward, easy to devolve, easy, in some kind of a Hindu or Buddhist universe, to become the ant and the spider and the frog. That's what I did. I went back. I retreated to the warrior. No difficulty there. I'm not going to encounter too many things that are so profound that I'm smitten or stunned by them. So dipping my little mental finger into other people's emotions and projecting them is child's play, really. I had the capacity once to be a philosophy professor. So that's the path not chosen."

．　．　．

One of my personal concerns in working on this book with Tony Serra was that I might step on his proverbial toes, in some way offend his sense of righteousness, and thus be ejected to kingdom come. It wouldn't be the first time he's done that. I took this opportunity to get to the bottom of that issue: "It's known that you're quick to excommunicate anyone from your life who crosses you. What do you have against forgiveness?"

Tony took a deep breath before answering this question, as if to re-structure his thought pattern.

"OK. Let me tell you. We talked about hate. As a warrior, I must carry hate. It's one of my banners. But *I* don't really have hate. As a *warrior,* I have hate. As a warrior, then, here's the credo with respect to for-giveness: You do not forget and you do not forgive. Never! Never! Never! And I'm very mindful of these fucking snitch lawyers who are sometimes my allies and my friends and my colleagues and when they roll someone, I've always got my eye on them. I don't forgive them for rolling someone and I don't forget.

"Remember, the warrior is forged from a fundamental premise that his life is always in jeopardy and that at any minute he can be defeated and killed. That's what the germ of it is. The contemporary term for this is paranoia, but it's really not that. You've got to be highly in tune with the natural selective forces if you're going to survive. Remember, war-riors don't survive. They live short lives. They return to their family on their shield and are, in principle, respected. Like war veterans."

"What about forgiveness in your personal life?" I asked.

"Forget personal life. To raise your kids, you must forget and forgive. When I'm at my highest level, it's easy to understand, to appreciate, that with wisdom, one could understand how things occur, that is, taking into account all of the causative factors, all of the karmic factors, all of the random factors. You can see it.

"Ordinarily, we're looking at a piece of the puzzle, just one little tiny piece. Does it look green? Does it fit on the end? We don't even know. But there comes a point where you see all the pieces in harmony or in unity, and therefore you see the form of the whole.

"I can appreciate that there are religious and philosophic people who can reach that stage, people who are called 'enlightened' in the East. And I can appreciate that, at this stage there would be no moral judg-ment, no goods or bads. It's a fact of nature that raccoons eat chickens. Well, from the perspective of a chicken, that's a terrible thing. From the perspective of a raccoon—let's say a pregnant one—it's the guiding force of her life. So there's this relativistic perspective of these emotions.

"Forgiveness implies a perceived transgression. Well, at a higher level there are no such things as transgressions. I'm going to use an analogy to explain this 'no-transgression' point. You're at the symphony. The musicians are tuning their instruments. The orchestra is about to start. There's a dissonant sound. The chair of the violinist slips, and just as the orchestra begins there is this sudden *screech*. A terrible screech! Oh! That's bad! That's dissonance. That's invasion. That sound is tyranny.

"I'm trying to draw an analogy to social and political levels in a way we don't ordinarily think of. In this instance, could you forgive? Probably with understanding, you'd rise to a position where you'd say, 'Look, even though the violinist destroyed the harmony of the moment—it was ghastly; it just destroyed the fabric of the event—we see that it wasn't really his fault, because the chair fell over.' We can try to decide whether or not that's karma. After all, *he* was in the chair; someone else wasn't. But you'd sense that, in the overall picture, he would be innocent of the dissonance—the discord, the disharmony, that he perpetrated on his group. You'd understand that it was a random thing in which his volition, as we see volition, wasn't involved. And you'd forgive.

"That's my personal view. I can rise to that level, where there's no *reason* to forgive. Everything is seen in its causal relationship. You see the god Shiva. The act of destruction is *the act* of creativity. I see the yin-yang. So in my higher moments, I *believe* in that concept and therefore I forgive everything. Or what proceeds that is that there's nothing to forgive. The perceived transgression is *only* an illusion. Everything is *always* in perfect harmony. Everything is always *totally* explicable."

•   •   •

Returning to the microcosm of issues that I can relate to, I brought Tony back to square one. "A warrior's life is highly principled, highly self-centered. Yet you're a family man and you've always been in partnership with a woman. How do you deal with the foibles and needs of family life and relationships?"

He was quick to answer. "We all have foibles. Family, relationships, those are my foibles. A warrior *qua* warrior should have no family, because he must devote himself to each battle and he must die, thus he's the worst kind of family man. Even a sailor on the high seas who visits his family every three years could be considered better than a warrior, because the warrior is out there 'killing' symbolically. He comes back to a family that completely contradicts the state of mind and the behavior that he has to manifest. It's not good for the children.

"I think the statistics show that good trial lawyers are isolated and most of the time, in the common parlance, they're fucked up! They're so focused on their own little world that they don't have anything left over for anyone else. And what the warrior usually does is suck them into his trip, because that's all there is for him, and he devours them, he exploits them, he cannibalizes them.

"*My* sojourns into domesticity—children and the women in my life— are, for a warrior, an aberration, a self-contradiction, a *definite* limitation and weakness. But I never purported to be, I don't know, the Platonic definition of a warrior. I'm very weak, or whatever you want to call it. What really happens to most of us is we get used to the affections and associations of a woman and family *before* we evolve to warrior status, before we're cognizant that we're warriors.

"Maybe at *this* stage of my life, when I realize what the main thrust of my life has been, in retrospect I can say it was wrong, and a limitation, and a self-indulgence. But I don't recommend judging one state of mind by a different state of mind. I don't think it means much to say 'I erred' in hindsight. What it means is that in a later stage of life, I'm focusing on something else."

. . .

Going for one last probe, I presented this question. "Your role is to use the power of your words as your weapon and your armor. If you were stripped of this role, what would remain?"

Tony responded, "I think I understand what you mean. Stripped of the semantics of argument, or the semantics of conflict, who would I be? This is a concept that I haven't really visited at all, but I've run into it. The word *logos* comes to mind. It's a Greek word, translated in the Bible as 'In the beginning was the word.' Logos means language.

"Now, this leads me to believe that, metaphysically, logos is the substratum of existence. Remember that I'm a self-made Platonist, so what would that mean to me as a Platonist? It means that the only way we have of identifying the 'ideal,' the perfect forms, is to circumscribe them semantically.

"For example, what is *good*? The only way we're going to be able to discuss the meaning of good is through verbal communication. It wasn't always so. Tribal people, labeled 'savages,' might voice sounds to welcome the sunrise. To us this sounds like yelling and screaming; to them it means *good*. They're communicating through their chanting the concept of the 'good' symbolized in the rising sun.

"We in the Western world, and in many parts of the world, are channeled into semantics. It's my impression that logos, or the metaphysical substratum of language—words, verbiage, symbols, metaphors—is very close to what is basic, fundamental, ontological existence. We look into ourselves; obviously, there's a zone beyond words and that's the true stratum. Logos is the substratum, but the true stratum isn't words, isn't any form of perception. It's a white light. It doesn't have any particularization. But very close for us humans is the substratum of logos, so when we look into ourselves, before we get to the white light, before we get to the purity of nothingness, we see the realm of words. We're trapped in it. We created it, the semantic index of understanding, the semantic index to ultimately obtaining enlightenment. That's our vice. That's the real distinction between the Western world and the Eastern world: We rely on words so much. And so, when I look into myself, I see a flurry of words: word concept, word idea, word description, word explanation. I don't see a sunset; I see someone's tribute, some poem, to a sunset.

"You say words are this role—or the way I use words is a role. Well, no, it's deeper than a role. In my little garden of the imagination, beyond a warrior's words, I see all kinds of beautiful things. I've read a lot of children's poetry, and then I see a bird and I put it together, children laughing. So I'm not filled with snakes and nails and puppy-dog tails. I have this secret gift of being titillated by different pieces of the sensorium, little lights and sounds and chirps. I'm quite happy smoking a joint, sitting by the fire, closing my eyes, and entertaining myself. I find it utterly fascinating. All of these probes are for some dark hole, some festering sore blister in my psyche from which all of this spews. I don't see it. *I don't see it!* That's why, I think, I can still laugh at this life. Some of these lawyers my age are very cynical, very cold fuckers! And I can still laugh. I can still smile at existence."

Tony Serra was indeed smiling. Was it because he'd just journeyed through his own fecund imagination, from the bullfighter-lawyer confronting constant death and rebirth at the horns of unmorphined bulls and the zealot potato farmer working night and day for potatoes to feed humanity to the wheel of Samsara being reborn as a poet sage holding court with frogs and a wannabe Sir Lancelot who's so busy saving the world that he has no time to spend with his family and whose altruism is so pure that he has no money to pay the rent, from the junkie of neon sensorium getting his kicks by shooting up the emotions of desperate criminals to the trial warrior riding hard on the thundering hooves of his own words?

Or was it because this interview—and this book—was finally over and he could now enjoy the sanity of a quiet walk on the beach?

Chapter 19

Superman, Sisyphus, and Serra

N o portrait of J. Tony Serra would be complete without a brief discussion on the likeness of the radical lawyer to the superhero Superman and the Greek's archetypal Sisyphus.

America is a culture of hero worship. Superman embodies the hero
inside the common man. Where the voices of disparity call, Superman
appears. In Clark Kent, the call to serve a greater cause awakens su-
perhuman powers that prevail over adversity. He sheds his work-a-day
appearance and becomes bigger than life to rescue the moment. When
summoned to the rescue of someone victimized by an unfair socio-political system, so too does Tony Serra become bigger than life.

Sisyphus is a character in Greek mythology who can also be likened
to Serra. Sisyphus's punishment for angering the gods was to push a
huge boulder uphill from the underworld to the top of a mountain slope
every day. (Recall, Serra painted his room black at Stanford and placed a
huge boulder in the center of it.) Every day, Sisyphus dutifully attended
to his "punishment." Sisyphus locked himself into position, with his feet
dug into the earth and his shoulders braced up against the boulder, and
began his task anew. The boulder cast its shadow upon Sisyphus as a

constant reminder of the darkness of its primal origin, the underworld. The sheer weight of the boulder ultimately overcame him and it rolled back to the underworld. The gods could conceive of nothing more hopeless and futile and cruel than performing an impossible, repetitive, relentless task that was doomed to failure, forever.

I see the underworld as the environment inhabited by Serra's clients: the underdogs, the maligned, the downtrodden, the disenfranchised. These inhabitants are in a primal struggle for survival. In my metaphor, the boulder is consciousness, comprised of the heavy elements of crime, which to some degree everyone experiences: anger, hatred, revenge, jealousy, addiction, and heat of passion, as well as other qualities that get relegated to dark and hidden subterranean realms considered socially unacceptable.

Serra's plight of pushing this boulder up the mountain is to move these elements out from their delegated darkness into the light, into the higher realm of understanding, of compassionate consciousness. The mountain represents the justice system. Serra overcomes his fate of hopeless daily drudgery by becoming one with his task, by joining forces with it, and knowing that although he may never reach the top of the mountain, which symbolizes freedom, he does manage to push his boulder of consciousness a little farther each time, thus advancing the evolution of understanding a bit more with every attempt.

This boulder seems to possess a life of its own. I envision Sisyphus running after it as it rolls back down the mountain to once more lodge itself in the darkness of the underworld. Each day his desperate obsession is to haul it back into the light again.

Just as Serra represents the mythical superpowers possessed by everyman, as well as the eternal struggle of fighting the forces of gravity, so too does his boulder represent the qualities of everyman in the daily struggle to attain higher ground, which begins with compassionate understanding, the goal of which is freedom.

• • •

The many years that I interacted with Tony Serra were some of the most growth-inducing of my life. They were glorious and they were tough. But when I unfasten myself from the humdrum lockstep of daily struggles and catch a glimpse of the larger picture, I always think of him as this big man—with big hands and a big voice and a big ego and a big heart and a big fury who has carved a big swath through the rising tide of injustice in America. I envision him searing through life like some kind of meteorite, careening across the heavens, stirring up the furies and shedding poetry in his wake.

Index

About the Author

Paulette Frankl, daughter of Austrian-born world-renowned Art Deco designer Paul T. Frankl, has been an artist all her life. Her first public art exhibit was at the age of seven in a joint show with her father for the sophisticated art world in Los Angeles, California.

Ms. Frankl is a graduate of Stanford University, where she obtained a bachelor's degree in art and languages. She studied art at the Skowhegan School of Painting and Sculpture in Skowhegan, Maine, where her work was awarded for its originality.

Frankl has lived and worked in United States and Europe as a photojournalist, fine-arts artist, and graphic artist for magazines. Her work includes a cover on France's "Réalités." As a photo-journalist in Europe, she was a staff photographer for Gruner & Jahr in their publications, "Twen" and "Eltern." The German magazine "Geo" profiled her lifestyle in California in the seventies.

Frankl's courtroom art has been aired on CNN, NBC, CBS, ABC, Fox TV, NNS, WGN-TV, and Talk America. It has taken her all the way to the United States Supreme Court in Washington, D.C.

In *Lust for Justice* Frankl combines her love of language and her perceptive insights honed from years of performance in pantomime with her innate visual perception to produce a painterly style of writing and a story-telling style of art. The challenge of capturing the multi-faceted persona of J. Tony Serra on paper demanded the creation of its own unique style of courtroom art. Frankl's art combines the visual with the emotional to engender a live force in an original style she calls *Perceptualism*.

Frankl says about her art, "Words and brush strokes have much in common: they must be carefully chosen, applied with deliberation, and they must convey either in and of themselves or by juxtaposition the full impact of the statement intended. Words and brush strokes, like Haiku, convey much more than the sum of their parts."

As a performance artist in the field of mime and magic, she was featured on Italian television at Carnival in Venice. She has also appeared in *Sunset* magazine. Her creative association with Marcel Marceau as collaborator and muse spanned thirty-five years. Frankl worked as a professional magician in the magic capital of America, Las Vegas, Nevada.

A native Californian, Ms. Frankl currently resides in Santa Fe, New Mexico. Her fine art was in a show of XV Santa Fe Artists at the Las Vegas Art Museum in 2005.

More of Frankl's art can be seen on her website: www.pauletteart. com.

J. TONY SERRA

Currriculum vitae

Lifelong resident of Bay Area, mostly San Francisco.

Family: Two brothers: Richard Serra and Rudy Serra, nationally prominent sculptors in New York City.

Five children: Ivory, Shelter, Chime, Wonder, and Lilac. All have university and/or post-graduate degrees; all are successful in fields of sculpture, photography, off-Broadway acting and playwright, movie production, and fashion.

EDUCATION

San Francisco public schools

Bank of America Giannini Award for most promising graduating student in field of English

Stanford University, Bachelor of Arts, Philosophy

U.C. Berkeley, Boalt Hall School of Law, LLB

Counter-culture lawyer

45+ years practicing criminal defense, specializing in jury trials

NOTEWORTHY CASES

Huey Newton—Black Panthers (murder of prostitute)

White Panthers

Russell Little—SLA

NWLF

Hell's Angels

Chol Soo Lee

Hooty Croy

Brownie Mary

Ellie Nesler

Bear Lincoln

Sara Jane Olson a k a Kathleen Soliah (SLA)
Judi Bari & Darryl Cherney v. FBI
Michael Bortin (SLA)
Rick Tabish (Las Vegas "Binion" case)
Rod Coronado (E.L.F.)
BALCO (representing Barry Bonds' trainer, Greg Anderson)

AWARDS

Runner-up, "Best Lawyer in America", *American Lawyer* magazine, 1982
Drug Policy Foundation Achievement in the Field of Law, 1992
Boalt Hall "Alumnus of the Year," (approx.) 1993
Charles Garry Award, 1994
ACLU Benjamin Dreyfus Civil Liberties Award, 1997
California Attorneys for Criminal Justice, 2000
    Ten Best Criminal Defense Attorneys of Century
Lifetime Achievement Award, 2003
    McFetridge-American Inn of Court
Co-Awardee, "2003 Trial Lawyer of the Year"
    Trial Lawyers for Public Justice
Certificate of Honor, December 1, 2005
    Board of Supervisors, City & County of San Francisco
Lawyer of the Year, 2005
    Criminal Trial Lawyers Association of Northern California
2005 Gideon Equal Justice Award
    San Francisco Public Defender's and the SF Private
    Defense Bar
2008 NORML—Lester Grinspoon Award
    For Outstanding Achievement in the Field of Marijuana Law Reform

Index of Images

ARTIST'S STATEMENT:

To my knowledge, this is the only time a courtroom artist has singled out one lawyer exclusively in order to create such a large body of work in and out of the courtroom.

—Paulette Frankl

Cover art stylized from a photo from the *Los Angeles Times* magazine, June 24, 1990, by Jeffrey Newberry. Article: "The Ballad of Hooty Croy" by David Talbot.

CHAPTER IMAGES:

ART MANUSCRIPT:

P1: Top: Capps case, July, 1995; Bottom: Rashid v. Houghton case; February,1994; Closing Arguments;

P2: Top: Bear Lincoln case September 1997; Top and Center: Closing Arguments

P3: Left: J. Tony Serra; Right: Richard Serra stylized from a photo by Mario Sorrenti for *W* magazine, May 2007

P4: Top: Brownie Mary hearing October 9, 1992; Bottom: Balbir Singh Lally case November 1994

P5: Top: Espenal case September 1994 Closing Arguments; Bottom: Cordova case January 1995

P6: Top: Balbir Singh Lally case November 1994; Bottom: Doheny Case: August 1995 Dr. Jeffry Gutstadt witness

P7: Ellie Nesler trial August-September 1993 Top: Closing Arguments

P8: Ellie Nesler trial: August-September 1993

P9: Top: Ellie Nesler trial: L-R: Daniel Driver, Willie Nesler, Ellie Nesler; Bottom: Defeat

P10: Contempt of Court: United States of America v. J. Tony Serra: Top: Palmer Hoovestal defense; Below: Gerry Spence witness

P11: Ted Binion Murder retrial: Top: October-November 2004

The images from Chapters 1, 2, 4, 6, 8, and 13 are random sketches in my collection and are not associated to specific cases.

PHOTO SECTION

P12: Top: J. Tony Serra; Bottom: National Association of Criminal Defense Lawyers

P13: Top: JTS at Contempt of Court trial; Top R: Bear Lincoln trial: Photo by Nick Wilson; Lower L: Bear Lincoln case: Lucille Lincoln, Paulette Frankl, Bia; Center R: Bernadette Zambrano, Diana Samuelson

P14: Top: Diana Samuelson; Center & Bottom: Tony Serra's office Pier 5 The Embarcadero

P15: Top L-R Secretaries Penelope Rose, Stephanie Brown; Center: Serra's North Beach apartment; Bottom: Serra at Office Halloween party

P16: Bear Lincoln case: Eukaia; Bottom: Paulette Frankl, Bolinas